Genealogy Online, 5th Edition

To Rachel
Happy Hunting!
Elizabeth Powell Crowe
2001

Genealogy Online, 5th Edition

Elizabeth Powell Crowe

Osborne/McGraw-Hill

New York   Chicago   San Francisco
Lisbon   London   Madrid   Mexico City
Milan   New Delhi   San Juan
Seoul   Singapore   Sydney   Toronto

Osborne/**McGraw-Hill**
2600 Tenth Street
Berkeley, California 94710
U.S.A.

To arrange bulk purchase discounts for sales promotions, premiums, or
fund-raisers, please contact Osborne/**McGraw-Hill** at the above address. For
information on translations or book distributors outside the U.S.A., please see
the International Contact Information page immediately following the index.

Genealogy Online, 5th Edition

  34567890 DOC DOC 01987654321
ISBN 0-07-213114-4

Publisher: Brandon A. Nordin
Vice President &
Associate Publisher: Scott Rogers
Acqusition Editor: Michael Sprague
Project Editor: Monika Faltiss
Acquisitions Coordinator: Paulina Pobocha
Copy Editor: Mike McGee
Proofreaders: Pat Mannion, Pam Vevea
Indexer: Valerie Robbins
Computer Designers: Roberta Steele, Michelle Galicia, Melinda Moore Lytle
Illustrator: Lyssa Sieben-Wald
Series Design: Gary Corrigan
Cover Designer: William Voss

This book was composed with Corel VENTURA™ Publisher.

To my mother Frances Spencer Powell.

About the Author

Elizabeth Powell-Crowe is the author of three books, including *Genealogy Online AOL Edition*. Besides previous best selling editions, she also wrote *Information for Sale* with John Everett, and *The Electronic Traveller*, both for McGraw-Hill. She has been a contributing editor for *Computer Currents* magazine and the author of numerous articles in both popular and technical publications. She lives in Huntsville, Alabama with her husband Mark and her children Marianne and Matthew.

Contents at a Glance

Part I
The Basics

1 What You Need 3

2 Software 19

3 Beginning a Genealogy Project 55

Part II
The Internet

4 Usenet 69

5 Genealogy Mailing Lists 89

6 The World Wide Web 113

7 Chat: Hail Thy Fellow on the Net! 149

8 Using Search Sites for Genealogy 173

Part III
The "Must See" Online Resources

9 RootsWeb 199

10 The Ancestry.com Family of Sites 211

11 Everton's 223

12 Online Library Card Catalogs 231

13 Library of Congress and NARA 243

14 The Church of Jesus Christ of Latter-day Saints 257

15 America Online's Golden Gate Genealogy Forum 271

16 CompuServe's Genealogy Forums 299

17 International Genealogy Resources 317

18 GenServ 335

A Forms of Genealogical Data 349

B Internet Error Messages 359

Glossary 367

Index 387

Contents

Acknowledgments xvii
Introduction xix

PART I
The Basics

1 What You Need 3
    Get Set Up 4
        Modems 4
        Wherefore UART? 7
        ISDN and xDSL 8
        DSL: Not Quite 31 Flavors 11
        Internet Appliances 13
        Choosing an ISP 14
        Baby Steps 16
        Wrapping Up 18

2 Software 19
    What Makes the Web Tick 20
        Browsers 21
        Other Browsers 24

FTP 29
E-mail 31
The Legislative Front 33
Libbi's Spammer Twit List 36
Internet Mail Clients 41
Inoculations 47
Publishing on the Internet 48
Genealogical Standards 49

3 Beginning a Genealogy Project 55
Always Start with Yourself 56
Standards for Sound Genealogical Research 58
Sources and Proof 59
Standards for Use of Technology in Genealogical Research . . . 59
Standards for Sharing Information with Others 64

PART II
The Internet

4 Usenet 69
Complicated, but Useful 70
Usenet's Structure 71
Usenet History 73
The Software 74
Newsgroups of Interest to Online Genealogists 79
Binary Files on Usenet 82
Newsgroup FAQ Files 83
Net Etiquette and Tips on Usenet 83
Searching for Information Within Newsgroups 86
Beyond Usenet 87

5 Genealogy Mailing Lists 89
Proper Addressing 90
General Subscribing Tips 91
An In-depth Visit to ROOTS-L 91
Other Genealogy Mailing Lists 98

6 The World Wide Web 113
Browser Tips and Tricks 115
FTP 118
FTP Conventions 119
Four Score and Seven Sites to See 119
In-depth Explorations of Major Genealogical Web Sites 135
AfriGeneas 135

DearMYRTLE 138
Genealogy Home Page 142
National Genealogical Society 144
USGenWeb 145

7 Chat: Hail Thy Fellow on the Net! 149
Introduction 150
Important Warnings About Chat 152
How It Works 153
Security Risks in IRC 154
Chat Flavors 155
AOL Instant Messenger 155
ICQ 157
MSN Messenger Service 2.2 159
Microsoft Chat 160
mIRC 162
How to Chat 163
Some Common IRC Commands 164
Where to Chat 166
Chat Without a Chat Program! 168
Chat Etiquette 169
Chat Shorthand 172

8 Using Search Sites for Genealogy 173
Defining Terms 174
Searching with Savoir Faire 175
Using Boolean Terms 176
Search Sites 178
AltaVista (http://www.altavista.com) 178
Ancestry - GenPage Finder (http://www.ancestry.com) 179
AOL NetFind (http://search.aol.com) 180
AskJeeves (http://www.askjeeves.com) 181
Biography Guide (http://bioguide.congress.gov) 181
C|Net Search (http://www.search.com) 181
Excite (http://www.excite.com) 182
FastSearch (http://www.alltheweb.com) 182
GO/Infoseek (http://www.go.com/WebDir) 182
Genealogy Pages (http://www.genealogypages.com) 184
GeneaSearch.com (http://www.genealsearch.com) 184
GenealogyPortal.com (http://www.genealogyportal.com) 184
GenGateway (http://www.gengateway.com) 185
GenServ (http://www.genserv.com/) 185
GenSource (http://www.gensource.com) 186

GenealogySearch.com (http://genealogysearch.com) 186
Google (http://www.google.com) 187
HotBot (http://hotbot.lycos.com) 187
LookSmart (http://www.looksmart.com/) 187
Lycos (http://www.lycos.com/) 188
MetaCrawler (http://www.metacrawler.com/
    index_power.html) 189
Northern Light (www.northernlight.com) 189
Obituary Search Pages 189
Surname Web (http://other.surnameweb.org/search/) 190
SurnameSite (http://surnamesite.org) 191
Snap (http://www.snap.com/) 191
World Connect (http://worldconnect.rootsweb.com/) 191
Yahoo! (http://www.yahoo.com) 191
People Directories 193
File Search Sites 194
Searching for Information within Newsgroups 195

PART III
The "Must See" Online Resources

9 RootsWeb 199
Searching for Surnames 201
Other Search Engines 205
GenConnect 206
Web Sites 207
State Resource Pages 207
The HelpDesk 207
Newsletters 207
Mailing Lists 209
The Merger 210
More and More 210

10 The Ancestry.com Family of Sites 211
Ancestry.com 212
FamilyHistory.com 214
Message Boards 214
World Tree 216
Society Hall 217
MyFamily.com 217
Family Tree 218
History 219

Chats 220
Other Features 221
A Nice Collection of Sites 221

11 Everton's 223
Databases 225
Online Classes 227
Reference Library 227
Subscribing 228
A Valuable Resource 229

12 Online Library Card Catalogs 231
Connecting to Card Catalogs by Web Browser 233
A Sample OCC Search 234
Connecting to Card Catalogs by Telnet 239
Where to Find More Online Card Catalogs 240

13 Library of Congress and NARA 243
Library of Congress 244
American Memory 244
The Library Today 248
Research Tools 248
Exhibitions 248
NARA 249
The Genealogy Page 250
NARA Web Databases 250
Prologue 255
Some Experience Necessary 256

14 The Church of Jesus Christ of Latter-day Saints 257
FamilySearch Internet 258
A Run-through 259
Other Cool Stuff 262
Library 265
Other Resources 265
How to Use Information from LDS 266
Some Background 267
A Visit to an FHC 269

15 America Online's Golden Gate Genealogy Forum 271
Proprietary Content 272
Front End Software 272
Quick Jumps 272
Forums 273

Mail 273

Usenet 273

Files 273

Member Welcome Center 276

Beginners' Center 277

Message Boards 282

Genealogy Chat Center 287

File Libraries Center 289

Resource Center 290

Internet Center 290

Surnames Center 291

Reunions 292

Search the Forum 292

GenealogyForum.com 293

The Staff of the Genealogy Forum 294

16 CompuServe's Genealogy Forums 299

A Quick Overview 301

Go Genealogy 302

Forum Decorum 304

Sysops: The Forum Managers 306

A Tour 306

Profile: Dick Eastman, Genealogy Sysop 313

17 International Genealogy Resources 317

Introduction 318

A Success Story 318

Origins of Surnames 322

LDS Research Guides 325

WorldGenWeb 327

International Internet Genealogical Society 328

Asia 329

Europe 330

South America 332

Australia 332

Africa 333

North America 334

18 GenServ 335

The Original GEDCOM Exchange 336

GenServ is the Greatest! 337

How to export your GEDCOM 338

A Forms of Genealogical Data 349
   Ahnentafels, Tiny Tafels, and GEDCOMs 350
      Ahnentafels 350
      Tiny Tafels 352
      GEDCOMs 356

B Internet Error Messages 359
   Browser Error Messages 360
   FTP Error Messages 362
   Usenet Error Messages 363
   E-Mail Error Messages 364

   Glossary 367

   Index 387

Acknowledgments

As with any book, this one was made possible by the efforts of many people besides the author. First, I would like to thank every person mentioned and quoted in this edition of the book. Obviously, without all your help, the book would still just be a dream.

Very special thanks to Cliff Manis, Terry Morgan, and DearMYRTLE for helping me out of many a dead end. Thanks also to all the fine folks at McGraw-Hill who sweated out a cold season to get this book out.

To my family and friends, who patiently waited for me to emerge from the writing frenzy, and especially Marianne, Matthew and Mark, who were the best support a writing mom and wife ever had, a big thank you.

But most of all I want to thank my mother, Frances Spencer Powell, who urged and encouraged me, babysat and researched for me, and traveled and travailed with me ever since I first got the idea to write a book about online genealogy.

Introduction

"I've gotten more genealogy done in one year on Prodigy than I did in 20 years on my own!" my mother exclaimed. This quote, from a 30-year genealogy veteran, shows how technology has changed this popular hobby. The mind-boggling deluge of data needed to trace one's family tree has finally found a knife to whittle it down to size: the computer. A reader of the previous edition of *Genealogy Online* wrote to me:

"Libbi, I can't begin to tell you how much benefit I've gotten from *Genealogy Online*! After reading your book, I began an online search for John's and my ancestors. Since both of our mothers also had an interest in genealogy and had already prepared quite a bit of information that they passed to us, I was starting with most branches of our combined families in the early 1800's and working backwards from there, when records were sparse.

With the knowledge I gained from your book, I've been able to trace many branches of our combined family back several more generations! I've found out that my husband and kids are related to George Washington and Wild Bill Hickok. The Hickok connection was always in the family folklore, but I've been able to provide the missing link.

I've traced one line back to the 1400's in England, and have recently learned that another line is available back to the 800's. I've traced our roots back to the very same rural county in Virginia where John's brother now lives, just a short distance from the original family farm. Through the Internet, I've made connections with two of my mother's cousins and two of John's fourth cousins, and we are collectively working to share family information and document our heritage.

I've had so much fun, but I've had to learn to be patient when searching. Sometimes the most obscure reference is the one that provides the missing link you're searching for. Without *Genealogy Online*, I wouldn't have even known where to get started on my search. With the help of your book, we now have several hundred more years worth of family history!"

This book will help you understand that there's a rich community of information out there—information that can help you find where those missing ancestors are lurking. Some of the sources are free, some cheap, some dear. However, until you know about them, they're worthless to you. Once you know, you can decide for yourself whether to use them.

For Those New to Genealogy

When you study your own genealogy, you trace your place in history. Your results can be shown in charts, trees, circles, quilts, scrapbooks or even a published hardback book. In the process, you are bound to learn about history, law, sociology, and eugenics. Most amateur genealogists find that history is much more exciting when they see exactly how it affected and shaped their own families.

A major appeal of genealogy is that it provides people with a sense of continuity and belonging. This sense of belonging extends to other genealogists, for it is almost impossible to research any family line by yourself. Genealogy can be used to research medical histories, confirm your rights to an inheritance, or to qualify for certain scholarships. Overall, however, genealogy for most people is just a fascinating hobby.

It's not as hard to find some information as you might think. Almost any self-respecting public library, no matter how small, has a local history and genealogy section. Some libraries have entire floors dedicated to those subjects.

The Church of Jesus Christ of Latter-day Saints (the Mormons) has collected an extensive bank of genealogical data (official registers of births, marriages, and deaths, and related documents), probably the greatest such collection in existence. Church members use these records in order to bring their ancestors posthumously into the church. The index to their information is now on the Internet.

The federal government has recently started to put much of its data, such as death records, veterans' records and so on, in machine-readable databases, which could then be accessible via an Internet.

The U.S. alone has numerous genealogical societies that trace people's descent. Some of these are national, but many more are local or regional, such as the Tennessee Valley Genealogical Society or the New England Historical Society. Others are specific to certain names. Many patriotic organizations, such as the Daughters of the Confederacy, limit membership to descendants of a particular historical group.

A recent cover article in *CompuServe* magazine highlighted the uses of their online forum for genealogy, where forum leader Dick Eastman said thousands of users visit a week. The article then proceeded to describe how the forum helped one woman find her natural father, how stories about ancestors are swapped, and the sort of informational files uploaded to the library.

Where Computers Come in

Databases, online services, online card catalogs, and bulletin boards are changing the "brick wall syndrome", that frustrating phase of any lineage search where the information needed seems unavailable. Genealogists who have faced the challenges and triumphed are online, helping others.

There's no denying that the computer has changed just about everything in our lives, and the avocation and vocation of genealogical research is no exception. Further, a wonderful new resource for computers, the Internet, has come into being and is still developing at a pace that's dizzying. This book will explore many different networks, services, and Web sites that can help you in your pursuit of your ancestry.

Stories about how online communities have helped people in their genealogical research abound. Here are some examples:

DearMYRTLE Finds a Patriot

DearMYRTLE, a daily genealogy columnist on the Internet (see Chapter 7 or http://members.aol.com/dearmyrtle/), was helping a friend move files, data, and programs from an old computer to a new one. In the course of the conversation DearMYRTLE's friend wondered aloud what online genealogy could do for him but expressed doubt anything useful could turn up online.

Then the conversation turned to the first of the new U.S. quarters, the one with the Delaware patriot Cesar Rodney on the reverse.

"Who was he?" asked DearMYRTLE's friend.

"All right," she replied, "let's run a test. Your wife here will look him up in the Encyclopaedia Britannica. You look him up on your old computer using Microsoft Encarta 97. I'll look him up on the Internet with your new computer."

The friend and his wife both found short text mentions that Rodney had signed the Declaration of Independence and led the Delaware Militia. Just as quickly, DearMYRTLE had found the Web site of the Historical Society of Delaware (http://hsd.org/george.htm) with a short biography on him, and a copy of a letter from George Washington to Rodney discussing troop movements, along with two others written by Delaware patriots Caesar Rodney and Jacob Broom!

Now THAT'S how online research can help you!

Nancy's Story

Nancy is a friend of mine from high school who knows more about computers and the Internet than I do but not quite as much about genealogy. When her stepmother died recently, Nancy got a large box of her father's memorabilia and photos. In August 1998, we spent some time at the beach together and using her laptop computer, I showed her some good genealogy sites on the Internet.

I didn't think much more about it until she called me in early 1999 with considerable excitement. She had not only found the USGENWEB (http://www.usgenweb.org) site for her father's home county in Texas, but she also found out that the moderator of the site had known both her father and her grandfather. She was scanning in the old photos and emailing them to the fellow, and he was identifying people left and right. One photo was of Nancy's grandfather as a child, another showed her father as a teenager. Every day the USGENWEB sysop was helping her fill in more holes in her family history.

What is a Hoosier? Genealogy has the Answer

Randy Hooser of Huntsville, Alabama has been working on his genealogy for years. One result has been his work with a University of Indiana Professor to publish a White Paper in Februray 1999 to prove his family is the origin of the nickname "Hoosier". A fascinating story, the migration of Randy's family involves religious and political movements of this nation's history. You can see the results of his research on his web site, http://www.geocities.com/Heartland/Flats/7822/. In it he postulates that his pioneer ancestors, being usually the farthest West of civilization, were the origin of the nickname "Hoosier".

However, that's not the only use for Randy's web site. Randy used it to plan a big family reunion in Indiana in 2000, to exchange genealogical data among the cousins, and to publish a newsletter. An e-mail list with all his known relatives keeps everyone up to date on births, marriages, and deaths among those living and similar data on ancestors as the family historians find them.

Regular family meetings take place on Randy's Hooser message board. Unlike chat (see Chapter 7), the family members post messages to the site's message board. In this way, Randy is using the Internet for past, present, and future generations of his family.

Some Conceptual Background About Online Genealogy

Genealogists have had publications to turn to for many years. From local/regional publications such as the Tennessee Valley Genealogical Society's *Valley Leaves* to the venerated *Genealogical Helper*, a wealth of information has been printed to help genealogists find others working on the same ancestral lines, publish interesting tidbits, and help each other with vexing research problems.

For not quite so long, but for some time now, they have also had computers and genealogical database programs to help them track, organize, analyze, and share their genealogical information. For a while there was a dearth of such programs, then a widening choice of formats, and then finally a standard in the GEDCOM. Everyone was plugging away, gathering and storing information. They all had more information than they could use, some of it germane to their own lineages, some of it not, but surely useful to someone, so why throw it away?

So, here were all these collections of data, and all these users wanting to share that data. Soon a problem arose: how to transfer data, for example, from a CP/M to Windows-based machine or to a Mac? In other fields, people were faced with the same problems. Astronomers, teachers, and the military were all doing the same thing genealogists were on different subjects.

The answer was to create new ways to communicate. Electronic mail systems (e-mail), bulletin board systems (BBS), and the Internet all came into being to solve the problem of getting data from one place to another. By using phone lines and protocols (way of transmitting data), regardless of the machinery and proprietary software involved, people could exchange data.

Electronic Mail

Electronic mail systems are simply a way to send text from one place to another, just as regular mail does. Through a variety of different programs, that text can be private messages, public postings of articles, text files, graphics, even sounds.

However, please take that "private messages" phrase with a grain of salt. I'll make this point several times in this book: posting something to a list, echo, or board means that many, many people will read it. Posting something to a certain person at his or her e-mail address means you and that person will read it, but so will the people who run the system to which you posted the text. As of this writing, no law or court case has established that electronic mail is as private as first-class mail. One or two court cases, indeed, have held the opposite: when something is posted to a company-owned, company-run, electronic mail system, the text is considered the property of the company.

An e-mail system might be a part of an Internet, a bulletin board, or a pay-per-use commercial service; it might even be part of a combination of these. Alternatively, it might stand alone, as a company-run e-mail service does. You need to carefully check out any e-mail service you use, its costs and distribution.

Bulletin Boards

In previous editions, I spent many words on bulletin board systems (BBS), which were dial-up services for exchanging files, messages and real-time comments. They were usually hosted in someone's home. Dial-up BBS still exist, but for this edition I have eliminated them from the text in favor of Usenet, e-mail, and online forums. Many of these BBS have folded, others have become Internet service providers, some are still running, but they are not nearly as popular as they used to be.

Networks and Echoes

Connections of computers are called networks. The connection may be constant, or intermittent, but the point is that computers in different locations can share information. Although BBS networks still exist, this edition will be concerned more with the Internet.

These networks are not unlike the Internet in purpose. However, when you get to the Internet, the functions and services are expanded to the extreme, and ever-changing.

The Internet

The Internet, with a capital "I", is more of a concept than an entity. The concept is, hook up lots of computers running the same protocol (way of communicating digital data) and let people communicate over their computers with pictures, words, sounds and whatever else they can digitize. The Internet is a network of networks to implement that idea. There are several smaller "internets" with government, educational or research purposes that connect to the Internet at certain points.

A network is a group of computers working together through some connection, intermittent or continuous. The connection can be phone wires (most common) but also can be cables, or radio, satellite, or other wireless connections. The Internet is a set of computers connected all the time, (the "backbone") to which your computer can connect any time, and through which your data can travel. The data is sent with a protocol called TCP/IP. It makes sure the data goes in the most efficient (not necessarily the shortest) route available at the moment.

The backbone consists of companies such as America Online, MCI and AT&T, universities, research institutions and government organizations; all running computers connected with the Internet Protocols. Every facet of the communications industry, in other words, gives some support to the Internet.

At first, you couldn't use the Internet unless you were an employee or student at one of the previously mentioned places, and your connection was probably free, supported by tax and research dollars. There were a few exceptions to this. Some entrepreneurs paid for an Internet connection at one of those places and then sold access: they are Internet service providers. Then the government decided it had done enough to get the Information Superhighway paved, and bowed out. The infrastructure was opened to commercial use, and the number of Internet service providers went from a few dozen to about a thousand.

Today a great deal of scientific, educational, and technical research still goes on over the Internet, but entertainment and hobby use has grown phenomenally. The Internet is a resource, a method of research, and a "place" called cyberspace all at the same time.

Much more is involved in how the Internet developed and works today than this book can cover. For the genealogy hobbyist, it's enough to understand that the Internet is a worldwide connection of computers; you can connect to it, and it has a wealth of information and many people willing to share on it.

How to Use the Internet

To use the Internet you use different services. All of these services started out as text-based programs. Most of them are now available in some Windows or Macintosh graphical user interface. The main Internet services are:

- ◆ Chat—typing conversations, in real time, over a network with someone. If you liked CB radio, you'll like online chat. Though it's popular, I haven't found much use for it in genealogy, except on the commercial online services. The chapters dealing with CIS, AOL, Prodigy, and MSN note the genealogy chat services (sometimes called "conference") they offer.

♦ E-mail—sending and receiving messages at your individual Internet account's address.

♦ Finger—sending a test signal to a person's e-mail address. If that person has written a text file to respond to a finger command, the file will be returned to you. Some systems will also tell you if that person is logged onto the Internet right now or the last time that person logged onto the system.

♦ FTP—file transfer protocol is how you get files, programs, pictures and other data from another site to yours, or to send those things to another site. Anonymous ftp is a system where a lot of files are stored at a certain computer, and anyone is welcome to download them. You simply log in as "anonymous" or "ftp" and give your e-mail address as the password.

♦ Ping—sending a test signal to a specific computer on the Internet. Useful for when you cannot connect to a WWW, telnet, or other Internet site; ping will tell you if the computer is down, or if the computer is running but busy. Windows 95 comes with a ping program, but you have to drop to the MSDOS prompt to use it.

♦ Telnet—a text-based system of running a distant computer from your own. Once you log in, you must know and use the commands at that remote computer, but you can run programs and services such as ftp from telnet connections. The most common use for genealogists is to look at library card catalogs. Windows 95 comes with a telnet program, but there are graphical user interfaces that are better.

♦ Usenet—also called "Internet bulletin boards", Usenet newsgroups number in the thousands. They are organized by topic, and when you post a message to one, you are talking to the whole world, usually. Usenet is not e-mail; it's many-to-many or one-to-many communication.

♦ World Wide Web—an interface called a browser ties together all these services, except ping and finger. It's the easiest way to use the Internet.

A Quick Look at this Book

This book will give you a basic education in the online world. Nevertheless, please be aware that what is written here was current as of late 2000. Since that time, commercial online services and the Internet will have added, expanded, revised, and changed what they offer, as well as how and when they offer it. The only constant in the online world for the last five years has been change, and at an exponential rate. So, be prepared for adventures!

Section I, The Basics

Chapter 1, What You Need—A look at hardware and connections, this chapter helps you prepare to go online.

Chapter 2, Software—A look at the programs that will help you with online genealogy.

Chapter 3, Beginning a Genealogy Project—This chapter discusses the basics for beginning genealogy research, online or offline.

Section II, The Internet

Chapter 4, Usenet—How to find genealogy information on the Internet message system called Usenet.

Chapter 5, Mailing Lists—Internet mailing lists help you discuss genealogy with others around the word.

Chapter 6, The World Wide Web—You will learn how to surf for genealogy information and several important sites to get you started.

Chapter 7, Chat: Hail Thy Fellow on the Net!—Find out how to have real time conversations, even attend genealogy classes, using the Internet.

Chapter 8, Using Search Sites for Genealogy—How to use search engines to find what you want.

Section III, The "Must See" Online Resources

Chapter 9, RootsWeb—The original online genealogy heaven.

Chapter 10, The Ancestry.com Family of Sites—A suite of sites aimed at the beginning to intermediate genealogist.

Chapter 11, Everton's—One of the most respected publishers in genealogy has a Web presence worth visiting.

Chapter 12, Online Card Catalogs—How to search libraries all over the world from your desk.

Chapter 13, Library of Congress and NARA—These government sites have links to secondary and primary sources.

Chapter 14, The Church of Jesus Christ of Latter-day Saints—How to use FamilySearch, an index to some LDS genealogy data.

Chapter 15, America Online's Golden Gate Genealogy Forum—Helps people in all phases of their genealogy search.

Chapter 16, CompuServe's Genealogy Forums—Divided into sections by geography and topics, these discussion groups and file libraries are still one of the best resources online.

Chapter 17, International Genealogy Resources—Once you get "back to the boat", where do you go from there? A case study and a small list of resources will help you continue your search.

Chapter 18, GenServ—An example of a GEDCOM exchange site, where you can swap data with other genealogists near and far.

Appendix A, Forms of Genealogical Data

Appendix B, Internet Error Messages

Glossary

Index

Part I

The Basics

Chapter 1
What You Need

Online genealogy is only different from the old-fashioned kind in the type of tools you use. Instead of using a photocopier, you'll make copies on your printer. Instead of sending queries in an envelope, you'll send them by e-mail. Instead of reading an article in a magazine, you'll read it in a browser. And instead of going to the library in a car, you might visit it by modem.

Please understand that I don't mean to imply you will never do things the old-fashioned way again. Of course you will. You'll just find yourself using these online techniques very often, sometimes before you try to do research the traditional way. They are new tools for age-old genealogical tasks.

You will have to learn the ins and outs of hardware, software, and techniques for online information exchange in order to get the most out of the experience. In this section, the chapters will cover hardware considerations, software you might want to use, and online techniques and tips you should know.

Get Set Up

In this chapter, you will learn what you need to get connected to the Internet. In order to use the Internet, you need a way to connect your computer to the wires. You can do this through a modem, or through a digital data service such as an ISDN or Digital Subscriber Line, which requires different equipment. In my experience, most people will use a modem. Digital connections, which are covered in the next section, are coming on fast, but most people begin with a good old dial-up connection.

Note

Telephone lines have very little electrical resistance. You should always disconnect it from the wall during a thunderstorm. If you don't, your modem, computer, and printer could be damaged by a lightning strike. The added measure of installing a surge protector on your phone lines wouldn't hurt.

Modems

A modem is a gadget that converts the data of your computer system into sounds, which are then sent via a phone line (or a cable physically connecting two computers) to another computer. That's modulation. The other computer, with its modem, translates these sounds back into computer-readable signals. That's demodulation. The modulator/demodulator, or modem, makes it possible for computers to "talk to each other."

> ## Note
>
> *A modem, incidentally, changes the data from digital to analog to digital. If you have a digital connection, this isn't necessary, but you still have to get the data from your computer into the wire. That's important later on when we discuss ISDN and xDSL.*

Most modems on the market today are capable of receiving information at up to 56,000 bits of data per second (referred to as 56Kbps) and transmitting it at up to 36Kbps. The reason it's faster coming in than going out is that the wiring in your house ends and begins with analog transmission. Once it gets to your phone company's equipment, it becomes all digital.

A modem will compress the data according to a protocol. The protocol used must be the same for both the devices sending and receiving the data. When such protocols are grouped together and approved by the International Telecommunications Union, they become a "standard." When you buy a modem, be sure it meets the V.90 ITU standard. Though this is the latest technology, it includes past technologies within it. So a V.90 modem will be able to talk to other V.90 modems, as well as to older modems that don't have the standard yet.

> ## Note
>
> *A protocol is a standard set of formats and procedures for the exchange of information between systems. There have been many modem protocols in the past, with the latest being V.90.*

You will find hundreds of makes and models of modems, ranging in price from under $100 to more than $1,000. Some are "internal," that is, they fit into a slot inside your computer. Others are "external," meaning they're housed in a case outside your computer, where they sit on your desk, and have lights on the front to show you the status of various functions. External modems must have their own power supply along with the case, so they tend to be slightly more expensive. An external modem also requires a high quality cable to connect it to the communications port on your computer. Be sure to ask if one is included when you purchase an external modem. If not, make sure you pick one up.

Other important features to consider when selecting a modem include:

- *Fax capabilities, fax speed, and fax software.* Being able to send and receive faxes can be a convenience if the software is user-friendly. Many modems have this built-in and include software to run it. Also, Windows 95 and 98 can be installed with Windows Fax functions. Unless you have a scanner as well, you won't be able to fax anything you didn't create on your computer. But even without a scanner, you can use your fax modem as a printer and send anything you create on your computer as a fax. This can be a real convenience.

- *Flash Upgrade Modem technology.* Since their emergence 15 years ago, modems have been constantly changing and evolving. Customers, however, soon got tired of being told every 18 months that their modems were obsolete, with the only solution being they shell out another $200 for a new one. As a result, the flash upgrade was developed. This is a special program that rewrites the chip in the modem called read-only memory (ROM). The ROM holds permanent information for the modem such as the V.90 standard. Someday that standard will be replaced by a newer one, and if your modem has flash upgrade capability, then you can upgrade without getting a new modem. This is definitely much more expedient!

- *Extras such as software or hardware that allow two computers to use one modem, or that enable two computers to connect to share data.* One such gizmo is the OfficeConnect 56K LAN modem from 3Com. At about $200, it's pricey for a modem, but a bargain for a LAN. Right this minute, my tower Gateway and my SOLO laptop are both on the Internet. I'm typing this *and* answering e-mail while my laptop is searching for mentions of "genealogy" with the word "online" out on the Internet. It works great on my

Gateway (although PC Magazine's labs found other brands where it didn't work so well). My main problem has been Windows 98's insistence on dialing with the old modem instead of using the LAN. Apparently, AOL resets it every time it's used. Other than that, I'm doing back-flips over this thing. When I take my laptop somewhere for research, I simply bring it home, plug it into the LAN and boot it up. Then transferring work and files from one to another is as simple as drag and drop.

Wherefore UART?

If your computer is more than 4 years old, the UART is a consideration. The UART (Universal Asynchronous Transmitter and Receiver) is the part of the computer that sends the data out the wire. Internal modems have built-in UARTs. External modems, however, use the UART in your computer.

If you are using an external modem, therefore, it is crucial you understand what type of UART your COMM port is using. An internal modem probably will be equipped with a suitable UART, but checking it out wouldn't hurt. Also, if your computer is more than five years old, you may have to replace the UART to make your modern modem work its best anyway.

How do you find out what kind you have?

Run a program on your Windows computer called MSD.EXE (Microsoft System Diagnostics). Search your computer for it; it's probably in the DOS directory if your computer is more than three years old. Run the program in DOS, not Windows. (It can produce incorrect results if run from Windows or in a DOS session under Windows.) Select the PORTS option. If MSD reports a 16550x type of UART (where X is one or more letters), chances are, you'll be fine. However, if MSD reports an 8250 or 16450 type of UART, the UART is an older model. All is not lost, however. If you have a serial card (or motherboard) with a socket for the 8250 or 16450 UART, you can replace the chip with a 16550A. Add-on high speed data communications cards with 16550A (or equivalent) UARTs are also available at your local computer store at prices ranging from $20 to $75 depending upon the number of ports and other features.

ISDN and xDSL

The modem isn't the only way to connect to Internet services, nor is it the fastest. The alternatives, ISDN and Digital Subscriber Line (DSL), are so innovative and expensive I hesitate to mention them, but in the interests of completeness, I feel I must. This will be a very short introduction; if you want to try to jump into digital communications with your computer, you'll have to read much more than this brief description before you're ready.

Note ──────────────────────────────────

With all digital connections, two things are true: First, they offer continuous connection to the Internet. Second, because of this continuous connection, you will be vulnerable to certain attacks on your system. This will be discussed in the section on viruses in Chapter 2.

ISDN

The phone companies currently marketing ISDN (Integrated Services Digital Networks) to their customers would like you to believe that faster is better and that's all there is to it. ISDN is a new kind of connection that has three channels, A, B, and Data, to carry your signals. Phone companies have been promising for years that ISDN would replace our old (and reliable) analog phone lines. With an ISDN line hooked up to your PC, phone, fax, and what-have-you, you can send and receive just about any kind of data—voice, documents, graphics, sound, even the full-motion video necessary for movies or teleconferencing—over the line at speeds up to 64,000 bits per second (BPS).

Another selling point is versatility. With the right equipment and software on your end, a single ISDN line can support two phone numbers. In effect, you could get a video phone call from Grandma on one line, while transmitting a report to your company on the other. ISDN also lets your phone be a little smarter, because the "ring" sent down an ISDN line could tell your phone who's calling, the type of call (data or speech), the number dialed, and so on. Your intelligent phone could analyze this information and act appropriately. For example, your phone could be programmed to answer calls from certain numbers only, or to answer specific calls on specific lines, such as all fax calls on line two.

Unfortunately, ISDN isn't cheap, although prices are falling each month. Even though you'd treat an ISDN line like your old analog phone line—being billed for long distance charges, call waiting features, and so on—it comes with a passel of complications. Cost, for one thing.

Although an ISDN line costs as little as $20 a month in California, it's considerably more expensive in the East. Moreover, installation runs about $200. An ISDN line would eliminate the need for a modem after all, a MODulator-DEModulator is designed to turn digital data into analog and back again, and ISDN is all-digital. Yet hooking up your PC to an ISDN line will require a special adapter that can cost up to $1,000 or more, depending on the application. Moreover, using your existing fax machine, telephone, and so on, requires buying bridging devices and still more software. The alternative is to buy all new, ISDN-smart equipment. 3COM, Adtran, and many other companies are starting to offer consumer-priced equipment like this. So if you shop hard enough, you may find something in your price range.

Another consideration: the ISDN system is powered by your household current, not the phone company's. If the power to your ISDN system goes out, you're unreachable. This is why many businesses that have jumped on the ISDN bandwagon also buy a separate power source for their ISDN system, and keep an old analog line around, just in case of thunderstorms, brownouts, and earthquakes.

The price tag for your local telephone company is also steep, and no doubt some of that cost will find its way onto your monthly bill. For starters, all the "switches" in your phone company's central office have to be replaced with digital switches that can recognize ISDN. The new switches also have to be within 3.5 miles of your house. Therefore, the cost on both sides of the ISDN connection is high.

Consequently, communities that have adopted ISDN have often found themselves isolated digital islands in an analog sea. But the Baby Bells have been selling ISDN hard the last year or two, so many major cities in the U.S. have it, as well as smaller communities, such as Chapel Hill, North Carolina and Huntsville, Alabama. The web of ISDN communities is growing, so that sending and receiving data at blinding speeds from point A to point B across country may be possible fairly soon. Just not yet.

Criticizing ISDN is easy—after all, adopting it involves more than a few leaps of faith. Many companies that you'd expect to be taking the ISDN leap—such as commercial online services—are moving very slowly to implement ISDN. You're lucky if you can find an Internet service provider who has an ISDN link. Nevertheless, ISDN may be coming to a town near you.

The idea of high-speed, multi-channel phone lines is appealing. But like most cutting edge technologies that don't offer immediate, quantum gains in productivity, ISDN won't make serious inroads until it's as ubiquitous, invisible, and cheap as cable TV. Personally, I'll wait till then.

xDSL

Then there's xDSL, or Digital Subscriber Line, with the "x" being a letter that designates a type. Types include asymmetric, rate adaptive, very high, single line and all sorts of other flavors. There are those who will tell you, dump your modem. Forget ISDN. Leave the cable attached to your TV. If you believe the boosters, we could all be surfing the Net merrily at megabits per second using some form of Digital Subscriber Line (DSL).

What all the various DSL versions have in common is they're much faster than modems. They use plain old telephone lines to carry data at up to 51 megabits per second (Mbps), and they're not cheap (yet).

How does Digital Subscriber Line do its magic? Naturally, you need Digital Subscriber Line (DSL) modems at both ends of the connection. Using everything from digital signal processing to fancy compression algorithms, Digital Subscriber Line shoots data over your phone line at a much different frequency than that used by voices and standard modems. And while DSL is using your existing phone line to transmit data, it also lets you talk over it, because your voice is travelling at different frequencies than the data.

As you might suspect, getting on the DSL track requires new hardware and services from your local phone company. Although you don't have to order a new physical line, you do have to order DSL service from your local Bell (assuming your local Bell offers DSL service; many don't). You also need to buy a DSL modem and, in some cases, a splitter, which lets the phone line carry both DSL data transmissions and your voice. For Internet access, you'll need to order a DSL account from your local Internet Service Provider (America Online offers Digital Subscriber Line (DSL) access).

DSL: Not Quite 31 Flavors

The several different types of digital subscriber lines have their strengths and weaknesses. Here's a quick summary:

ADSL. Asymmetric DSL. As the name implies, downloads data faster (from 1.5 megabits to 9 megabits per second, depending on the provider) than it sends it (about 640Kbps). That rate is slow compared to some DSL methods, but downloading is still 20 times faster than with a 56Kbps modem. Chances are, the DSL your local phone company installs will be ADSL. There are two catches. You'll need a device called a splitter (which can cost up to $200) and ADSL signals can only travel about 3.4 miles. That means every three miles or so your phone company must install a repeater to push the signal along. Given such costs, your phone company may opt to provide ADSL only in limited areas.

UDSL or UADSL. Universal DSL is ADSL without splitters, but it limits download/upload speeds to 1.5Mbps and 640Kbps, respectively. Some people call this service ADSL light.

RADSL. Rate-adaptive DSL allows two DSL modems connected to one another to adjust their speed to line conditions. The connection is typically 600Kbps to 7Mbps in the download direction and 128Kbps to 1Mbps in the upload direction, but there's no distance limitation.

VDSL. Very-high-bit-rate DSL is the Godzilla of DSL technologies. It can download data at up to 52Mbps and upload it at speeds approaching 2.3Mbps. The only problem is it's limited to about 4,500 feet. That makes it a good solution for moving data in-house or perhaps bringing HDTV signals from the curb to your house.

HDSL. High-bit-rate DSL uses two twisted pairs of copper wire (instead of ADSL's single twisted pair, the configuration found in most homes) to send and receive data at 1.544Mbps or 2.048Mbps. The distance limit is about 2.5 miles. Because of the wiring requirements, HDSL is best suited for office connections, such as linking Internet servers and linking LANs in different buildings.

SDSL. Single-line DSL is as fast as HDSL, but it uses one twisted pair of copper wires. Its distance limit is about 10,000 feet, which makes it a good solution for local area networking.

Hold the Phone?

Chances are consumers will be using UDSL and businesses will opt for ADSL. But when will DSL become more widely available and affordable? At the moment, various phone companies around the country are doing trials.

For example, BellSouth has been offering ADSL in limited areas of Birmingham, Ala., for about six months now and has declared the experiment a success. (For information, see http://fast1.corp.bellsouth.net/adsl/, see Figure 1-1.)

But don't rush out and sign up just yet. For starters, make sure your Bell even offers DSL. Second, make sure your ISP offers matching service (I suspect most will go the ADSL light route). Third, make sure the DSL modem you buy is appropriate to the service you're getting: Different flavors of DSL require different modems.

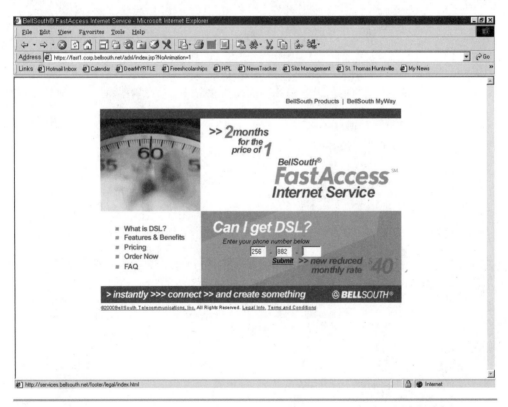

FIGURE 1-1. *Many local phone companies have DSL information pages*

Don't forget that DSL speeds can vary wildly, due to local conditions. That 52Mbps line may actually only deliver 13Mbps. Remember, too, that various standards have yet to be ironed out. Most versions of DSL are incompatible with each other. Also, no doubt there will be bugs in the DSL hardware and in Windows' attempts to work with DSL. Besides, it won't be cheap.

Consider U.S. West's (www.uswestcom.com) ADSL offerings. The company's MegaHome residential service, limited to 256Kbps, costs $40 per month. The MegaBit 7Mbps download/1Mbps upload service costs $840 per month, not counting installation or the cost of hardware.

In short, DSL isn't likely to displace ISDN, T1, or Ethernet connections just yet, but it does offer the promise of bringing multimedia—full-motion video, high-definition TV, and more—into homes and businesses. Whether that promise will be fulfilled is still unknown.

Note

> *To learn more about DSL, check out the ADSL Forum at www.adsl.com and TeleChoice at www.telechoice.com.*

Internet Appliances

Cable Internet boxes, hand-held Internet access devices, and cell phones with e-mail access are popping up all over. They can offer you convenience when traveling, or when researching in the library, but they are of limited usefulness for genealogists. The reason for my attitude is this: most such Internet appliances are only designed to *display* information to you. Saving, printing or compiling the information is limited because the memory and attachments are often limited. In light of the fact that the whole point of online genealogy is to exchange information, these one trick ponies are only half the show.

The exception to this rule is the palm-top computer (especially those models with Internet connections), which has become popular with genealogists. Besides its usefulness when it comes to note-taking, retrieving e-mail, and, if it has the proper port, uploading and downloading information to desktop or laptop computers, some surprisingly functional software for these devices is available.

Some examples are:

◆ *The GEDPalm* (http://www.ghcssoftware.com/gedpalm.htm)
which lets you browse a GEDCOM (see glossary), and could
prove very useful on a trip to the library. See Figure 1-2 for
some screen shots. The program even has its own discussion
list (http://www.rootsweb.com/ ~ jfuller/gen_mail_ software.
html#GenPalm).

◆ *MyRoots* (http://sites.netscape.net/tapperware/MyRoots/).
This is a genealogical database for the Palm Pilot.

◆ *The Pocket Family Researcher* (http://www.world4you.com/
genealogy/palmtop/), a genealogical database for Windows
CE-based machines.

◆ *Relations 2.3* (http://members.home.net/msdsoft/relations2.html),
a database configured for Newton palm devices.

A list of such programs is maintained on Cyndi's List at http://
www.cyndislist.com/software.htm#Palm.

Choosing an ISP

Like choosing a mate, you should know what you want before you
start looking for an Internet service provider. Your choice isn't final,
of course—but you don't want to hopscotch from one e-mail address
to another, either. So, go into this knowing that Internet providers are
as different as dog breeds. All of them will get you onto the Net, but
access speeds, services, software, and other goodies will vary. Before
you lay down any cash, ask yourself some basic questions:

◆ What services do I need?

◆ How often do I need them?

◆ How fast do I need them?

◆ How many hassles am I willing to put up with to save money?

◆ How much am I willing to pay?

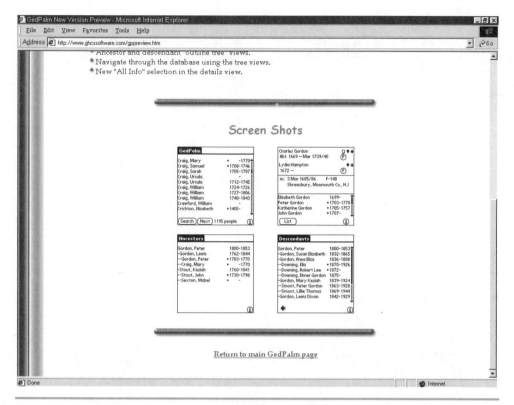

FIGURE 1-2. *GEDPalm is just one genealogy program for personal digital assistants*

Just keep in mind that there are trade-offs no matter what provider you finally choose. For example, you may find there is a price break for slower and less direct connections, or a premium necessary to dial into your account from various places in the country. In addition, you may find that companies consider support extremely expensive to provide, so if you sign up with a full service provider, it will cost a bit more.

You may save money by choosing only what you need. However, in the end you may find you need the whole shebang. While some users are happy with just electronic mail, to uncover all the genealogical treasures out there, you'll need considerably more features, such as a Web browser to fetch sound, pictures, and online animation. Consequently, you'll also need a provider that offers high-speed Internet connection.

When it comes to services, insist on the whole range: e-mail, telnet, Usenet news groups, ftp, gopher, and more—in short, everything the Internet has to offer. Even if the ISP service is austere, it should at least come with a technical support service.

Go Shopping

Make a list of two or three Internet Service Providers and contact them. Ask these questions and listen for these answers:

- ♦ Do you offer 56kbps and faster access? The answer should be yes. The faster, the better, because the genealogical information out there is immense.

- ♦ If you decide digital access is for you, ask the Internet service provider if such access is available for your neighborhood. If so, what is the cost?

Baby Steps

As I mentioned earlier, the commercial online services now offer Internet access; and for your first online forays they are probably your best bet. Once online with CompuServe, America Online, or a similar service, you'll quickly learn the ropes and familiarize yourself with what's out there, after which you may decide you want an Internet Service Provider (ISP) instead. To find a local Internet Service Provider, look in your Yellow Pages. Or, use AOL, CompuServe, or Prodigy to find one of several sites that let you search for an ISP by area, cost, or other factors. Two such sites are:

- ♦ http://www.isps.com   From a publisher called CMP Net. Lets you search for an ISP by area code, name, price, and national and toll-free services.

- ♦ http://www.thelist.internet.com   From Meckler Media. This is a buyer's guide to ISPs.

♦ For dial-up accounts, will I get busy signals if I call during prime time in the evening? In other words, how many high-speed lines does the provider have? How many customers log in on average during prime time? (And test them on their answer: dial them up just after supper!) Their response should be that you can get on any time you want; they have enough lines or enough ISDN capability to handle their current customer base.

♦ Do you offer anything else besides Internet access, such as BBS echoes and file collections? The answer should be yes; this is part of support.

♦ Can I use a graphical third-party front end like Netscape to access your system? Do you provide this software? Both answers should be yes. If the first answer is no, then you have to deal with a text-oriented UNIX system, and the provider should supply a written manual. If there's no manual or menu system, this should be a really cheap service.

♦ Which message readers can I use with Usenet newsgroups? The answer should be a client that runs on your machine, that they can provide you. If the answer is "pine," "rn," or "nn," beware! These are arcane UNIX newsreaders, text-based and a real pain to use. Windows and Mac-based user-friendly readers like Free Agent or Outlook Express are better; new browsers such as Microsoft Internet Explorer and Netscape Navigator include newsreaders as part of the program.

♦ What's the capacity of private e-mail boxes? Here, the answer should be at least 100K of space. Bigger is better. If you subscribe to even a few genealogical mail lists and newsgroups, your mailbox could be stuffed quickly. Even worse, if your mailbox is limited to 100 messages, you might miss important mail.

♦ Will my connection be SLIP or PPP? PPP is better: it's newer, faster, and more reliable than SLIP, but if SLIP is all you can get, take it.

♦ Do you provide access to all Usenet newsgroups, or just a selection? The answer should be all. This is very important when it comes to some of the more arcane genealogical newsgroups.

♦ When do you schedule downtime for maintenance? How heavily loaded is the system? Good luck getting straight answers to either question, but they should at least reassure you that downtimes will be announced in advance somehow. For the real scoop, nose around Internet discussion areas and ask users of the service for the low-down.

♦ Do you have Points of Presence (POPs) across the country, so if I'm on the road, I can still reach you with a local (or toll-free) call? You hope the answer is "Yes." But reality may dictate you get Internet accounts from two different providers—one for home, and one for the road.

♦ How do you charge? A flat monthly fee for unlimited connect time is the ideal answer. Second best: a flat fee with a generous allotment of online time and a low hourly fee ($1 to $3) for use beyond that allotment. Beware of hourly based connect charges, which can add up in a hurry.

Really smart Internet Service Providers offer a complete manual, training classes, and online news featuring phone number changes, service enhancements, and other information of interest to users.

With prices ranging from $10 a month for telnet access to $260 a month for an always-open direct line, there's something out there for everyone. The trick is knowing what you want, asking tough questions of prospective Internet providers, and finding a company that will give you what you need. Don't forget to compare the answers to these questions with the national Internet Service Providers, and to check up on how prices have changed every few months.

Wrapping Up

To get online you'll need the following:

♦ A computer (with lots of disk space!)

♦ A connection device, whether a modem or a digital device

♦ An Internet service provider

♦ The correct software

Coincidentally, the correct software just happens to be the subject of the next chapter.

Chapter 2

Software

Once you have your hardware in place, and you know how you are going to connect, you need to look at your software. As noted before, many Internet service providers (ISPs) include software as part of the package. AOL, CompuServe, Prodigy, Mindspring, Netcom and most other national Internet service providers have front-end software that includes the communications software, browser, ftp, mail and other programs you need.

The software you use to access the World Wide Web will often be called "clients." These programs send signals to other computers, called "servers," and instruct them to display files and information to you, or run programs for you. The resulting display may be e-mail, a Web page, or a GEDCOM you want to download. The program the clients run may be a search engine or a chat site.

What Makes the Web Tick

What makes a modem work is your communications software. Think of it as the inner workings of a watch. The watch displays the time, which to you is the whole point of the thing; but to a watchmaker, the workings determine the value of the watch. So it is with the software: mostly, you just want the clients to contact the servers and tell you what you want to know. Nevertheless, you also should know a little bit about how these things tick.

There are two basic types of communications programs: serial communications programs and TCP/IP stacks. The former constitutes older technology that was used for dialing into Bulletin Board systems and some commercial online services. You can still find it on the market today, and it works very well for direct linking with another computer, if, for instance, you want to send your data files to your cousin directly, not over the Internet.

TCP/IP, on the other hand, is the chief communications format for the Internet, proving to be the standard way of connecting one computer to another. Windows 95 with the Plus! package has a TCP/IP stack built into it, while Windows 98 has it without the Plus! package. There are versions for DOS, Macintosh, and many other platforms, too. An example of using TCP/IP in Windows 98 is in Figure 2-1.

In many cases, you won't have to worry about finding communications software for your modem; it will find you. Most of the commercial services have front-end software to connect to their service.

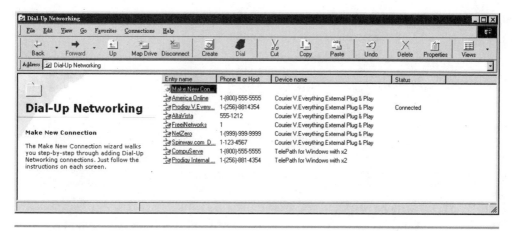

FIGURE 2-1. *Dial-Up Networking in Windows 98 is handled through your TCP/IP stack*

America Online, CompuServe Information Service, Prodigy Internet, and other ISPs will usually supply you with the software you need.

Find a good Internet service provider, as outlined in the previous chapter. The best ones will include a package of software, manuals, and handholding to get you started.

Browsers

Ten years ago, the Internet was a lot harder to use. For each function (or "Internet service") you needed to know about a different program, with a different set of arcane commands. Just learning the jargon was a challenge.

To prove my point, here are a few examples: To transfer a file, you used file transfer protocol or "ftp." To find the file you wanted to get by ftp, you might use a search program called "archie." To run a computer on the Internet by remote control, you used "telnet." To look at documents on a system, say, a university's information system, you might use a menu-based display program called a "gopher." To search the gophers all over the world for a specific document, you might use "veronica," or if you just wanted to search one gopher, you'd use "jughead." Then, if you wanted to talk to someone about it, you used your "chat" client to contact a server for an "Internet relay chat" session.

You get the idea. Still, once you got the hang of it, using the Internet was so fun it was almost addicting.

Finally, a Swiss research group, CERN, decided to try to pull all these different services into one interface, with a single protocol. At first, their new program, called a "browser," was text-based, too, just as the entire Internet was. Very soon, however, graphic interfaces were added, making the browsers even easier to use.

As a result, for most people today, "the Internet" is the "World Wide Web," an attempt to link information all over the world via online resources. Of course, genealogists are involved in this, too!

Browser-Speak

Even though the World Wide Web has made the Internet easier to use, the jargon has not gone away. The Web has its own lexicon, and these terms can be confusing. Here are a few expressions you should know before you get going:

HTML is the language that turns a text document into a WWW-browsable one. Many shareware and commercial products have popped up in the past year to help you create HTML documents, but with a good handbook on the subject, you can create HTML code in any word or text processor.

URL means "uniform resource locator." It is basically an address on the World Wide Web with the format access method://machine.name/directory/file. Access method can be ftp, http, gopher or some other Internet service. The machine name is the computer that holds what you are after. The directory and file are the location of the object on that computer; if you just type something.com, you will get a default file called index.html.

To use a URL, you either click on a link, or you type the URL in your browser's address box. This will cause your browser to load the page, or as it's said in Web-speak, "go" to a site.

A page is a set of files presented to you in the browser in one display. The basic page itself is written in HTML, and if you looked at it (using the menu View and the selection Source in your browser), you would see simple ASCII text, with embedded commands to tell the browser how things should look to you. Some text will be designated a "headline," while other text might tell the browser to show a picture in a certain place. The most important part of this coding scheme, called "HTTP" for hypertext transfer protocol, is the link.

A link is a pointer to another file, and the term for linking files is hypertext. Hypertext is a system of embedding pointers in text, presented to you usually as underlined colored words or a picture, that will prompt the browser to display another file, either on that same site, or somewhere else on the Internet. When the cursor changes from an arrow to a hand, you are pointing your mouse at a link.

If you click on a link, you will be taken to that document, perhaps at another site. Depending on the type of file chosen, the link may take you to a sound bite, if you have a sound card. Or a picture, if you have VGA graphics.

(WARNING: sound and pictures across the Internet are still VERY SLOW on dial-up connections as of this writing!)

What we love about browsers is that they combine many Internet services: sending and receiving e-mail, reading and posting to Usenet, or transferring files with ftp and gopher.

Which Browser Should I Use?

I'm often asked, "Which is the best browser?" I can only reply that this is like asking, "Which is the best car?" It all depends on your taste, habits, and budget.

The current leaders in the browser wars are Netscape Navigator and Microsoft Internet Explorer, and entire books are devoted to helping you get the most out of them. The major online services and Internet service providers have lined up with one or the other for their customers to use.

Microsoft Internet Explorer is free, but it makes major changes to your operating system and therefore sometimes causes trouble with other programs. Netscape Navigator is not free (about $40 as of this writing) but it has a nice user interface, is easy to use and is the most popular. Others such as Opera, Mosaic and Ariadne are less feature-packed, but they are free and very easy to use, and sometimes much faster. See the following sidebar titled *Other Browsers* for information on these.

Netscape Navigator and Microsoft Internet Explorer are chock full of features but they are also what I call "hardware hogs": they need super-duper hardware and lots of disk space to run. If you have an older or smaller machine (in terms of RAM and hard disk drive size), check out some other browsers in the sidebar. They have fewer features, but

Other Browsers

CELLO Cello was around before Mozilla (aka Netscape Navigator) was an egg. It's a nice little Windows browser, but it's strictly no-nonsense. Cello has exactly three buttons on the toolbar: Up (or Back in other browsers), Stop, and Home. You can choose the font for displaying Web pages and other basic preferences, but you can forget about colored text, frames, plug-ins, Java, and all that. Cello doesn't support forms, either, so you can't respond to online surveys or register with Web sites. And to add helper applications, you have to manually edit its INI file with Notepad.

Still in version 1.01 (it hasn't changed since 1994), Cello may be showing its age. But if you want to zip around the Web without stumbling over multimedia, this is your program. And naturally, Cello is light on your system. It needs about 4MB of RAM, takes up just 1MB of hard disk space, and can even run on a 386SX PC. Try that with Navigator or Internet Explorer. You can download Cello free from Cornell University at http://www.law.cornell.edu/cello/cellotop.html/.

MOSAIC NCSA's Mosaic was one of the first graphical browsers, and it's still one of the best. But like Cello, Mosaic is lean and mean, requiring just a 386 SX PC with 4MB of RAM to run. It takes up about 2.5MB of disk space. You can download it from http://www.ncsa.uiuc.edu/newtest/index.ncsa.html?Info = http://www.ncsa.uiuc.edu/SDG/Software/Mosaic/NCSAMosaicHome.html,Nav = /newtest/ncsaNav.html,navIcon = ncsaNav,infoIcon = infoNode for Windows, Macintosh and Xwindow systems.

Mosaic doesn't use plug-ins, and setting programs to view pictures, play sounds and so forth requires editing Mosaic's INI file. But Mosaic can be personalized in so many ways, from display colors to sounds for events, it's hard to beat. Mosaic lets you cache Web pages to disk or RAM and define which MIME types (pictures, sounds) should be used. Mosaic also lets you chat and exchange files with other Mosaic users via a host Web site, which is great for training and demonstrations!

Mosaic can even retrieve Web pages for you automatically. Using the Autosurf feature, you simply enter an URL and Mosaic will follow a series of links from that page, storing each page in the cache. You control the number of pages downloaded, how many levels of links are followed, and whether Mosaic retrieves pages from the current server only or moves on to others as well. You can download a whole Web site while you're at lunch and view the pages offline when you get back. Mosaic's built-in, stand-alone viewer is an ideal way to open HTML files stored on your hard disk.

OPERA   Opera 2.1 is a $30 shareware browser that supports tables, forms, frames, background sounds, video, and other Web doodads but not Navigator plug-ins. Opera can open several Web pages in separate windows at once, letting you cascade the windows or view them side by side. You can set preferences for everything from turning off frames to sounds for "file not found" messages and other events. You can even have Opera display links as raised text or 3-D icons. Opera also has a nice, built-in, mail-out function. But best of all, Opera is fast, even at the most graphics-intensive sites. Opera will run on a 386SX with 8MB of memory or better and takes up about 1.5MB on your hard drive. It's available for Windows and Windows 95 in Norwegian, Swedish, Spanish, and English. You can download it at http://opera.nta.no/download.html.

ARIADNE   This 32-bit browser for Windows supports the Cyrillic alphabet and has loads of features you can use right here in the United States, including built-in e-mail, page caching, and slick bookmark functions. Ariadne also supports Microsoft Internet Explorer extensions such as background music and scrolling banners. Unfortunately, it doesn't use Navigator plug-ins. And for Java support, you have to install Sun's Java Development Kit.

Ariadne is fast and seems fairly stable on my system. It takes up about 2MB of hard disk space and uses 4MB of RAM. You can download a free preview version at http://www.open-sft.com/ariadne/.

And that's not all! New browsers appear regularly. To keep up with what's new, haunt The Ultimate Collection of Winsock Software (TUCOWS) at www.tucows.com and Stroud's Consummate Winsock Apps page at www.cwsapps.com. Stroud's also tracks new Mac software, check www.icorp.net/stroud/macwww.html.

take up much less room on your hard disk and in your RAM. For a comprehensive list, visit http://www.tucows.com and search for "browser."

My advice is to test-drive a few of them (most allow you to try before you buy) and see which one suits you best.

A Guided Tour of a Browser

DearMYRTLE's page is shown in Figure 2-2 in Netscape Navigator Version 6, and in Microsoft Internet Explorer 5 in Figure 2-3. To see this page in your browser, type this in the address box:

http://www.dearmyrtle.com

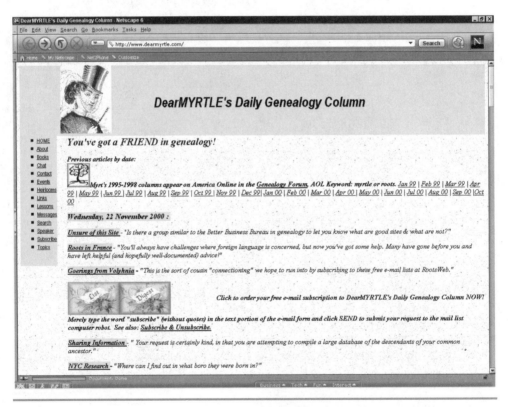

FIGURE 2-2. *This is a typical page in the Netscape Navigator browser*

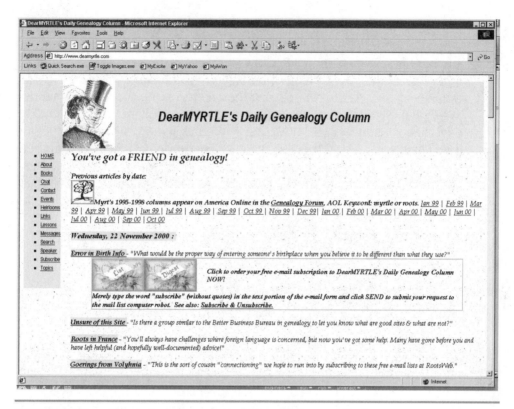

FIGURE 2-3. *This is the same page in Microsoft Internet Explorer*

You can also use the menu option File | Open and type the URL in the dialog box.

You'll note the differences in one browser's rendition from the other's; this is something to consider when you start publishing on the Web, as discussed later in this chapter.

Let's look at the Netscape screen in Figure 2-2. First, you can see the browser's title bar at the top of the screen. This tells you the title of the Web page you're viewing. The title is often the same as the page's first headline, but it can be different. When you save a Web page's address (URL) in your bookmark file, the name associated with the URL is usually taken from the title. Sadly, many Web developers don't realize this and name their pages something uninformative such as My Page or Link.

Next is the browser's menu bar. Most browsers will have File, Edit, View, Go, Bookmarks (or "Hotlist" or "Favorites"), Options, and maybe a few others. Usually under File you can save or open a page, among other commands. Edit menu options allow you to search for a word or save something to the clipboard; generally the same sort of commands in any Edit Windows menu. View menu options will let you re-load the page or see details of the HTML. Go is the navigation command; clicking it will give you a list of the sites you've visited today, or a box to input a specific URL. Bookmark is for remembering the URL of good sites. The Tasks menu lets you switch to other Netscape components such as the Mail program. The Help menu gives you access to online documentation about the program.

Below the menu bar is the toolbar. Most browser toolbars let you move backward and forward through Web pages, reload a page, travel to a home page, print a page, stop the current load action, and so on. They are simply one-click shortcuts to the commands in the menu bar.

At the end of this toolbar is the Netscape icon. Whenever you're loading a page, you'll see an animation of comets raining down on the poor little Netscape planet. If you double click the N, you'll be taken immediately to Netscape's home page at http://home.netscape.com.

On this URL box, and on its far left is the Bookmarks Icon. Click this, and a menu will pop up allowing you to save the location's address so you can come back later. Afterward, you can create different folders in order to sort and organize your bookmarks. Next to it is a small bookmark icon. Click and drag this to your desktop and a bookmark is created at the spot where you released the mouse button; this creates what's called a "shortcut" to that site (at least in Windows 95 and 98). Double-click that shortcut and your browser automatically takes you to the page. Microsoft Internet Explorer has a similar icon that does the same thing.

Take special note of the Location box, where you actually enter a Web site's address. If you need to copy a URL to your clipboard, you can just double-click, press the CONTROL key at the same time you press the "c" key (expressed as CONTROL + C), and it's ready to be pasted elsewhere. Are your fingers tired of typing http://www? Just type the unique part of the URL (such as genealogy.com) and the browser will fill in the first part. Type in an FTP site like ftp.symantec.com, and the browser will insert the necessary ftp://. If you click the down arrow on the right side of the Location box, you'll see a list of the last 15 or so

URLs typed in this way. This feature is handy if you can't remember that neat place you visited yesterday. Place the pointer in the Location box and press the DOWN ARROW key. You'll hop to the next URL in the list.

The next toolbar is your Personal toolbar. You can click and drag bookmarks to it for ready reference, *and* it comes with pages Netscape thinks are cool, worthwhile sites. For example, NetSearch takes you to a page of Web search engines. The People button, meanwhile, transports you to a form for searching online white pages, while Software takes you to the Navigator software site where a new version of the program is posted almost weekly! (Microsoft Internet Explorer has similar buttons.) Should you wish to change any of the buttons, you can always delete the buttons on this toolbar that came with the program and add your own.

Below this toolbar, and taking up most of the screen, is Netscape's active window, where the current Web page is displayed.

Finally, let's go to the bottom of the screen. At far right at the bottom is a little open lock. In Navigator, this means the page you're viewing has no built-in security. That's not a problem in this case, because you're not filling out a form or providing any information. If the page had a form, the little open lock would indicate that someone else could see your answers. When a secure site is being viewed, you'll see a solid blue line at the top of the screen and a closed lock. Every browser notes security in different ways. Get to know yours well.

Below the display part, you'll find the status line. This line tells you how much of a page the browser has loaded. Move your mouse pointer over links on a page and you'll see the associated URLs displayed here, too. If the site's developer is versed in Java, a message may even scroll across this box like a ticker tape. Next to the status line is a "thermometer" bar, another visual cue that shows how long you have to wait for an operation to finish.

Over to the far left at the bottom of the screen are icons that take you to other parts of Netscape Communicator like the mail program, HTML editor, and so on.

FTP

File Transfer Protocol (ftp) is how files are sent and received from many places on the Internet. When receiving a file, say a photograph or a program, your browser handles that just fine. No worries. However, if you want to upload (send) a file, you should use an ftp program. Some browsers can handle sending, but an ftp program does it faster and easier.

Programs for ftp abound on the Internet. Some of the more popular ones include CuteFTP, ActifFTP, LeechFTP. My favorite has always been WS_FTP. You can try the limited edition for free if it's for home, educational, or non-profit use. A screen shot of the program is shown in Figure 2-4.

Why I love it: WS_FTP makes downloading files from an Internet FTP server or maintaining your Web site easy. You can select multiple files and/or directories and transfer them with a single click. WS_FTP lets you tell it what local directory and remote directory to log into for each connection by default. It automatically keeps a log that you can

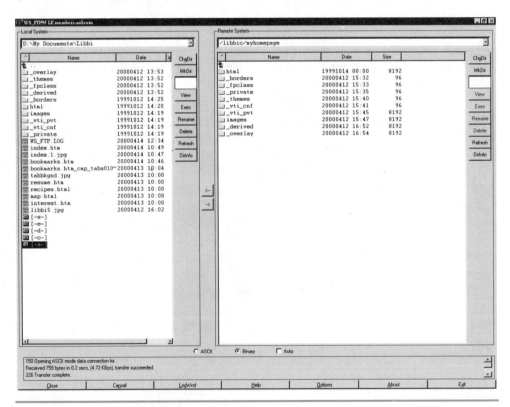

FIGURE 2-4. *WS_FTP is free for home use*

save and view to see if there was a problem during a transfer, or just to remind yourself what you sent and what you got. Many of the display features can be personalized, such as directory sorting and window layout. It comes with a ready-to-use list of popular public FTP sites, and adding new ones is as simple as filling out a form. The Limited Edition doesn't offer some advanced features (e.g., resuming interrupted downloads), but it's free to qualifying users, easy to use, and well documented. It's what I use every day.

To set up a connection, click the button on the bottom left which says "Open" before you connect to an FTP site and "Close" while you are connected.

Type in the address of the site, for example, ftp.cac.psu.edu and the opening directory, space/genealogy/ftp/. Then enter the appropriate directory on your machine for the default on the left side.

Note

Create a directory called "DOWNLOAD" and put all your downloaded files there. Then run a virus-check on any files before you open them.

For an anonymous ftp site, your e-mail address will be automatically entered as the password. Now all you have to do is highlight any files or folders and click the arrow to show which direction they should go: left, to bring them to your machine; right, to send yours there. I've taught people to use WS_FTP in less than 15 minutes.

E-mail

Reading mail is the biggest part of online life. Some of the best information, and even friendships, come through e-mail. If you are on any Internet service provider, a mail reader makes life much easier. The mail readers in browsers tend to have fewer features than the stand-alone mail clients. In order to get the most out of electronic mail, or e-mail, you need to get a few techniques under your belt.

Filters

The programs I'll be reviewing next all have the ability to let you filter your e-mail. This is a very important feature. A filter is an action you want the mail program to take when a message matches certain conditions. You can have an e-mail program reply to, copy, move or destroy a message based on such things as the sender, the subject line, or words found in the text. You can have the e-mail program do all that before you read your mail, or even before the e-mail gets downloaded from the Internet service provider's mail server.

If you have never dealt with e-mail, this may seem like a lot of "bells and whistles," but believe me, when you start getting involved in really active mail lists (see Chapter 5), you're going to want to be able to sort your mail by geography, surname, and time period, at least!

Furthermore, there will be some people you just don't want to hear from. You can have your mail filters set up to simply delete mail from those people. Which brings up the next important topic, spam protection.

Spam Protection

Long ago (ok, less than 10 years ago) only academics and researchers used the Internet, and they liked it that way. They didn't want the general public and, most of all, general businesses to get to play on the Web. Once the Internet was opened to the public, they warned, the demons of advertising would hound us. Ads would flood our mailboxes, clog the bandwidth with their shilling and hawking, and make the Internet much less useful and fun. Well, we opened Pandora's box anyway and the result was junk e-mail. The old "netheads" were right after all, and the "spammers" are now upon us.

"Spammers" is the Net slang term for people who send unsolicited e-mail to advertise. "Spammers" get their name from an old Monty Python skit where people in a restaurant are prevented from having a normal conversation because some folks at the next table insist on loudly praising Spam. The uninvited e-mail advertisements you receive are often called "spam," because, as in the skit, they rudely interrupt you during more enjoyable activities. The Hormel folks, understandably, don't like the term and prefer the more accurate and official "unsolicited bulk e-mail," to describe this annoyance. Let's call it UBE for short.

UBE could constitute endless messages regarding get-rich-quick ideas, pyramid schemes, vitamins, you name it. Sometimes the pitch is disguised as a newsletter, and might include some bogus return address. But whatever the guise, the purpose is the same: They are using your paid online account for their own advertising.

Why You Get Spam

Any time you post a message to a Usenet newsgroup, use a public chat room on America Online, CompuServe, or the Internet, or supply an online service with your profile, the UBE guys are there collecting your e-mail address and any other information they can find. Then they sort the addresses and sell them, causing you to get junk e-mail.

Naturally, they know that not everyone will be pleased to hear from them, so they disguise themselves with bogus From: and Reply to: lines. You can try to reply and "remove" or "unsubscribe" yourself from their lists, but it seldom works. The return addresses either don't exist or aren't designed to receive mail. To reach the culprits and get off their lists, you have to do some detective work.

What to Do

Frankly, I'm intensely opposed to this noxious form of telemarketing (can you tell?). The first step is for everyone who uses the Internet to write to Congress and have this practice stopped. If Washington can pass a law controlling junk faxes, why can't it do the same for junk e-mail?

Second, learn to protect yourself. One extreme measure would be to never use chat, post to Usenet, use a forum on AOL or CompuServe or a bulletin board on Prodigy, or post your member profile online. But then, online life would be pretty dull, wouldn't it?

A less harsh solution is to create two e-mail accounts: one public and one private. You use the public one for Usenet, chat, anonymous FTP, and so on. The other you keep hidden like an unlisted phone number, only giving it out to people you really want to hear from. Then all you have to do is check your private e-mail box whenever you feel like it, and ask your Internet service provider to delete any mail that comes to the public one.

The Legislative Front

UBE is sent by folks who claim it's their First Amendment right to use a service you paid for to advertise their stuff to you. Congress is currently considering that claim, and whether they can protect us from these twerps. You can keep abreast of it at the Center For Democracy and Technology's "Junk E-mail" pages, URL: http://www.junkemail.org/bills/.

If you use an e-mail program like Eudora or Pegasus, you can alternatively filter out all the junk. Both programs can, based on a message's address, subject line, or body text, drop e-mail into specific folders. Whenever I get junk e-mail, I copy the address, header, and any catch phrase like "money-making opportunity" to a filter. The next time I get a message from the spammer, it's dumped into my Trash folder and deleted. (In Eudora, for example, select Tools|Filters, enter the e-mail address, check the Transfer To box and select Trash.) For some suggestions on who to add to your twit filter, see the sidebar *"Libbi's Spammer Twit List."* Another good source for names and strategies (some of which I suspect aren't quite legal) is the Internet Black List at www-math.uni-paderborn.de/∼axel/BL/#spam.

And what about America Online and CompuServe users? AOL can now automatically intercept incoming e-mail from known UBE senders, thanks to a recent court decision. The controls are set by default. To turn them off, use the keyword: PREFERRED MAIL. Of course, AOL's action keeps out only so much UBE. If you get junk e-mail from an AOL account, forward it to TOSSPAM. AOL's staff will tell that person to stop sending you e-mail. You can also control what you get by entering the keyword: MAIL CONTROLS. Click on the icon that says "Set Up Mail Controls" and choose the screen name, clicking Edit. The Mail Controls window gives you several options, the first three being:

1. Allow all e-mail

2. Allow e-mail only from AOL members

3. Block all e-mail

I don't use these because the first is too open, and the second and third are too restrictive. Plus, many UBE senders use AOL screen names. "Allow e-mail from all AOL members, and only from the listed Internet domains and addresses" is the one I use, because I have to be able to receive e-mail from AOL's ever-changing public relations staff. "Allow e-mail from the listed AOL member, Internet domains and addresses" is the best choice for most people. The drawbacks are that you are limited to 100 such names, and this will filter out e-mail based on the From: field (not the subject or the text of the message). Still, I have found it workable. You can insert a specific address like Libbic@prodigy.net in the list. In addition, if you know a certain domain (such as rootsweb.com or ancestry.com) will only send you mail you want, you can simply put the part of the address after the @ and any mail from that ISP will get through. You can even put in a top-level domain; for example, any address that ends in .gov or .edu is allowed on my list. I figure if I receive any UBE from a government or educational institution, I can quickly report it and have it taken care of!

The last choice, "Block e-mail from the listed AOL members, Internet domains and addresses" is totally useless because of the 100-name limit on the list. Considering there are hundreds of thousands of UBE senders out there, this would be like trying to plug a fire hydrant with a golf tee.

CompuServe doesn't offer as many options for blocking UBE, but it's always been against the rules for CIS members to send advertising to other CIS members. If you do, CIS can terminate your account. As for non-CIS mail, you can set your e-mail preference to never receive or send any Internet mail, but that's hardly a solution.

Desperate Measures

Is junk e-mail still deluging you? You can try to track down the culprits, even though they try to disguise their true whereabouts. Don't look at the "From" or even the "Reply To" lines. Look at the lines that say "Comments: Authenticated sender is:" or "Received," see Figure 2-5. These lines will tell you the route of the message from your mailbox back to its origin. Once you have a domain name (like yxt2@srdinc.com), you at least know which ISP the message originated on.

```
Headers ------------------------------
Return-Path: <yxt2@srdinc.com>
Received: from  rly-yc04.mx.aol.com (rly-yc04.mail.aol.com [172.18.149.36])
by air-yc05.mail.aol.com (v56.24) with SMTP; Sat, 06 Feb 1999 18:40:50 -0500
Received: from ntserver1.agency1 ([204.95.231.66])
by rly-yc04.mx.aol.com (8.8.8/8.8.5/AOL-4.0.0)
with ESMTP id QAA04730;  Sat, 6 Feb 1999 16:59:33 -0500 (EST)
Date: Sat, 6 Feb 1999 16:59:33 -0500 (EST)
From: yxt2@srdinc.com
Message-Id: 199902062159.QAA04730@rly-yc04.mx.aol.com
Received: from 501 (hil-qbu-ppv-vty33.as.wcom.NET
[209.154.56.33]) by ntserver1.agency1 with SMTP
(Microsoft Exchange Internet Mail Service Version 5.5.1960.3)
id 1K1TF9GW; Sat, 6 Feb 1999 16:58:27 -0500
To: ntnalv3s@aol.comSubject: Out to lunch
```

FIGURE 2-5.   *Look carefully at e-mail headers to track down a message's origin.*
Then complain to the Internet service provider that it was sent on

Send a message to the ISP using the format postmaster@provider.com. Politely explain that you don't want to receive any more messages from the perpetrator. Do this consistently, and the UBE sender's privileges might be revoked.

Note

Do not insult or scold the Internet service provider. It may not know the client is using the account this way. Assume the Internet service provider is on your side when you write.

At the moment, there is no surefire, legal way to shut these scoundrels up as they fill our e-mail boxes, clog the already crowded Internet, and cost us extra toll charges. Although recent court decisions indicate more controls are coming, who knows when they will ever come to pass. Instead, be prepared. Use the strategies outlined above and as a result your e-mail box should have less digital clutter.

Note

Two FAQs on this subject are posted on the Web. The E-mail Abuse FAQ is at http://members.aol.com/emailfaq/emailfaq.html#5b. The Net-Abuse FAQ is at http://www.cybernothing.org/faqs/net-abuse-faq.html.

Libbi's Spammer Twit List

Which junk e-mailers should you filter out? Well, each time you get a piece of unsolicited bulk e-mail, add that sender's entire domain (what's after the @) to your filter list. To help you, here's a starter list.

- ◆ 1Cust40.tnt2.sdg1.da.uu.net
- ◆ 202.188.95.1
- ◆ 205.176.181.63
- ◆ 212.250.196.101

- aaaflyhi@aol.com
- advanix.net
- aravinthan.force9.co.uk
- a-z-marketing.com
- bball@exchangecom.net
- brichards@mailexcite.com
- cb-s.co.uk
- chinachannel.net
- cn.net
- cuffs.com
- cyberemag.com
- cyberfiber.net
- cyberpr0m0.co
- cyberpr0m0ti0ns.com
- cyberprom0.com
- cyberpromo.com
- 194.202.128.76
- cyberpromotions.com
- dial-access.att.net
- dialup-171.apc.net
- emailers1@juno.com
- foticomm.com
- Friendsnnn@aol.com
- globalfn.com
- gothere.net

- hosted2u.net
- inetsvs.com
- inter.net.il
- jeffg@crushnet.com
- keyholding.co.uk
- legend.co.uk
- listnet.net
- m-22569@mailbox.swip.net
- metronet.de
- mike1@est1-rave.co.uk
- netseek@dial.pipex.com
- news.newswire.microsoft.com
- nnn@nnn.com
- online.sh.cn
- p4a@juno.com
- pacificcoasts.net
- postnet.com
- progress.com
- propertyworld.co.uk
- renee358@hotmail.com
- rhaney19@ally.ios.com
- rsdesigns.force9.co.uk
- save-net.com
- SIMPLE1GIL@aol.com 550
- smartwall.taldem.com

- sosglb.com

- srdinc.com

- stlnet.com

- sub-mit-it.com

- tankards.com

- tas74883@yahoo.com

- tech-center.com

- telcom.co.nz

- telintar.net.ar

- top-10.com

- UCanDoItac@aol.com

- userk663.uk.uudial.com

- usr11-dialup6.mta.198.3.99.199.excite.com

- web-style.com

- xlg02@dial.pipex.com

- yougotmail.com

- youvegotmail.com

- zeus.scolo.net

File Attachments and Formats

Judging from the comments of my readers, nothing causes more gnashing of teeth to new Internet users than file attachments. You get a message that looks like gobbledygook, or has some filename like foobar.mim, and you don't know what to do with it.

The Internet is so big and powerful that we sometimes lose sight of its limitations. For example, e-mail—the Net's original reason for being—is limited to transmitting the 128 alphanumeric characters (the ones on your keyboard) of the basic ASCII set. Just about every computer, large and small, uses ASCII, which is why e-mail (and Usenet newsgroups) are limited to these characters.

Yet how does one send the photograph of an ancestor to a newsgroup on Usenet? The secret has to do with the processes of "encoding" and "decoding." Like Little Orphan Annie's Secret Decoder Ring, encoding schemes turn binary files (such as .EXE files, graphics, spreadsheets, and formatted documents) into strings of text that, when properly decoded on the other end, resume their original form.

The downside: An encoded file can be 25 to 100 percent larger than the original file.

There are many different encoding schemes used on the Internet. As with file transfer protocols, you must know which scheme your correspondent used so you can properly decode the file you've received. The key schemes and their file extensions follow.

♦ UUENCODE (.UUE, .UU) is one such scheme; its name comes from "UNIX to UNIX Encoding," and it's a very common, very old method. UUencoded files are deciphered with UUDECODE.

♦ XXENCODE (.XXE). This is a slightly different version of UUENCODE, created for later versions of UNIX.

♦ BINHEX (.HQX, .HEX) originated on the Mac, but you can now find BINHEX encoders and decoders for the PC.

♦ MIME (.MME, .MM). The Multipurpose Internet Mail Extensions scheme is the new kid on the block, and unlike its peers, it specifies the kind of file being sent. This allows many e-mail and Web browser programs to recognize what's in a certain MIMEd file and display its contents with the appropriate helper application.

When you receive a coded file, how do you translate it? If you're using a fairly decent e-mail program like Outlook, Pegasus, or Eudora, or you are using AOL, and you get a MIME or BINHEX file, you usually don't have to do anything—the software's built-in decoders will do the job for you. However, if you get a file that's been coded with another format, you'll need a third-party program to do the dirty work for you. I've noted some sources later in this section.

"But wait," says a reader. "I sometimes get a coded file that has another coded file within in it. In my e-mail program, I see this huge ream of nonsense text. What do I do?" Look closely, and you'll see instructions in this mess of text: probably the words "copy below this line" and "copy above this line."

Select the text between these lines and paste it into a word processor. Save the file as text only, with the .UUE file extension (because this is a UUENCODED file). Then run a Uudecode program, and the hidden file will emerge.

> ### Note
>
> *Sometimes a large UUENCODED file is split into a number of e-mail messages, usually labeled FILE1.UUE, FILE2.UUE, and so on. Carefully cut and paste the contents of these files, from the first message to the last, into a single file. Then follow the steps in the text.*

Which programs decode (and encode) attached files? You can search the shareware sites for the latest offerings. Two I recommend:

♦ UUE.ZIP (at http://shareware.cnet.com/shareware/0-13628-500-1268763.html?tag = st.sw.13628_501_1.lst.titledetail) is free, simple, fast, and small. It doesn't do anything but deal with UUENCODE.

♦ WinZIP (at http://www.winzip.com) costs $29 but handles many kinds of files, including Uuencode, but also most compression formats. It's worth the money.

Internet Mail Clients

Mail reading programs (also known as "clients") are everywhere, and some do quite a bit of fancy stuff. But to get you started I recommend you try one the following:

♦ Eudora 4.3

♦ Pegasus

♦ Microsoft Outlook 2000

Eudora 4.3 (http://www.eudora.com)

Qualcomm rolled out Eudora 4.3 in early 2000. This newest version lets you choose to pay for all its powerful features, use them for free (by putting up with some ads), or install an ad-free "lite" version (see Figure 2-6). If you're a Eudora Pro 4.2 user, the update is available at www.eudora.com/pro_email/updaters.html. Eudora works great with the default settings, but you can tweak the program to do many things automatically. Here's how.

Scheduled Pick-Ups Eudora's simplest automation feature is checking mail at regular intervals. You can set this option during installation, but if you missed it, select Tools | Options and click the Checking Mail icon in the left scrolling window. Type a number in the "Check for mail every [ ] minute(s)" box.

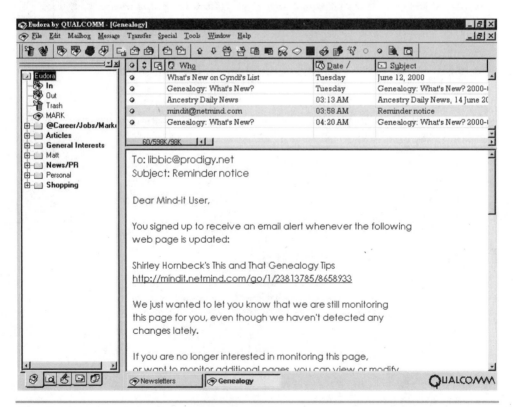

FIGURE 2-6. *Eudora is available for free, with ads, or for $49 without ads*

Eudora can also do the dialing when checking mail. Select Tools |
Options, scroll down to the Internet Dialup icon. Select "Have Eudora
connect using dial-up networking," and pick the proper connection in
the drop-down Entry box. To have Eudora hang up, check the "Hang-up
after receiving and sending" option. The "Close connection on exit"
option will disconnect the Internet connection every time you close
the program.

The Many Faces of Eudora   Many users have more than one e-mail
account. As long as the accounts are POP or IMAP compliant, Eudora
can check them for mail. Each account's information is stored as a
"personality;" the dominant personality is the one you set up during
install. To add others, click Tools | Personalities. Right-click in the
Personalities window to the left and choose New. A wizard walks you
through the steps to create a new account (or personality), but you must
enter your mail server, login name, and password information manually.
If you have the information stored in another mail program, such as
Outlook or Netscape, Eudora can import the settings. Just click the
second radio button in the wizard's opening window.

Once the personality is created, modify its settings by right-clicking
it and choosing Properties. If you don't want to automatically check this
account's mail, uncheck the Check Mail box. You can also set default
stationery and a default signature for this personality here.

Custom Stationery and Signatures   A signature is a bit of text or
graphics that you append to outgoing messages. I have three: one with
my full contact info, one with just my name, and one with a business
signature. Once saved, they're listed in a drop-down box in Eudora's
toolbar. The default listing is < none >.

However, you can assign an account its own signature. When I
compose a message with that personality (return address), for example,
the signature will appear unless I choose a different one or "none" in
the drop-down box. To create a different signature, right-click on the
Personality (click on the little tab that has a face on it in the left pane,
where you usually see the mailboxes). Choose Properties, select Default
Signature from the drop-down box, choose the signature, and click OK.

Stationery is basically a standard message that you can save and use
over and over, like a template. To create stationery, select Tools |
Stationery. Right-click anywhere inside the small Stationery window to
the left and choose New. Eudora opens an e-mail message-like

composition window. Enter the desired text, fill in the headers (Subject, CC, etc.,) as you would with an e-mail message, and set any options in the toolbar (such as return receipt).

When you're done, choose File | Save As Stationery. The default file name is whatever you entered in the Subject line, but you can enter a different file name. Click Save to save the file in your Stationery folder. To use the stationery when creating a message, choose Message | New Message With and click the name of the stationery. You can also use a filter to reply to messages automatically with stationery.

Filters: One For You, One For Me   A filter forces Eudora to examine incoming messages, compare them to criteria you define, and take appropriate action before you read them. That action could be to delete a message, put it in a specific folder, play a sound, run a program, or answer it automatically with stationery, among other things. The criteria could be based on the message's headers or text in the body of the message. The more filters you have, the longer it takes for Eudora to display all your messages after retrieving them. But having messages sorted and dealt with before you read them saves considerable time.

The simplest way to create a filter is to open a message, right-click in the body, and choose Make Filter. By default, the contents of the From: field are automatically put in the Match Conditions box part, and the message is transferred to a new mailbox.

You can change these defaults before you choose Create Filter by clicking in the appropriate areas. You can also change the Match Conditions to look for words in the subject field or transfer a message to the Trash.

If you want to impose still more filters and actions, click on the Add Details button. Here you can choose up to three Match Conditions and up to five different actions for each filter. It's also here that you can set up an automated response to incoming messages and reply with stationery that you created earlier.

So, if a message contains the phrase "Powell genealogy" in the subject or body, it could be automatically answered with stationery you saved that includes the Powell GEDCOM. If the incoming message is dated during your vacation, it could be automatically answered with stationery that says, "I'm on vacation, sipping a cocktail with a little umbrella in it. Catch you on the flip side!" (Of course, you'd have to set Eudora to dial up, receive mail, and sign off once a day while you were gone.)

Each new filter is automatically added to the bottom of the filter list, and is processed in the order listed. You can rearrange the order of the filters by dragging them up and down on the list, but you can't, unfortunately, actually search the filters, something I hope Qualcomm adds to future Eudora releases. To get Eudora Pro, call Qualcomm Inc.; 800/238-3672, 619/658-1292. The list price is $49.

Pegasus (http://www.pegasus.usa.com/)

Pegasus Mail has all the features of Eudora and more. In fact, because it has so many more features, it's a little harder to learn at first, but once you get the hang of it, Pegasus Mail is just wonderful. It is an extremely intuitive, great-looking mail program with integrated address books and mailing lists. The program itself is free, but if you want a printed manual to help you learn all the features, it costs $40.

Extensive drag and drop capabilities also help make Pegasus Mail easy to use. You can attach or include a file in a message with Pegasus Mail but there are so many wonderful options to choose from in this regard that it may take you a few times to sort it all out.

Pegasus also includes a spelling checker, advanced filtering controls for incoming messages, and a feature that lets you minimize Pegasus while it continues to check mail at regular intervals and notify you through a sound file whenever a new message arrives. Most functions are one click off the menu bar, and you can change your setting easily from the Configuration menu. One of the best features of Pegasus Mail is how wonderful it is to use off-line; you only have to connect to post and retrieve. In addition, when sending a message or replying to one, you have the option of sending a copy to both the recipient and yourself or just to the recipient, not to mention the ability to review or delete queued mail. The price is nice, too... it's free!

To download Pegasus mail, go to the Pegasus home page, http://www.pegasus.usa.com/.

Microsoft Outlook 2000

This program not only reads e-mail, but also Usenet (see Chapter 4), and can keep track of e-mail addresses, just like Pegasus and Eudora, while acting the part of a full-fledged contact manager. A sample screen is shown in Figure 2-7. The filtering capabilities are as good as Eudora's and the sorting of messages into folders and subfolders is superior. You can color-code as well as file, save, delete, copy or forward messages with the filters. You can even flag items for follow-up, put someone in the address book by right-clicking on their e-mail address, plus lots of other cool things. Add to this a calendar, note filing system, and journal, and it's a pretty impressive package.

Like Pegasus, the only reason Outlook is more difficult to use than Eudora is because of its many features. Once you get the hang of it, it's a good program, even if it does take up a lot of disk space and memory compared to Eudora.

Note

Outlook uses something called "stationery," but it's markedly different from Eudora's "stationery." In this case, it's an HTML file with graphics and font definitions so you can, for example, have the company's logo embedded in any message, and change all the type to blue if you want. Stationery in Outlook mainly exists to make your messages pretty.

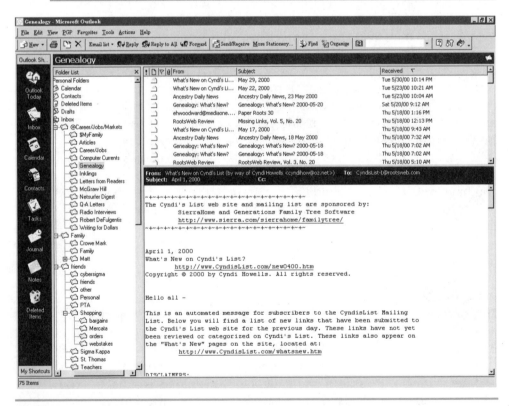

FIGURE 2-7. *Microsoft Outlook is part of the Microsoft Office suite. It does a lot more than just e-mail*

The main drawback to using this program is that most of the e-mail-based viruses are written to exploit Microsoft Office's features. If you are going to use Outlook, you have no choice but to use a virus protection program that checks e-mail (and to keep that program updated weekly). Indeed, no matter what e-mail program you use, you need to check all attachments for viruses.

With this nifty segue, it's time to discuss virus protection software.

Inoculations

No journey is without risk. Whenever you enter the jungle of "cyberspace," that dreaded microorganism, the computer virus, might be lurking about. Not only that, but your activities may attract Trojan horses and worms, too. So, keep a sharp eye out.

A virus is a program hidden on a disk or within a file that can damage your data or computer in some way. Some viruses simply display a message or a joke, while others will wipe out your entire hard drive. Therefore, I strongly recommend you inoculate your computer before using any mode of electronic travel.

One breed of computer virus is the Trojan horse. This is a program that seems to be useful and harmless when it first arrives, but that may secretly be destroying data or breaking down the security on your system. It differs from a virus only in that it does not propagate itself as a virus does.

A worm is a program that will cause your computer to freeze or crash as it sucks up all your available resources, like system memory. It can make copies of itself, and spreads through connected systems.

Programs to detect and remove these exotic virtual creatures are in your local computer store, and on various online services. Some are shareware, while others are more costly, but if the program manages to delete a virus before it harms your system, it's worth the price.

The two major virus protection suites are Norton Anti-Virus and McAfee Anti-Virus, which include one free year of virus updates, available to you once or twice a month. Whatever program you buy, however, be sure to keep it updated.

Even if you have virus protection software, you need to take precautions. Make a backup of everything important to you: data, letters, and so on, and resave it no less than once a month. The virus protection software will offer to make a "recover disk"; do so. It will save you much time and trouble later on down the line, should your system need to be restored. Generally, when you download, look for an indication that the files have been checked for viruses. If not, reconsider downloading from that site. If someone mails or hands you a diskette with data, always run a virus check on the disk before you do anything else. Once a virus is copied onto your hard disk, removing it can be a major headache. In addition, make sure you run a virus check on your hard drive at least twice a month, just to be certain. This should be part of your regular tune-up and maintenance.

Virus protection is good, but if you opt for a high-speed, continuous connection such as DSL or cable Internet, you'll also need a firewall that will help protect you from hackers, Trojan horses, and worms. A firewall is a piece of software, hardware, or combination of both that forms an electronic boundary preventing unauthorized access to a computer or network. It can also be a computer whose sole purpose is to be a buffer between your main computer and the Internet. It controls what goes out and what comes in, according to how the user has set it up.

Example firewall programs are ZoneAlarm by Zone Labs, BlackICE Defender from NetworkICE, or Internet Security 2000 by Symantec Corp. A detailed description of how firewalls work can be found on Shields Up, a Web site devoted to broadband security created by programmer Steve Gibson, head of Gibson Research Corp. (http://www.grc.com) of Laguna Hills, Calif. Run the tests. You'll be surprised.

Publishing on the Internet

Sooner or later you are going to want to share what you've found, perhaps by publishing it on the Internet. To do this, you need a server; most ISPs include an allotment of disk space on their servers for their users. Check with your ISP to see how much you have.

Furthermore, there are dozens of sites out there offering up to 10 megabytes of space for free: AOL's Hometown, Yahoo!, Xoom, Angelfire, and more. Most of these are free, as long as you allow them to display an ad on the visitor's screen.

Finally, there are genealogy specific sites, such as RootsWeb and MyFamily.com with free space for non-commercial use.

Many genealogy database programs will translate your genealogy data into HTML format, so you can publish them on the World Wide Web. Furthermore, there are several web sites, such as MyFamily.com, which will put the information you have into HTML automatically; all you have to do is upload the GEDCOM. Finally, you can use an HTML editor to create the layout and design yourself. In short, publishing on the Internet is very doable, as well as enjoyable.

However, I should warn you that not everyone may be thrilled to be part of your project. Some people get upset just at finding their names published online without their written permission. Some genealogists consider anything published, whether it's online or in hard copy, to be "false" unless the documentation proving it to be true is included in the publication. Still others feel that sharing their hard work without getting data and/or payment in return is a bad idea. For these and other reasons, you may want to:

1. Publish data only on deceased people.

2. Publish only enough data to encourage people to write you with their data.

3. Use a program that can cite your sources as well as your data.

In short, you need to be careful about what you post on the Web, and how. The National Genealogical Society recently adopted a set of standards for publishing genealogy on the Internet. With their permission, I have included them in their entirety, in the following sidebar titled, *Genealogical Standards*. Keep these guidelines in mind as you prepare your data for publishing on the Web.

Genealogical Standards

The following text includes guidelines for publishing Web pages on the Internet as recommended by the National Genealogical Society, May 2000. Appreciating that publishing information through Internet Web sites and Web pages shares many similarities with print publishing, considerate family historians—

♦ apply a single title to an entire Web site, as they would to a book, placing it both in the < TITLE > HTML tag that appears at the top of the Web browser window for each Web page to be viewed, and also in the body of the Web document on the home, title or index page.

- explain the purposes and objectives of their Web sites, placing the explanation near the top of the title page or including a link from that page to a special page about the reason for the site.

- display a footer at the bottom of each Web page which contains the Web site title, page title, author's name, author's contact information, date of last revision, and a copyright statement.

- provide complete contact information, including, at a minimum, a name and e-mail address, and preferably some means for long-term contact, like a postal address.

- assist visitors by providing on each page navigational links that lead visitors to other important pages on the Web site, or return them to the home page.

- adhere to the NGS "Standards for Sharing Information with Others" (see Chapter 3) regarding copyright, attribution, privacy, and the sharing of sensitive information.

- include unambiguous source citations for the research data provided on the site, and if not complete descriptions, then offer full citations upon request.

- label photographic and scanned images within the graphic itself, with a fuller explanation, if required, in text adjacent to the graphic.

- identify transcribed, extracted or abstracted data as such, and provide appropriate source citations.

- include identifying dates and locations when providing information about specific surnames or individuals.

- respect the rights of others who do not wish information about themselves to be published, referenced, or linked on a Web site.

♦ provide Web site access to all potential visitors by avoiding enhanced technical capabilities that may not be available to all users, remembering that not all computers are created equal.

♦ avoid using features that distract from the productive use of the Web site, like ones that reduce legibility, strain the eyes, dazzle the vision, or otherwise detract from the visitor's ability to easily read, study, comprehend, or print the online publication.

♦ maintain their online publications at frequent intervals, changing the content to keep the information current, the links valid, and the Web site in good working order.

♦ preserve and archive for future researchers their online publications and communications that have lasting value, using both electronic and paper duplication.

Using a Genealogy Program to Publish

Almost every good genealogy program now includes a way to publish on the Web. Ultimate Family Tree, Family Origins, Family Tree Maker, The Master Genealogist, Generations Family Tree, and Ancestral Quest are just a few of the programs that can turn your genealogical database into HTML. Most of them simply create a standard tree-branching chart with links to the individuals' data; others may create a set of family group sheets. Many of them allow you to have "still living" replace the vital statistics for certain people. In many of these programs, the process is as simple as creating a printed report; you simply choose "HTML" as the format.

However, some of the programs do not give you a choice of where you post your data. Family Tree Maker, for example, will publish your data on the FTM site. Once there it will become part of the FTM database, which is periodically burned onto CD-ROMS and sold in stores. Simply by posting your data on the site, you give them permission to do so. Quite a bit of discussion and debate is ongoing about this privatization of publicly available data. Some say it will be the end of amateur genealogy; others feel it's a way to preserve data that might be lost to disaster or neglect. It's left up to you as to whether you want to post to a site that will reuse your data for its own profit.

That is one reason I strongly urge you to visit local genealogy groups that have "show and tell" nights for genealogy software. Try several programs before you buy one. Ask questions about how and where it will publish your work on the Web. Furthermore, some genealogy programs let you record your sources, notes, and anecdotes to go along with your data. This ability to record and cite sources is essential, in my opinion, for any genealogy program; don't choose one without it.

Notice the programs' metaphors and try to find one that works the way you think. For example, some programs use a scrapbook metaphor where you are entering a "page" per person with details, pictures, even sound clips. Others have an index card metaphor, which feels very much like the good old-fashioned way of recording your data. Still others use a family group sheet form. Buy one that uses a format you find easy and comfortable to use.

Then look at the output. Besides HTML, some genealogy programs can output New England Historical and Genealogical Society formats, narratives in a book form, fan charts, even murals with pictures. And, of course, you won't buy any program that doesn't have the ability to export and import GEDCOM files. Be aware, however, that there are subtle differences in how each program handles GEDCOM; translation from one to another is rarely perfect.

Think about your goals in genealogy and pick a program that can help you meet them.

Using a GEDCOM to HTML Program to Publish

Then there are programs that take a GEDCOM from any program on the market and turn it into HTML. The inexpensive program ($10) GedPage (http://www.frontiernet.net/ ~ rjacob/gedpage.htm) will turn GEDCOM files into very attractive HTML. You can choose a version for Macintosh or Windows (3.1 and up). The output is formatted as Family Group Sheets, as shown in Figure 2-8.

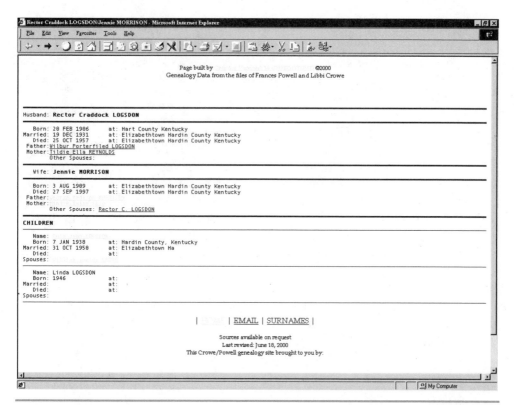

Husband: **Rector Craddock LOGSDON**

Born:	28 FEB 1986	at: Hart County Kentucky
Married:	19 DEC 1931	at: Elizabethtown Hardin County Kentucky
Died:	25 OCT 1957	at: Elizabethtown Hardin County Kentucky
Father:	Wilbur Porterfiled LOGSDON	
Mother:	Tildie Ella REYNOLDS	
	Other Spouses:	

Wife: **Jennie MORRISON**

Born:	3 AUG 1989	at: Elizabethtown Hardin County Kentucky
Died:	27 SEP 1997	at: Elizabethtown Hardin County Kentucky
Father:		
Mother:		
	Other Spouses: Rector C. LOGSDON	

CHILDREN

Name:		
Born:	7 JAN 1938	at: Hardin County, Kentucky
Married:	31 OCT 1958	at: Elizabethtown Ha
Died:		at:
Spouses:		

Name:	Linda LOGSDON	
Born:	1946	at:
Married:		at:
Died:		at:
Spouses:		

| | EMAIL | SURNAMES |

Sources available on request
Last revised: June 18, 2000
This Crowe/Powell genealogy site brought to you by:

FIGURE 2-8. *GedPage produces a readable, if simple, set of pages from a GEDCOM*

Note

Because a GEDCOM usually doesn't include sources and citations, this page does not conform completely to the NGS guidelines.

Using this program is simplicity itself. First, create a GEDCOM. Then change the files HEADER.HTM and FOOTER.HTM to say what you want, generally your contact information. (You can do this in any text editor. Simply replace the text and leave anything within the < > brackets alone.) Start GedPage, and fill in the blanks for the URL, the e-mail address, then choose colors if you like. Click Create Page. In a few seconds, a set of pages for the database will be created. Then you use an ftp program to upload the pages to your site.

This program is just one example; there are others out there. Check out Cyndi's List for an up-to-date list of programs: http://www.CyndisList.com/software.htm.

Using an HTML Editor

For the real do-it-yourselfer, HTML editors can help you create your own site from the ground up. Most modern HTML editors work just like word processors, in fact, Word 2000 can save any document file in HTML format, complete with links and graphics. Microsoft Internet Explorer and Netscape both come with simple, useful HTML editors as part of the package. Microsoft Internet Explorer can be installed with Front Page Express and Netscape with the Composer module; both being fairly easy to use. Once you are done, the programs can post the results for you; simply choose "Publish" under the File menu.

Using a Web Site to Publish

MyFamily.com (Chapter 10), RootsWeb (Chapter 9), and other sites give you an opportunity to publish to the Web. I'll show you how in the chapters that cover these sites.

Chapter 3

Beginning a Genealogy Project

Many folks, like my mom, come to online genealogy after years of doing it the old-fashioned way. They know what they are looking for, and simply want to use online tools to help them in their search.

But maybe *you* are as new to genealogy as you are to the online world. In that case, I'd like to give you a brief overview of how to proceed.

Always Start with Yourself

Begin with what you know for certain: Your own vital statistics, and those of the people living with you. Gather up the documentation that proves your birth, marriage, graduation and things you own. Write down family stories, legends and events as you remember them. Gather up photos and identify the people in them (and the date the photos were taken, if possible). These are primary sources: data recorded close to the time and place of the event.

Now, determine how you are going to keep track of it. You can fill out family group sheets or pedigree charts, record the data in a genealogy program, use index cards, or whatever suits you. Most people feel finding a good genealogy program, which will allow you to record your sources (as noted in Chapter 2), is the way to go. Your paper sources can be scanned into digital form or stored in good old filing cabinets. Remember to keep information that may, at first, seem unrelated to your family lines. You never know. Later on down the line, a connection may appear, or you may be able to trade that data with someone who has what you need!

Most of the genealogy programs on the market today will print out family group sheets and other report formats and blank forms so you can take them to the library or to a genealogy conference for quick reference, or display them at family reunions. Many can also handle video and sound recordings. Whichever program you choose, be certain you record a source for each fact, and keep families together in your system.

Pick a surname to pursue. Now that you have a system for storing and comparing what you have, you are ready to begin gathering more data on that surname. Begin by interviewing family members: parents, aunts, uncles, cousins, and in-laws. Ask them for stories, names, dates, and places of the people and events in the family. Where possible, get documents to back up what you are told. Family Bibles, newspapers, diaries, wills and letters can help here.

A good question to ask at this point is whether any genealogy of the family has been published. Understand that such a work is still a secondary source, not a primary source, but it may clear up a lot of puzzles for you.

Visit a Family History Center and the FamilySearch site, which has indexes to the Church of Jesus Christ of Latter-day Saints' (LDS) genealogy information (see Chapter 14). This includes:

- IGI—The event-based International Genealogical Index (the largest single database in the world)

- Ancestral File—A patron-submitted pedigree format genealogy

- OPR—Old Parochial Register

All of the previous databases are made up of research done by LDS members, but may include data on people who are not members.

Record all you find in your system of choice. It's tedious, but necessary. Get someone to proof your entries (it's so easy to type 1939 when you meant 1993!).

Now you have enough information to start asking intelligent questions in queries to magazines and mail lists (see Chapter 5). You have enough data to answer questions in chat rooms and Usenet groups (see Chapter 7 and Chapter 4). And most of all, you have enough names, dates, and places to start using search engines to find World Wide Web and FTP sites (see Chapter 8 and Chapter 6).

As you gather more and more information, remember to check what you find against what is considered good practice for genealogists. The National Genealogical Society has a set of standards for research, shown in the following sidebar titled, *Standards for Sound Genealogical Research* and reprinted here with permission. You can also find these on the Web at the NGS Web site located at: http://www.ngsgenealogy.org/.

Standards for Sound Genealogical Research

As recommended by the National Genealogical Society, always remembering they are engaged in a quest for truth, family history researchers consistently—

♦ record the source for each item of information they collect.

♦ test every hypothesis or theory against credible evidence, and reject those that are not supported by the evidence.

♦ seek original records, or reproduced images of them when there is reasonable assurance they have not been altered, as the basis for their research conclusions.

♦ use compilations, communications and published works, whether paper or electronic, primarily for their value as guides to locating the original records.

♦ state something as a fact only when it is supported by convincing evidence, and identify the evidence when communicating the fact to others.

♦ limit with words like "probable" or "possible" any statement that is based on less-than-convincing evidence, and state the reasons for concluding that it is probable or possible.

♦ avoid misleading other researchers by either intentionally or carelessly distributing or publishing inaccurate information.

♦ state carefully and honestly the results of their own research, and acknowledge all use of other researchers' work.

♦ recognize the collegial nature of genealogical research by making their work available to others through publication, or by placing copies in appropriate libraries or repositories, and by welcoming critical comment.

♦ consider with open minds new evidence or the comments of others on their work and the conclusions they have reached.

Sources and Proof

Most serious genealogists who discuss online sources want to know
if you can "trust" what you find on the Internet. Again, the National
Genealogical Society has a set of standards to go by, shown in the next
sidebar titled, *Standards for Use of Technology in Genealogical Research*
and reprinted here with permission.

Standards for Use of Technology in Genealogical Research

As recommended by the National Genealogical Society, mindful
that computers are tools, genealogists take full responsibility for
their work, and therefore they—

♦ learn the capabilities and limits of their equipment and
  software, and use them only when they are the most
  appropriate tools for a purpose.

♦ refuse to let computer software automatically embellish
  their work.

♦ treat compiled information from on-line sources or digital
  data bases like that from other published sources, useful
  primarily as a guide to locating original records, but not as
  evidence for a conclusion or assertion.

♦ accept digital images or enhancements of an original record
  as a satisfactory substitute for the original only when there is
  reasonable assurance that the image accurately reproduces
  the unaltered original.

♦ cite sources for data obtained online or from digital media
  with the same care that is appropriate for sources on paper
  and other traditional media, and enter data into a digital
  database only when its source can remain associated with it.

♦ always cite the sources for information or data posted online
  or sent to others, naming the author of a digital file as its
  immediate source, while crediting original sources cited
  within the file.

- ◆ preserve the integrity of their own data bases by evaluating the reliability of downloaded data before incorporating it into their own files.

- ◆ provide, whenever they alter data received in digital form, a description of the change that will accompany the altered data whenever it is shared with others.

- ◆ actively oppose the proliferation of error, rumor and fraud by personally verifying or correcting information, or noting it as unverified, before passing it on to others.

- ◆ treat people on-line as courteously and civilly as they would treat them face-to-face, not separated by networks and anonymity.

- ◆ accept that technology has not changed the principles of genealogical research, only some of the procedures.

©1997 by National Genealogical Society. Permission is granted to copy or publish this material provided it is reproduced in its entirety, including this notice.

Many professional genealogists I know simply do not accept what is found on the Internet as proof of genealogy, period. Their attitude is that a source is not a primary source unless you have held the original document in your hand, and it is not proof unless supported by at least one other original document that you have held in your hand. To them, seeing a picture of a scanned original will on the Internet is not "proof."

For example, you can see in Figure 3-1, the *Mayflower* passenger list has been scanned in at Caleb Johnson's site, *Mayflower* Passenger List, http://members.aol.com/calebj/passenger.html. Do you consider this a "primary source?" A "secondary source?" Or just a good clue?

Others are even angry with those who publish their genealogy data on the Internet without citing each source in detail. Once when I was at a conference teaching a class on how to publish genealogy on the Internet, a very respected genealogist took me to task over dinner. "Web pages without supporting documentation are lies!" she insisted. "You're telling people to publish lies, because if it's not proven by genealogical standards, it might not be true!"

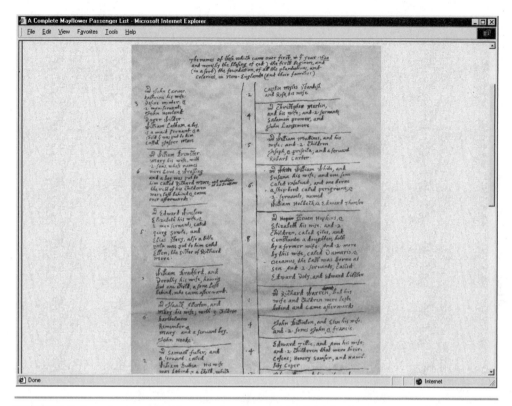

FIGURE 3-1. *Is a scanned image of a document an original source to you?*

I have to admit that I don't quite see it that way. In my opinion, you must evaluate what you find on the Internet just as you evaluate what you find in a library, courthouse, or archive. Many a genealogy book has been published with errors; so will online genealogies be. On the World Wide Web, there are no real editors. You will find all kinds of information and sources on the Internet, from casual references in messages to documented genealogy to original records transcribed into HTML. The range is astounding. But the same can be true of vanity-published genealogies found in libraries.

You *will* be able to find some limited primary materials online. People are scanning and transcribing original documents onto the Internet, such as the Library of Virginia and the National Park Service. You will also find online a growing treasure trove of public vital records, indexes, and scanned images of Government Land Office land patents at http://www.glorecords.blm.gov/and more (see Figure 3-2).

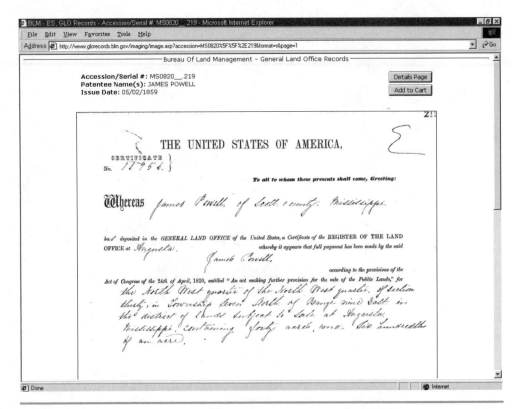

FIGURE 3-2. *The Bureau of Land Management can show you land patents online*

Don't be put off by those who sneer at the Internet, saying nothing of real value can be found there. That may have been true just a few years ago, but not today. Now, you will find that scanned images of census records are going online at both the Census site (http://www.census.gov) as well as at volunteer projects such as the USGenWeb Digital Census Project. Looking at these records in HTML is as good as, or better than, looking at them in microfilm or microfiche, in my opinion.

Nevertheless, secondary sources are much more common. The main value of these secondary sources on the Internet is finding other genealogists who are researching the same lines. Additionally, you may uncover leads to finding primary and secondary sources offline, and, very rarely, get a glance at an actual data source, perhaps even a primary source. Simply *knowing* that a source exists can be a breakthrough.

Other people are putting their family trees online, and while it is true many of these data files don't have the disk space available to include complete documentation, most people who do so are willing to provide pertinent details to anyone who has data to exchange with them.

Therefore, I still believe in publishing and exchanging data over the Internet. However, you must use good judgment.

The criteria for the evaluation of resources on the Web must be the same you would use for any other source of information. Be aware that the fact that something is on a computer does not make it infallible. Garbage in, garbage out. With that in mind, ask yourself some questions in evaluating online genealogy sites.

Who created it? You will find resources on the Internet from libraries, research institutions, and organizations such as the National Genealogical Society, not to mention government resources and those from universities. Sources such as these give you more confidence in their data than, say, resources from a hobbyist, for example. Publications and software companies also publish genealogical information, but you must read carefully at the site to determine whether they've actually researched this information or simply accepted anything their customers threw at them. Finally, you will find tons of "family traditions" and while traditions usually have a grain of truth to them, they're usually not unvarnished.

How long ago? The more often a page is updated, the better you can feel about the data it holds. Of course, a page listing the census for a certain county in 1850 need not be updated every week, but a pedigree put online should be updated periodically as the author finds more data.

Where does the information come from? If the page in question doesn't give any sources, you will want to contact the page author to acquire the necessary information. If there *are* sources, of course you must decide if you can trust them, for many a genealogical error has been printed in books, magazines, and online.

In what form is the information? A simple GEDCOM published as a Web page can be useful for the beginner, but ideally, one wants an index to any genealogical resource, regardless of form. If a site has no search function, no table of contents or even a "document map" (a graphic leading you to different parts of the site), it's much less useful than it could be.

How well does the author use and define genealogical terms? Is it clear the author knows the difference between a yeoman farmer and a yeoman sailor? Does the author seem to be knowledgeable about genealogy? Another problem with online pages is whether the page author understands the problems of dates, both badly recorded dates and the 1752 calendar change. There are certain sites that can help you with calendar problems.

Does the information make sense compared to what you already know? If you have documentary evidence that contradicts what you see on a Web page, treat it as you would a mistake in a printed genealogy or magazine: tell the author about your data and see whether the two versions can be reconciled. And that sort of exchange, after all, is what online genealogy is all about!

With that in mind, it would help to become familiar with the National Genealogical Society's Standards for Sharing Information with Others, reproduced by permission in the next sidebar. Judge what you find on the Internet by these standards; hold yourself to them as you exchange information; and help keep the data on the Internet as accurate as we can make it.

After you have these standards firmly in mind, a good system to help you track what you know, how you know it, what you don't know, and the surnames you need, is just a matter of searching for the facts regarding each individual as you go along.

And the Internet can help!

Standards for Sharing Information with Others

Being conscious of the fact that sharing information or data with others, whether through speech, documents or electronic media, is essential to family history research, the National Geneological Society recommends that responsible family historians should consistently—

♦ respect the restrictions on sharing information that arise from the rights of another as an author, originator or compiler; as a living private person; or as a party to a mutual agreement.

- observe meticulously the legal rights of copyright owners, copying or distributing any part of their works only with their permission, or to the limited extent specifically allowed under the law's "fair use" exceptions.

- identify the sources for all ideas, information and data from others, and the form in which they were received, recognizing that the unattributed use of another's intellectual work is plagiarism.

- respect the authorship rights of senders of letters, electronic mail and data files, forwarding or disseminating them further only with the sender's permission.

- inform people who provide information about their families as to the ways it may be used, observing any conditions they impose and respecting any reservations they may express regarding the use of particular items.

- require some evidence of consent before assuming that living people are agreeable to further sharing of information about themselves.

- convey personal identifying information about living people—like age, home address, occupation or activities—only in ways that those concerned have expressly agreed to.

- recognize that legal rights of privacy may limit the extent to which information from publicly available sources may be further used, disseminated or published.

- communicate no information to others that is known to be false, or without making reasonable efforts to determine its truth, particularly information that may be derogatory.

- are sensitive to the hurt that revelations of criminal, immoral, bizarre or irresponsible behavior may bring to family members.

True Story: A Beginner Tries the Shot-Gun Approach

Just two months ago my mother shared some old obits with me that intrigued me enough to send me off on a search for my family's roots. I started at the Roots Web site with a meta search, then sent e-mails to anyone who had posted the name I was pursuing in the state of origin cited in the obit. This constituted over 50 messages. A real shot-gun approach. I received countless replies indicating there was no family connection. Then one day I got a response from a man who turned out to be my mother's cousin. He himself had been researching his family line for the last two years. He sent me census and marriage records, even a will from 1843 that gave new direction to my search.

In pursuing information on my father, whom my mother divorced when I was two months old (I never saw him again), I was able to identify his parents' names from an SS 5 application and subsequently track down state census listings containing not only their birth dates but the birth dates of their parents. All of which has aided me invaluably in the search for my family's roots.

Having been researching only a short while, I have found the online genealogy community to be very helpful, and more than willing to share information with newbies like myself. The amount of information online has blown me away.

—Sue Crumpton

Part II

The Internet

Chapter 4

Usenet

Over the years, Usenet has been called an "Internet bulletin board," an "Internet news service," and many other things, but my particular definition of it is this: Usenet is an Internet service where messages to the world are posted. E-mail messages may give you the ear of a specific person or group, and forums and bulletin boards may open you to an even wider audience, but when you post to Usenet, you post your messages to the whole world.

Usenet isn't an organization per se, nor is it in any one place. Lots of machines carry the messages, receiving them and sending them on down the line. In the end, your Usenet feed comes from your Internet service provider.

Note

Throughout this chapter you'll find references to mailing lists and Web sites; an example of just how interconnected genealogy resources on the Internet can be. Stay tuned. In later chapters, you'll learn everything you need to know about mail lists and Web sites to make your research efforts that much easier.

Like so many things concerning the online world, Usenet has its own Frequently Asked Questions (FAQ) file. It is updated about once a month, and thereafter posted to the newsgroups news.announce.newusers, news.admin.misc, and news.answers, as well as the Web site http://www.faqs.org/faqs/ (see Figure 4-1). Much of what those sites say is contained in this chapter, but reading them won't hurt!

Complicated, but Useful

The first thing to understand about Usenet is that it's hard to understand. Don't be discouraged about that. It has been said that many Usenet flame wars arise because the users themselves don't comprehend the nature of the network. And these flames, by necessity, come from people who are actually using Usenet. Imagine, then, how hard it is for those unfamiliar with Usenet to understand it! On the other hand, it should be comforting to the novice that so many people are successfully using Usenet without fully understanding it.

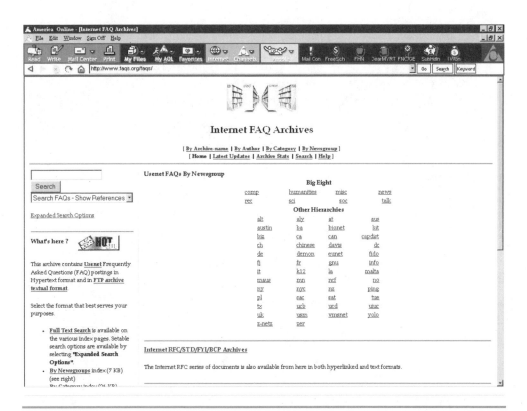

FIGURE 4-1. *Frequently Asked Questions and answers are at http://www.faqs.org/faqs*

One reason for the confusion is that Usenet is a part of the Internet, and for some people it's the only part they use. Yet it isn't the whole Internet, any more than Boston constitutes all of Massachusetts.

Usenet's Structure

Usenet's messages are sorted into thousands of "newsgroups," which are a bit like magazines (being that you subscribe to them), in some ways like late-night dorm discussions, and in other ways like symposia. A newsgroup is supposed to be a set of messages restricted to a certain subject, but abuses abound. Usenet's flavor depends on the newsgroups you subscribe to. Some newsgroups are wild; some very dull; most in-between.

A "moderated" newsgroup has a referee, who decides what messages get to go on that newsgroup. An "unmoderated" one (the most popular kind) isn't edited in any way, except that you'll get flamed (insulted) if you post a message off the proper topic.

There are eight major categories of newsgroups:

♦ COMP for computer-science-related topics

♦ HUMANITIES for the discussion of philosophy and the classics

♦ MISC for miscellaneous items

♦ NEWS for topics about Usenet itself

♦ REC for recreation, hobbies, and interests

♦ SCI for science not related to computers

♦ SOC for social interaction and hobbies. Most genealogy topics are in SOC

♦ TALK for general conversation

Tom Czarnik, who is a Usenet guru from way back, says, "Let's make a distinction between the Internet and Usenet. The Internet has come to mean the sum of the regional nets, while Usenet is a system for the exchange of newsgroups." Despite this clear separation, you'll often hear of "pictures sent over the Internet" or "messages on the Internet," even though they're talking about Usenet.

No person or group has control of Usenet as a whole. No one person authorizes who gets news feeds, which articles are propagated where, who can post articles, or anything else. These things are handled one newsgroup at a time. You won't find a Usenet Incorporated or even a Usenet User's Group. This means that, although the freedoms of expression and association are almost absolute, Usenet is not a democracy. It's anarchy, to put it frankly, something with little or no control placed on it except that exerted by the social pressures of those participating.

Therefore, sometimes Usenet is not fair—in part because it's hard to get everyone to agree to what *is* fair, and in part, because it's hard to stop people from proving themselves foolish.

Because all of this happens largely on a volunteer basis, you must understand that access to Usenet is not a right. After all, Usenet is not a public utility, at least not yet; there's no government monopoly and little or no government control, so far. Some Usenet sites are publicly funded or subsidized, but most aren't. And while many university campuses are connected—where much of the hard work of keeping Usenet going is done—it's not an academic network.

Moreover, although many people are connected through their workplace, Usenet is not a billboard for advertising. Those commercials that *are* tolerated are infrequent, informative, low-key, and preferably in direct response to a specific question. The only exception to this policy occurs in the .biz groups, where advertisements are accepted.

Keep in mind, too, that Usenet is not restricted to the US. There are many correspondents from around the globe—in places like Europe, Australia, and Japan—so be polite about grammar and spelling.

Usenet History

According to legend, Usenet began in 1979 when a group at Duke University in North Carolina sought a way to exchange research data with other interested universities. As a result, they acquainted themselves with UNIX, a blossoming operating system of the day. Soon they had written programs in UNIX that allowed them to exchange data and analysis with other universities running the same programs. The neat part was that they could send programs that had been changed into plain text (encoded), and then return them to their digital form (decoded) on the other end, allowing any type of data to be sent without clogging up the very limited bandwidth of the time.

Soon, they began using the program to send each other messages, discussing hardware problems, industry gossip, even how to fix certain bugs. Eventually the topics turned toward current events and shared interests.

Then they began routing the more interesting stuff through an automated program. The purpose of the program was to call other UNIX sites while people slept, leave packets of data and programs and messages, while simultaneously picking up packets destined for other places, then calling upon another site, and so on, and so on. Today, more than 500,000 articles a day are routed this way. Back in those pioneering days, however, having so much information to route meant that some sort of categorizing scheme became necessary. Because of this, messages were labeled according to their "newsgroup" and soon people began signing up for these newsgroups the way they subscribed to newspapers. About 100,000 new newsgroups later, we have the Usenet as it is today.

The Software

To read a Usenet newsgroup, you need a newsreader client. Many mail readers, such as Microsoft Outlook, include a newsreader. America Online, Netcom, CompuServe, Delphi, Microsoft Network, Portal, PSI, The Well, and many other commercial services offer their clients Usenet connections, as well as an appropriate newsreader.

You can, however, get to Usenet without a newsreader: several sites have the most recent postings available for search. One of these is deja.com (www.deja.com), see Figure 4-2. On the opening page, click on "Search Discussions," then on the next page, input your terms. A simple search for "genealogy" is illustrated in Figure 4-2.

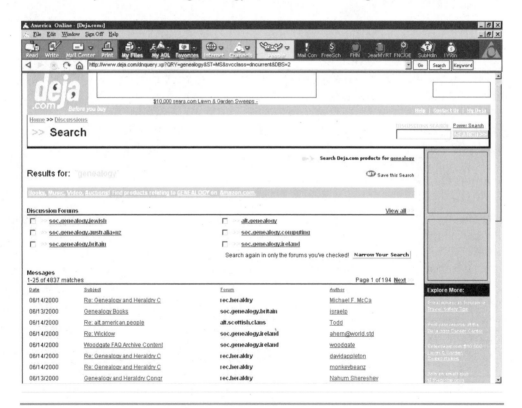

FIGURE 4-2. *At deja.com, you can read and post to Usenet from the Web; this page is the result of searching Usenet for "genealogy"*

You can also search Usenet postings at HotBot and other search engine sites. However, for most people, the most convenient way is to use a newsreader.

News Readers

In the "old days" (the first edition of this book!) we had to learn disagreeable, arcane UNIX commands and use unfriendly UNIX newsreaders to obtain the wonders of the Usenet. But, happily, times have changed. We now have a plethora of graphical newsreaders for any platform, be it Windows, Mac, UNIX, Xwindows or whatever. The online commercial services have all integrated newsreaders into their front-end software, too.

However, you may want to use a dedicated newsreader. Outlook Express, a free e-mail and newsreader client from Microsoft, is a popular choice. You can see an illustration of it in Figure 4-3.

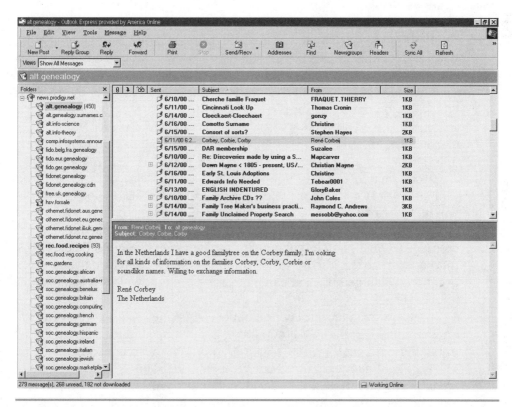

FIGURE 4-3.   *Outlook Express has a typical three-pane layout*

The first time you use Outlook Express to read Usenet, you have to tell the newsreader the name of your news server. Your Internet service provider tech support people should tell you what it is. It will be something like news.yourISP.com. For example, the news server at CompuServe is *news.compuserve.com*; the news server on Prodigy is *news.prodigy.com*. Generally, you have to be a signed-in customer to use an Internet service provider's news server: you can't get into CompuServe's news server if your connection is through Prodigy, for example.

Outlook Express' layout is very typical. The default is three panes of the window that show you information from your Usenet site. The left pane shows the names of the newsgroups. The upper right shows the message headers of a selected newsgroup. The lower pane shows the body of the selected message. Other newsreaders give you the option of changing this to a different layout (for example, stacking all three panes vertically).

The newsgroups pane will show you the newsgroups to which you have "subscribed" (that is, told the program you want to read regularly). You can set Outlook Express to hide the message headers of the postings you have already read, or to show them.

One nice component of this reader is the search feature. By using Edit | Find on the menu, or the "Find" button on the toolbar, you can search this list of newsgroup articles (alt.genealogy) for surnames or place names of interest. In addition, when your cursor is in the body of a message, you can search that message as well. A newsreader with a search function can save you tons of time and online charges.

Furthermore, you can set filters for the messages, just as you can for e-mail. You can click on Message in the menu bar, and choose Create New Rule for Message. Then you can choose to have subsequent messages (which match that sender, topic or message text) deleted, marked as read, highlighted with color, marked for following replies, or ignored all together. You can even have them downloaded as text to your disk.

In the newsreader display, the upper right pane is where information is given about current newsgroup messages (messages are called "articles" in Usenet parlance). Double-clicking on one of these lines opens the message in the lower pane. Subject lines in red denote messages that are unread, while previously viewed messages are displayed in black text. You can even change the color designations, if you so desire.

Replying and posting are accomplished by simply clicking on icons
on the toolbar at the top. You can reply by e-mail to just the person who
posted the message, or to the whole Usenet group.

Browsers

Reading Newsgroups with a Web browser (see Chapter 2) is another
way to go. Microsoft Internet Explorer uses Outlook Express. Netscape
Navigator has a news-reading window.

In Netscape Navigator 6, this means clicking on Edit|Mail|News
Account Setting and choosing the Newsgroup Servers as in Figure 4-4.
Click Add and put in the information for your news server (for example,
news.prodigy.net). Now, Netscape Navigator is ready to read news
for you.

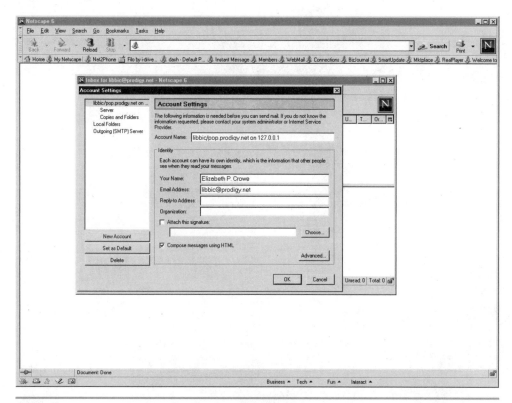

FIGURE 4-4.   *In Netscape Navigator, add the name of your Internet service
provider's news server in the Edit|Mail|News Account Settings screen*

In some other browsers, you may have to find the "helper programs" dialog box and add the news server and newsreader information.

Commercial Online Services

Microsoft Network, CompuServe, America Online, and the other major online services also have ways for you to read Usenet. Most of them involve reading online, while the meter is ticking.

AOL, however, has an option that lets you fetch newsgroup articles when you retrieve e-mail for off-line reading. First, you use the keyword USENET to choose your newsgroups. Simply click on the search newsgroup button, search for the genealogy groups you want, and click the subscribe button. Then close the window. Back at the AOL Usenet window, click on the Read Offline button in the upper right corner of the window. Put those that you wish to read offline in the right-hand pane of the window (see Figure 4-5).

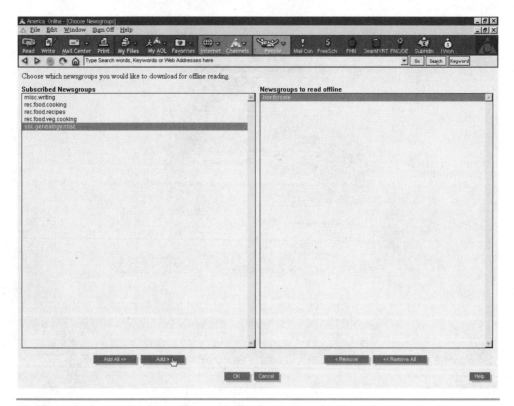

FIGURE 4-5.   *You can choose to read Usenet messages offline in AOL*

> *Note* ────────────────────────────────
>
> *Ever since AOL bought CompuServe, the two services' software has become more and more alike. This function and many others on AOL usually work just the same on CompuServe.*

Close that window and click on the menu Mail|Set Up Automatic AOL. Put check marks in the boxes about sending and receiving newsgroup messages. Now, whenever you run Automatic AOL to retrieve your AOL mail, you'll get the genealogy newsgroups you chose too. This will make the sessions longer but will take less online time than reading the newsgroups "live."

On CompuServe, it works the same way; on MSN, you will have to read Usenet online (as of this writing, anyway).

Newsgroups of Interest to Online Genealogists

Once upon a time, there was only one online genealogy Usenet newsgroup for genealogists: *soc.roots*. It soon became unwieldy, however, in trying to deal with an overwhelming array of genealogical topics, ranging from beginners' questions to historical epochs. Thankfully, after much discussion and soul-searching, we now have an embarrassment of riches in genealogical newsgroups:

♦ alt.adoption—A newsgroup that discusses adoption issues, including the search for birth parents.

♦ alt.genealogy—An older genealogy group (discussing more general topics); composed mostly of people who don't want to use *soc.genealogy.misc* for some reason. Copied to the *ALT-GENEALOGY* mailing list.

♦ alt.culture.cajun—Newsgroup devoted to discussions of Cajun history, genealogy, culture, and events.

♦ fido.eur.genealogy—A FidoNet echo copied to Usenet; meant for those researching European genealogy. FidoNet is a message network for dial-up bulletin board systems; some FidoNet discussion groups are copied to Usenet.

- fido.ger.genealogy—Same as *fido.eur.genealogy*, but intended for German genealogy research (with most messages posted in German).

- fr.rec.genealogie—Copied to the *GEN-FF-L* mailing list for the discussion of Francophone genealogy—the genealogy of French-speaking people. The primary language here is French.

- no.slekt—General genealogy topics, with most messages posted in Norwegian. Copied to the *NO.SLEKT* mailing list.

- no.slekt.programmer—Discussions of genealogical computer software; again, with most messages in Norwegian. Copied to the *NO.SLEKT.PROGRAMMER* mailing list.

- soc.genealogy.african—For the study of genealogy in Africa, and the African Diaspora.

- soc.genealogy.australia + nz—For genealogical research regarding Australia, New Zealand, and their territories.

- soc.genealogy.benelux—Genealogical discussions revolving around Luxembourg, Belgium, and the Netherlands.

- soc.genealogy.computing—Provides information about various genealogical programs and their corresponding bugs (including how-to instructions). Topics mostly concern software (with some hardware discussions). Copied to the *SOFTWARE.GENCMP-L* mailing list.

- soc.genealogy.french—Genealogy of French-speaking peoples (with most messages posted in French). Copied to the *GEN-FR-L* mailing list.

- soc.genealogy.german—Discussions of family history for those with Germanic backgrounds. Messages are mainly in German. Copied to the *GEN-DE-L* mailing list.

- soc.genealogy.hispanic—Genealogical discussions as related to Hispanics (some centering around Central and South American family lines), with many messages in Spanish.

- soc.genealogy.jewish—A moderated discussion of Judaic genealogy. Copied to the *JEWISHGEN* mailing list.

- soc.genealogy.marketplace—Buy, sell, and trade books; read about programs, seminars, etc., related to genealogy.

- soc.genealogy.medieval—Copied to the *GEN-MEDIEVAL* mailing list for genealogy and family history discussions among people researching individuals living during medieval times. Medieval times are loosely defined as the period from the breakup of the Western Roman Empire until the time public records relating to the general population began to be kept—roughly from AD 500 to AD 1600.

- soc.genealogy.methods—A general discussion of genealogy and methods of genealogical research. Copied to the *GENMTD-L* mailing list.

- soc.genealogy.misc—This is what became of *soc.roots*. It's essentially a general discussion of genealogy. Copies to the *GENMSC-L* mailing list; it's a catch-all for topics that don't fit into other *soc.genealogy.** categories.

- soc.genealogy.nordic—Genealogical products and services pertaining to Northern Europe.

- soc.genealogy.slavic—Slavic genealogy. Some messages in Slavic languages.

- soc.genealogy.surnames.global—A central database for sending queries about surnames from around the world. This newsgroup is moderated.

- soc.genealogy.uk + ireland—Copied to the *GENUKI-L* mailing list for the discussion of genealogy and family history. Also used for discussions among people researching ancestors, family members, or others who have a genealogical connection to people in any part of the British Isles (England, Wales, Ireland, Scotland, the Channel Isles, and the Isle of Man).

- soc.genealogy.west-indies—Covers Caribbean genealogy; most, but not all, of the messages are in English.

In addition to this list are several groups in the *soc.history.** hierarchies that discuss issues genealogists typically face, like records, sources, and so on.

Binary Files on Usenet

Some newsgroups carry binary files (recognizable because they usually have "binaries" in their names). This isn't seen so much on Usenet any more because the World Wide Web is far superior for trading sounds, pictures, and programs; still sometimes people do encode a binary file—which has non-text characters—into ASCII codes that can transfer on Usenet.

Caution

Viruses have been propagated on Usenet due to binary messages pretending to be pictures, sounds, movies or other binary file types. Be very cautious before downloading a binary file from Usenet.

Some newsreaders automatically take care of this for you. On AOL, you have to jump through a few hoops, however.

When you first join AOL, your account is set to the default to block all binary files in Usenet, because most of the groups that send binaries are pornographic. To turn this off, go to Keyword Parental Controls, click on Set Parental Controls Now, click on Custom Controls, and click on Newsgroups. Click on Newsgroups Controls, and Edit. Choose the Screen Name. Uncheck the box "Block binary downloads."

Encoded binary files are often broken up across several different messages. Gathering up the pieces, putting them together, and converting them to their original form used to be a real hassle. America Online's FileGrabber feature makes it very simple.

To get the most out of it, set the Complete Binaries Only preference. To do this, go to the Usenet window and click Read My Newsgroups. Click a newsgroup name in your list that contains the word "binary" or "binaries" to select it, then click the Preferences button and select the Complete Binaries Only preference. Note: You will unfortunately have to perform this operation newsgroup by newsgroup; the setting is not available in the Global Newsgroups Preferences window.

AOL's newsreader alerts you when you are viewing encoded data, and gives you three choices: download the file (the AOL software will automatically decode it for you), download the article that contains the code or piece of it (you will then have to decode the pieces yourself), or Cancel. (Remember, CompuServe is running basically the same software as AOL now, so all this works there, too.)

Again, I caution you: do not download and decode binaries on Usenet unless you know and trust the sender.

Newsgroup FAQ Files

Many newsgroups post files of information called Frequently Asked Questions (FAQs). About once a month, these get posted to their own newsgroup and to the newsgroup soc.answers. Look for a message called the Meta Genealogy FAQ, posted about the 22nd of each month to most of the soc.genealogy newsgroups. This message will show you how to get the FAQ files for the individual genealogy newsgroups.

Note

Remember, all this works the same on CompuServe now.

Net Etiquette and Tips on Usenet

Usenet is a fast-paced way of messaging. It's not quite so "instant" as chat (see Chapter 7) but you will find that new postings and responses appear more quickly than on a mail list (see Chapter 5). Sometimes you can get caught up in these almost real-time discussions, and forget the conventions.

Try to stay on topic in a newsgroup, or you might receive insulting messages, called flames. In general, the following topics are welcomed in genealogy newsgroups:

♦   Your family history information and requests for others to help you find additional sources and material. (Tiny tafels are often posted for this. A tiny tafel provides a standard way of describing a family database so the information can be scanned.)

♦   Information on upcoming genealogical meetings, workshops, symposia, reunions, etc.

♦   Reviews, criticisms, and comments regarding software or hardware you've used in your genealogy/family history efforts.

♦   Telling others about book shops around the world which contain publications or information about this subject.

♦   Almost any message about genealogy in general.

Remember that what you send is posted just as you sent it, unless the site (such as soc.genealogy.surnames) has a moderator who edits all incoming messages.

Participants in any genealogy newsgroup want the topics of discussion to relate directly to genealogy or family history. However, in some groups, the tacit agreement is that anything a subscriber thinks is appropriate *is appropriate*, as long as it relates to genealogy. To discern the lay of the land at a particular site, lurk for a while (read without posting) to discover if it tends to be more lax about off-topic posting.

Assume an attitude of courtesy among subscribers and readers. Remember that your postings and comments might be seen by as many as 20,000 readers on different networks throughout the entire world. Remember the rules I mentioned earlier:

Read carefully what you receive to be certain you understand the message before replying. Read what you've written carefully to ensure your message won't be misunderstood. As a matter of fact, routinely let a reply sit overnight, then read it again before sending. It will prevent that sinking feeling of regret when you realize what you posted was not what you meant.

Avoid sarcasm. If humor seems appropriate, clearly label it as such. A smiley face should indicate humor. It's easy to misunderstand what's being said when there's no tone of voice, facial expressions, or body language to go by.

Know your audience and double-check addresses. Make sure that the person or list of people to whom you're sending your message is the appropriate one(s) with whom to communicate.

Be tolerant of newcomers, as you will expect others to be tolerant of you. None of us were born knowing all about the Internet, nor Usenet. Do not abuse new users of computer networks for their lack of knowledge. As you become more expert, be patient as others first learn to paddle, then swim, then surf the net, just like you. Be an active participant in teaching them.

Avoid cluttering your messages with excessive emphasis (**, !!, > >, and so on). It can make the message hard to follow.

When you respond to a message, either include the relevant part of the original message or explicitly refer to the original's contents. People will commonly read your reply to the message before they read the original. (Remember the convention to precede each quoted line of the original message you include with the > character.)

In responses, do not quote more than necessary to make your point clear, and please, never quote the entire message. Learn what happens on your particular system when you reply to messages. Is the message sent to the originator of the message or to the list, and when is it sent? When responding to another message, your subject line should be the same, with RE: at the beginning.

Always include a precise subject line in your message. It should be something that gets their attention, and the only way to do that is to make sure it describes the main point of your message.

If you're seeking information about a family, include the surname in uppercase in the message subject. Many readers don't have time to read the contents of all messages.

Bad sample subject line:

Wondering if anyone is looking for JONES

Good samples:

Researching surname JONES

SPENCER: England > MA > NY > OH > IN > MS

Delaware BLIZZARDs pre-1845

? Civil War Records

In the good samples, note these conventions: surnames are in all caps, but nothing else is. A "greater than" sign (>) is used as an arrow to denote migration from one place to another. A date is always helpful. If your message is a question, indicate that in the subject line. Although passages in all uppercase are considered shouting, the exception to this rule in the case of genealogy is that surnames should be in uppercase, just as in any query.

Keep a message to only one subject. This allows readers to quickly decide whether they need to read the message in full. Second subjects within a single message are often missed.

Questions are often the exception to this rule. You may need to post a message that is full of questions on a subject. When you ask a question within such a message, end it with a ? and press the Enter key. That should be the end of that line. This makes it much easier for people to reply, because most newsreaders will quote the original message line by line.

Be specific, especially when asking questions. If you ask about a person, identify when and where the person might have lived. In questions concerning specific genealogical software, make it clear what sort of computer (PC/MS-DOS, PC/Windows, Apple Macintosh, etc.) is involved. The folks reading these newsgroups are very helpful but very busy, and are more likely to answer if they don't have to ask what you mean.

It is a good idea to put your name in the text of your message, along with your best e-mail address for a reply. However, you may want to disguise your e-mail address to prevent its being harvested for UBE (see Chapter 2). A good convention is:

```
Please reply to libbic "at" prodigy.net
```

The end of the message is a good place for your name and e-mail address.

Whenever any newsgroup posts a FAQ, **read it**. If you can't find a FAQ message or file, make one of your first questions on the group, "Where and when can I get the Frequently Asked Questions for this group?"

Sometimes (as when, in early 1994, rotten weather, an earthquake, and a national holiday all converged on a certain Monday) you'll find the Usenet news feed absolutely clogged with messages, because so many people found themselves unable or not required to go to work. In that case, you must choose what to read based on the subject line or sender, because it's impossible to read everything posted to the group that day. This is when a newsreader that lets you filter the messages for the subject headings is invaluable!

Searching for Information Within Newsgroups

You don't always have to read the whole newsgroup to find the information you need. There are several places where you can search newsgroups, one or several or all at a time. You can use several different search sites to search newsgroups, either by way of their messages (sometimes called articles) or the newsgroup's description. Good sites to use when searching for specific information within newsgroups are AOL's Netfind, InfoSeek (http://www.infoseek.com), and deja.com.

InfoSeek can access the last two weeks of activity for all Usenet newsgroups from its searchable database. Using a Web browser (see Chapter 4), go to http://www.infoseek.com. Use the drop-down box on the page to choose Usenet Newsgroups, and type in the surnames you want and +genealogy. InfoSeek Guide will return a list of the messages. Each message title is a link; click on it to read it. AOL's Netfind (www.aol.com) works much the same way. However, neither will let you narrow the search to specific newsgroups—they search them all. So, be prepared for a short wait!

Beyond Usenet

There's more to communicating with others on the Internet beyond Usenet, of course. For instance, some people find delivery to their own mailbox more convenient than Usenet. For that, we have mail lists, the subject of the next chapter.

Chapter 5

Genealogy
Mailing Lists

Electronic mailing lists are electronic discussion groups based on e-mail messages. All subscribers can send e-mail to the list, and receive e-mail from the list. Messages sent to the mailing list get forwarded to everyone who subscribes to the list. Replies to messages are also sent to the list, where they get forwarded to all participants. And so it goes.

Mailing lists can be completely automated, with a program taking care of subscribing people to the list, forwarding messages, and removing people from the list. Or humans can get into the loop, handling any and all of the mailing list functions that programs normally would. Such *moderated* mailing lists can take two forms: they can have restricted memberships where you have to be approved to subscribe, or the moderator(s) might let anyone join, reviewing each incoming message before it gets distributed, and preventing inappropriate material from making it onto the list.

There are plenty of mailing lists that focus specifically on genealogy. In addition, there are many more lists that, while not specifically for genealogists, cover topics of interest to genealogists—things like ethnic groups or historical events.

With a decent mail program (see Chapter 2), it's easy to participate in mailing lists.

Note

> *Throughout this chapter you'll find references to newsgroups and Web sites. This is just an example of how interconnected the genealogy resources on the Internet can be. You will learn everything you need to know about newsgroups and Web sites in other chapters.*

Proper Addressing

Each mail list has two e-mail addresses. You use one to subscribe or change how you use the mail list, and a different one to actually post messages to other subscribers. Some mail lists have a third address, used for certain administrative chores, such as reporting violations of the list's rules to the moderator. Names of several mail lists are included later in this chapter; the next few paragraphs explain how to use them.

General Subscribing Tips

Say you want to subscribe to the ROOTS-L genealogy mailing list, which requires that you send an e-mail to roots-l-request@rootsweb.org, with the message *subscribe*, to join the list. Here is how you do it.

♦ Click the Compose Mail icon in your mail program.

♦ In the To: box, type **roots-l-request@rootsweb.org**

♦ In the Message box, type **subscribe**. For some lists, you might have to add your full name; for others, the name of the list. In the case of ROOTS-L, all you need is "subscribe." Do not put any signature at the bottom.

♦ Click the Spell Check button to be sure there are no typos, then click the Send button.

An In-depth Visit to ROOTS-L

Imagine a worldwide, never-ending conversation about genealogy, where novices and experts exchange help, information, ideas, and gossip. Now imagine that this conversation is conducted by electronic mail (e-mail), so you don't have to worry about missing anything. You've just imagined ROOTS-L, the grandparent of genealogy mailing lists on the Internet.

ROOTS-L has spawned entire generations of newer genealogy mailing lists; some are large, some small, but this is the original. The home page at http://www.rootsweb.org/roots-l hosts thousands of mailing lists devoted to genealogy and history. (See Figure 5-1).

♦ In 2000, over 10,000 people were subscribed to ROOTS-L, so make sure you have a large e-mail box to handle the volume of messages you'll likely receive.

Note

If you ever decide to leave the list, you can unsubscribe by sending e-mail to roots-l-request@rootsweb.org, with the message UNSUBSCRIBE. Don't include anything else in the message: no signature block, no name or address, just the word "unsubscribe."

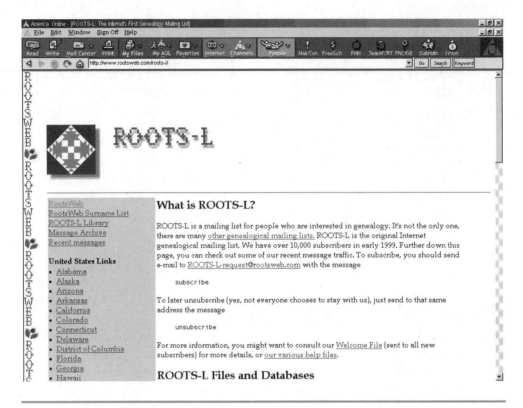

FIGURE 5-1. *The RootsWeb site has thousands of mail lists; ROOTS-L is the oldest*

Some ROOTS-L Rules

ROOTS-L clearly states all its rules in the welcome message. It would be wise to apply them to all mail lists you join, whether explicitly stated or not.

♦ Messages to people go to roots-l@rootsweb.org; commands to programs go to roots-l-request@rootsweb.org. (This is an important rule. My way of remembering it is to save the "request" address in my e-mail's address book under the name "ROOTS-L REQUEST" and the posting address under "ROOTS-L POST." When I'm ready to send a message to one or the other, I choose it from the address list just as I would a person's.)

♦ The list is not a place to refight old wars or discuss religion or politics.

♦ Advertising or selling a product is not, in general, acceptable. You can, however, post a new-product announcement.

♦ Make sure you spell the word *genealogy* correctly in all your messages.

♦ Don't post messages longer than about 150 lines unless you are sure they will be of very general interest.

♦ Don't include a "surname signature" in your messages. (These are lists of surnames that appear at the end of every message some people send. The surnames play havoc with the list archive searches, so don't use them.)

♦ Don't post copyrighted material like newspaper articles or e-mail messages sent to you by other people.

Communicating with People and Programs

I mentioned this rule earlier in the chapter, but people tend to get confused about this, so here are more details. If you're already sure you know where to send messages to subscribers of ROOTS-L, as opposed to sending commands to the ROOTS-L software, you can skip the rest of this section.

Sometimes it's hard to remember the distinction between the list server that runs a mailing list, and the list itself. This problem is common to most mailing lists. The list server gets all the commands: subscribe, unsubscribe, send message digests, etc., whereas the list gets messages you want to send to other people. For ROOTS-L, messages addressed to roots-l@rootsweb.org go to the mailing list. Messages addressed to roots-l-request@rootsweb.org get posted on the list for all to see.

So, if you wanted to request help finding information about your Aunt Tilly, you would send your message to roots-l@rootsweb.org. If you wanted to request a copy of the Roots Surname List (described in the next section), you would send your message to roots-l-request@rootsweb.org. If you need an index of all the files you can get by e-mail from RootsWeb, you send the command "list" roots-I-request@rootsweb.org ("eye" not "ell").

Available Files and Databases

ROOTS-L has tons of files and databases, and you can get these by e-mailing the appropriate commands to the list server that runs ROOTS-L. You can search the ROOTS-L Library for everything from a fabulous collection devoted to obtaining vital records, to useful tips for beginners, to book lists from the Library of Congress, and more. Some of the available files are:

- The Roots Surname List (RSL)—A list of over 350,000 surnames and contact information for the 50,000 people researching those surnames

- The Roots Location List (RLL)—A list of locations of special interest to individual researchers, along with contact information for those researchers

- U.S. Civil War Units—A file containing information about the military units that served in the United States Civil War

- The Irish-Canadian List—A list of Irish immigrants who settled in Canada, including (where available) dates and locations

- Books We Own—Books and other genealogical resources owned by Internet genealogists, in which, under certain conditions, the owners are willing to look up information

When you subscribe to ROOTS-L, you receive a long welcome message that tells you everything you need to know to get started with ROOTS-L, including how to ask the list server to e-mail files to you.

Note

You can also retrieve files yourself by going to the RootsWeb site and browsing for them.

Putting ROOTS-L to Work

Now that you are subscribed to ROOTS-L and know all the rules, it is time to learn how to put the list server to work. You can control your subscription from your e-mail program. Remember, however, that you can only control your subscription from the same e-mail account you subscribed with in the first place. The commands you send will be processed automatically by the list processor—if you remember to send them to roots-l-request@rootsweb.org. If you send your commands to roots-l@rootsweb.org, you'll just succeed in irritating the people running the list.

When you first subscribe to ROOTS-L, you are placed in *digest* mode. That means once or twice a day you will receive a large message from ROOTS-L containing a list of all the messages that have been posted to the list since the last digest message. For each topic, there is a topic number, a subject, and who posted it. Figure 5-2 shows a piece of a typical digest message.

Digests from ROOTS-L tend to be larger than many e-mail programs can view, including AOL. Instead of showing the whole message, you might get a display of only the first part of the message, or even a blank

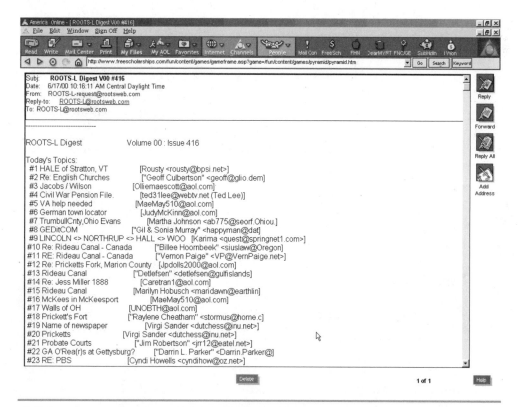

FIGURE 5-2. *ROOTS-L normally delivers in digest mode. Here it is shown in AOL's mail reader*

message with an icon noting an attachment. A copy of the entire message is converted into a text file, and stored as an attachment, which on AOL you have to download (most e-mail programs such as Eudora will download the attachment automatically unless you have set the default not to). From there, it's up to you to open the file with a word processor or text editor and read the messages.

You can get around this by telling the list server to give you each message separately by switching to *mail mode* or *index mode*. Instructions on how to switch modes are included in the files rootsl.welcome2 and rootsl.welcome3. To get them, send e-mail to roots-l-request@rootsweb.org, put the word "archive" (without the quotation marks) in the subject line, and include these commands in the message:

♦ get roots-l.welcome2

♦ get roots-l.welcome3

Note

In the previous addresses, the middle character after the dash is an l (a lowercase "L"), not a 1 (one). Don't include your name, tagline, signature or anything else besides the commands.

In index mode, all you'll get will be message subject lines, with associated message numbers. If you see a message with a subject line that interests you, send e-mail to roots-l-request@rootsweb.org. In this message, the subject should be: ARCHIVE. In the body of the message, you list the numbers of the messages you want to read—for instance, messages 103508 and 103509. As a result, the body of your message would look like this:

♦ get messages/103508

♦ get messages/103509

The commands must be in lowercase, you must use this slash / not this one \, and there is no space after the slash. Keep in mind, you can only include one request per line. So a complete message to the list server, asking for the full text of messages 103508 and 103509 would look like Figure 5-3.

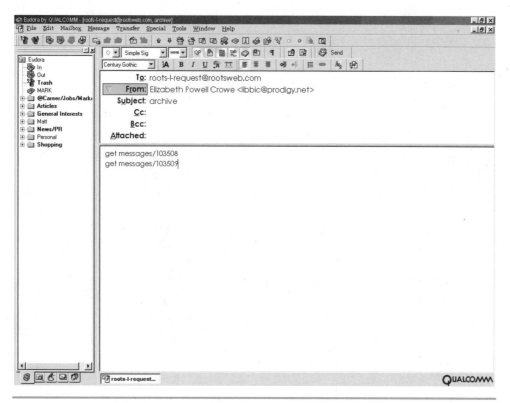

FIGURE 5-3. *An e-mail message (in Eudora) requesting the full text of two messages posted to ROOTS-L*

Losing Contact with a Mailing List

It's possible that you'll stop receiving messages from a mail list even though you didn't unsubscribe. There are two likely causes for this problem:

♦ Your Internet service provider could be having troubles with its e-mail service. Any service can have intermittent service problems; sometimes a whole section of the Internet might be out of order for a few minutes or hours (AOL has had such problems in the past). If all your e-mail has stopped arriving, not just mail from ROOTS-L, this could be the cause.

♦ You are using a different e-mail address than the one you used to subscribe to ROOTS-L. ROOTS-L will only send to the return address of the subscribe message.

If all else fails, just subscribe to ROOTS-L again. That should get the messages flowing for you.

Other Genealogy Mailing Lists

Once you've mastered how ROOTS-L works, you're ready to sample other mailing lists, because many of them work the same way. Over the next several pages, you'll find a small sample of genealogy-related mailing lists you can join. Where noted, the messages are copied ("gatewayed") to the specified Usenet newsgroup.

Not all mailing lists run on a list server. Some are managed *by hand*, so to speak. This means there is some person out there who receives all the messages, then forwards them to all the list subscribers. You subscribe to such lists by sending a politely worded message to an address such as afrigeneas-request@drum.ncsc.org. The message will go to the list owner, who will read it when he or she has the time, then add you to the list as soon as possible (assuming they decide they want to add you to their list).

You'll generally get a welcome message when you subscribe to a list. This message tells you the purpose of the list and other useful information.

Note

I make it a practice to save the welcome message as a text or word processing file for future reference. It saves you a lot of confusion and frustration later.

Sometimes a list is aimed at particular countries or regions. While these lists are not focused on genealogy, the list owners have indicated that genealogy is an acceptable, although in some cases unusual, subject for the list.

The mailing lists included here tackle many subjects, some addressing genealogy only indirectly. Several touch on heritage, culture, and the genealogy of particular ethnic groups. Others concentrate on specific family names or specific historical periods. Some address software and computer-related topics that may be of interest to online genealogists. The list here will get you started. Be on the lookout for messages that contain the names of other lists (which is when things can really snowball). Just remember to come up for air once in a while!

General Genealogy Lists

These are lists with general genealogy in mind—apart from any specific ethnic group, surname, region, or historical period—which are excellent for beginners.

◆ Adoptees—to share information, experiences, and feelings as related to adoption search, reunion, and other adoption-related issues. Membership is restricted to adoptees and adoptee-lites (people raised without one or both birth parents, but were never legally adopted). This list has an associated Web site, the Adoptees Internet Mailing List Web site at http://www.aiml.org (see Figure 5-4). To subscribe, go to the Web site, click the Subscribe icon, and fill out the form completely.

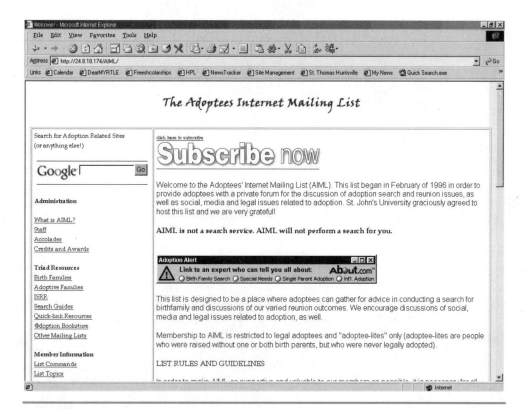

FIGURE 5-4. *The Adoptees Internet Mailing List is one of many mailing lists with an associated Web site*

♦ ADOPTION—Includes discussions of anything and everything connected with adoption. To subscribe, send e-mail to adoption-request@think.com with the message: SUBSCRIBE ADOPTION firstname lastname. The address for posting is adoption@think.com.

♦ ELIJAH-L—A list for members of the Church of Jesus Christ of Latter-day Saints where they can discuss ideas and experiences relating to genealogy in the LDS Church. There are documents and research aids at the Web site, http://www.genealogy.org/ ~holdiman/elijah-l/. Individuals not of the LDS faith are welcome to join as long as they respect the beliefs of the LDS faith and do not deliberately offend believers. To subscribe, write to byrondh@juno.com. Members share LDS-related genealogical ideas, tools, and approaches; LDS-related genealogical experiences and testimonies; and discuss answers to questions and scriptures related to both the LDS and genealogy.

♦ GENMSC-L—This group's messages also appear in the soc.genealogy.misc newsgroup for miscellaneous genealogical discussions that don't fit in one of the other soc.genealogy.* newsgroups. To post, send messages to GENMSC-L@rootsweb.org. To subscribe, send a message to genmsc-lt@rootsweb.org that says only Subscribe, with no subject and no other text.

♦ GENMTD—This group's messages also appear in the soc.genealogy.methods newsgroup. GENMTD discusses general genealogy research techniques and resources. To post a message, send it to genmtd-l-request@rootsweb.org. To subscribe, send a message that says only "subscribe" in the text to genmtd-l-request@rootsweb.org (mail mode), genmtd-d-request@rootsweb.org (digest mode), or genmtd-i-request@rootsweb.org (index mode).

♦ GEN-NEWBIE-L—A message exchange mailing list for the beginner, where the most basic genealogy questions are answered. This mailing list has an associated Web page at http://www.rootsweb.org/ ~newbie/ (see Figure 5-5). To subscribe, send an e-mail to gen-newbie-l-request@rootsweb.org with the message: SUBSCRIBE.

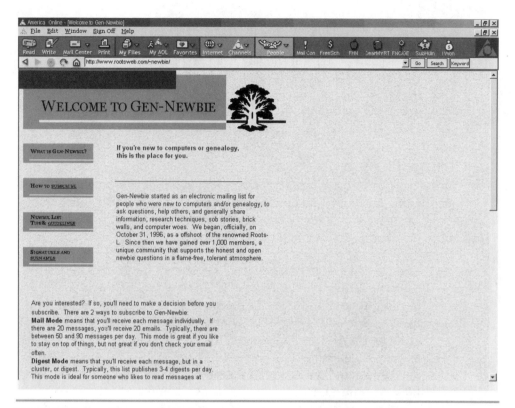

FIGURE 5-5. *If you are new to genealogy, or new to computers, Gen-Newbie is a great Web site to visit, and the mail list will be very helpful*

- NEW-GENLIST—Read this list to be advised of the newest mail lists. People post announcements, and John Fuller, the list owner, notes new lists periodically. You must be a subscriber to post to the list, however. To subscribe, send the word SUBSCRIBE as the only text in the body of a message to new-genlist-l-request@rootsweb.com (mail mode) or new-genlist-d-request@rootsweb.com (digest mode).

- NEW-GEN-URL—Read this list for announcements of new genealogy-related Web sites in order to save time locating new Web sites and locations of significant Web resources. Information on Web sites may be posted to the list even if the sites are not new; especially if they have been substantially revised or updated. Postings will contain the title, full name and e-mail address of the site owner; the URL (address) of the site; and a brief description of the contents of the site. Messages may also have a surname list if the site is a personal Web site. As usual, you must be a subscriber to post to the list. To subscribe, send the word SUBCRIBE as the sole text in a message to new-gen-url-l-request@rootsweb.com (mail mode) or new-gen-url-d-request@rootsweb.com (digest mode).

Ethnic Groups

These lists aren't specifically about genealogy, but cover the culture, history, and current events of particular ethnic groups. Most of them accept the occasional genealogy query, and they're great places to hang about if you want to learn a little bit about other people.

- ◆ AFRIGENEAS—This mailing list was created to discuss and promote family history research. There is an associated Web site at http://www.afrigeneas.com/; whereas archives of past messages reside at http://www.msstate.edu/listarchives/ afrigeneas/. AFRIGENEAS offers discussions on African ancestors, as well as genealogical interests, history, culture, and resources. Topics include, but are not limited to, surnames, records/events, how do I start, census, locations, people and places, and resources. Messages about research, queries, and resources go to afrigeneas@msstate.edu. Request to be added to the list by sending a message that says "subscribe afrigeneas" to majordomo@msstate.edu.

- ◆ BRAZIL—A mailing list for anyone with genealogical interest in Brazil; most of the messages are in Portuguese. The mailing address for postings is brazil-l@rootsweb.org. To subscribe, send the word SUBSCRIBE as the only text in the body of a message to brazil-l-request@rootsweb.org (mail mode) or brazil-d-request@rootsweb.org (digest mode).

- ◆ CHEROKEE-L—This list discusses Cherokee history and culture, with an associated Web site at http://www.io.com/~crberry/ CherokeeGenealogy/. To subscribe, send a message with both the subject and body containing only the word SUBSCRIBE to cherokeet-d-request@rootsweb.org.

♦ SURNAMES-CANADA-L—This is an echo of the soc.genealogy.surnames.canada newsgroup. To subscribe, send a message with the text SUBSCRIBE to SURNAMES-CANADA-L-request@rootsweb.org.

♦ GEN-DE-L—Mirrors the soc.genealogy.german newsgroup regarding the discussion of German genealogy. You subscribe by sending an e-mail to gen-de-l-request@rootsweb.org with the text: subscribe. The address for posting is gen-de-l@rootsweb.org.

♦ GEN-FF-L—Messages from the fr.rec.genealogie newsgroup are mirrored here. It discusses, in French, the genealogy of French-speaking peoples. To subscribe, send an e-mail with the word SUBSCRIBE as the only text to gen-fr-l-request@rootsweb.org (mail mode), gen-fr-d-request@rootsweb.org (digest mode), or gen-fr-i-request@rootsweb.org (index mode). The posting address is gen-fr-l@rootsweb.org.

♦ INDIAN-ROOTS-L—Discussions of Native American genealogical and historical research are held here. To subscribe, send an e-mail to listserv@listserv.indiana.edu with the message: SUB INDIAN-ROOTS-L firstname lastname.

♦ JEWISHGEN—This list is devoted to the discussion of Jewish genealogy. Mirrors the soc.genealogy.jewish newsgroup (JEWGEN is a synonym for JEWISH-GEN, and postings to both will give subscribers two copies of the same message). At the Web site—www.jewishgen.org—you'll find logs of special subgroups. To subscribe, send an e-mail to listserv@lyris.jewishgen.org that says subscribe jewishgen firstname lastname.

♦ PIE—Italian genealogy is the emphasis of this list and its companion Web site (http://www.cimorelli.com/pie/piehome.htm). PIE stands for Pursuing (Our Italian Names Together) In E-mail. The easiest way to subscribe is to go to http://www.cimorelli.com/pie/cfopie/subpie.htm and fill out the form.

Family Name Lists

The best place to find a mail list based on surnames of interest to you is to go to RootsWeb (http://www.rootsweb.org) and click the Mail Lists link from the home page. You usually have to request permission to join one of these lists. There are now literally thousands of them.

There are other name-specific lists all over the Net. I suggest you check out these sites to search for the surnames you are interested in.

Genealogy Resources on the Internet: Surnames
http://www.rootsweb.org/ ~ jfuller/gen_email.html

This page is a list of surname search/query mailing lists. Some are regional (such as SURNAMES-IRELAND). Others are very general, such as the Roots Surname List. Instructions for subscribing are included beside each list.

Genealogy Resources on the Internet: Mailing Lists
http://www.rootsweb.org/ ~ jfuller/gen_mail.html

Scroll down this page to the fifth entry: a categorized list of non-RootsWeb mailing lists.

Genealogy Listservers, Newsgroups & Special Home Pages
http://www.eskimo.com/ ~ chance/lists.html

This is a searchable list of resources involving surnames and localities. You can either click a letter for an alphabetized table of contents, or enter a name in the search box. It's not as complete as the Genealogy Resources on the Internet pages, but it seems to be updated often.

And, of course, there's always Cyndi's List at http://www.cyndislist.com/ mailing.htm

Historical Groups
These lists focus on historical events or groups that could be invaluable to you in your genealogy research.

- ♦ CIVIL-WAR—Contains discussions on the American Civil war, history, and other issues, including genealogy. Subscribe by sending the word SUBSCRIBE as the text message to civil-war-request@rootsweb.org (mail mode) or civil-war-d-request@rootsweb.org (digest mode). Post messages to civil-war@rootsweb.org.

- GEN-MEDIEVAL-L—These messages also appear in soc.genealogy.medieval for genealogy and family history discussions among people researching individuals alive during medieval times. The medieval era is loosely defined as AD 500 to AD 1500. To subscribe, send an e-mail message with the word SUBSCRIBE as the text to gen-medieval-l-request@rootsweb.org (mail mode), gen-medieval-d-request@rootsweb.org (digest mode), or gen-medieval-i-request@rootsweb.org (index mode). You can post messages to gen-medieval-l@rootsweb.org.

- MAYFLOWER—This list revolves about topics concerned with Mayflower descendents. The mailing address for postings is mayflower-l@rootsweb.org. To subscribe, send a message with the word SUBSCRIBE as the sole text to mayflower-l-request@ rootsweb.org (mail mode) or mayflower-d-request@rootsweb.org (digest mode).

- OVERLAND-TRAILS—Devoted to discussions concerning the history, preservation, and promotion of the Oregon, California, Santa Fe, and other historic trails in the Western United States. One project of particular interest to genealogists is a database containing all the names inscribed as graffiti on the various rocks along the trails. If one of your ancestors is rumored to have traveled such a trail, you may be able to confirm it by consulting this database. To subscribe, send an e-mail to listserv@calcite.rocky.edu with the message: SUBSCRIBE OVERLAND-TRAILS firstname lastname. The address for posting is overland-trails@calcite.rocky.edu. You must be a subscriber to post messages.

Regional Groups

RootsWeb has many mail lists for specific geographical locations; there's a separate list for almost every county in Ohio! Check out the RootsWeb mail list page (http://www.rootsweb.org/ ~ maillist/) for names and instructions.

These mailing lists focus on specific geographic areas.

- LISTSERV at Indiana University: This server has several different genealogy discussion lists, catalogued at http://listserv.indiana.edu/ archives/index.html. Many of them have searchable archives of old messages reaching back for years. To subscribe to each list, send a message to listerv@listserv.indiana.edu with the message SUB NAMEOFLIST YOUR NAME. A few of these lists are as follows:

- ARKANSAS-ROOTS-L—about 800 subscribers

- DEEP-SOUTH-ROOTS-L—about 1100 subscribers; discusses Alabama, Georgia, Florida, and Mississippi

- IA-NEB-ROOTS-L—for Iowa and Nebraska; about 500 subscribers

- INROOTS-L—for Indiana; about 800 subscribers

- INSCRIPTIONS-L—for discussions of tombstones; about 200 subscribers

- LOUISIANA-ROOTS-L—about 400 subscribers

- MID-ATLANTIC-ROOTS-L—for Deleware, Maryland, DC, and New Jersey; about 500 subscribers

- MISSOURI-ROOTS-L—about 800 subscribers

- NC-SC-ROOTS-L—about 1400 subscribers

- NEWYORK-ROOTS-L—about 500 subscribers

- NORTHEAST-ROOTS-L—covers New England; about 1100 subscribers

- OHIO-ROOTS-L—about 1000 subscribers

- PENNSYLVANIA-ROOTS-L—about 1000 subscribers

- TEXAHOMA-ROOTS-L—for Texas and Oklahoma; about 500 subscribers

- TNROOTS-L—for Tennessee-related genealogy; about 1200 subscribers

- VA-WVA-ROOTS-L—for the Virginias; about 850 subscribers

- WESTERN-ROOTS-L—for Hawaii, Alaska, Washington, Oregon, California, Nevada, Arizona, Utah, New Mexico, Idaho, Montana, and Wyoming; about 400 subscribers

Other interesting lists besides those at IU:

♦ MAGGIE_Ohio—This list acts as a forum for anyone interested in genealogy in the State of Ohio. The Web site is http://homepages.rootsweb.org/%7Emaggieoh/mco-proj.htm. Send the word SUBSCRIBE as the only text in a message to: Maggie_Ohio-D-request@rootsweb.org.

♦ KYROOTS—Discussions of Kentucky genealogy and historical research. To subscribe, send e-mail to listserv@lsv.uky.edu with the message: SUBSCRIBE KYROOTS.

Software Lists

These lists have information about genealogical software and computer standards (like GEDCOM) of interest to genealogists.

♦ GENCMP-L—A general discussion of genealogy and its relation to computers and computing. To subscribe, send an e-mail to GENCMP-L-request@rootsweb.org with "Subscribe GENCMP-L" in the Subject line.

♦ GEDCOM-L—A technical mailing list to discuss the GEDCOM specifications. If you aren't a computer programmer, a serious genealogical computer user, or haven't read the official GEDCOM specification, this list is definitely not for you. To subscribe, send an e-mail with the message: SUB GEDCOM-L firstname lastname. The address for posting is gedcom-l@listserv.nodak.edu.

♦ PAF—Mailing list for discussion of issues relating to the Personal Ancestral File genealogy program. Web site is http://www.innernet.org/paf/. To subscribe, send e-mail to majordomo@innernet.org with the message: SUBSCRIBE PAF.

E-mail Newsletters

Another e-mail resource is the newsletter. Unlike interactive mailing lists, newsletters are not interactive, they are meant to be read like a magazine. You can write letters to the editor if you like, but you won't often see them in the newsletters.

Some e-mail newsletters worthy of note are:

♦ Eastman's Genealogy Index (http://www.ancestry.com/home/ times.htm)—This is a weekly all-text newsletter on genealogy topics. A typical issue will cover reviews of genealogy computer programs, books, CD-ROMS, and television programs, as well as list news items of note to genealogists, and which Web sites are the best to visit. The reviews in this newsletter are specific (and honest, too!) without being verbose. Each issue is posted at the site listed above, as well as e-mailed to subscribers—you can also find back issues here. To subscribe, send an e-mail to subscribe@rootscomputing.com with the Subject: SUBSCRIBE.

♦ Treasure Maps Newsletter (http://www.firstct.com/fv/ sub.html)—Treasure Maps (Figure 5-6) is one of the best sites on the Web for novices. It is aimed at providing hands-on, how-to information to help you actually do research online. To keep track of the latest news on Treasure Maps, you might want to subscribe to their monthly newsletter. The newsletter also has genealogy information that hasn't been released yet. To subscribe, send an e-mail message to ragan@southeast.net with the subject: SUBSCRIBE TM. Within 24 hours, you should receive your first issue, as well as a help file telling you how to make the program work best.

♦ Genealogy Today Newsletter (http://www.enoch.com/genealogy/ newslet.htm)—This monthly newsletter contains tips, information, and meetings, as well as seminar announcements and queries. To subscribe, just send an e-mail to GenToday-L-request@ rootsweb.org with the word SUBSCRIBE as the sole text. You may also submit a query by e-mailing it to tfarris258@aol.com with "Query" in the Subject line.

♦ RootsWeb Review newsletter—Keeps you up to date on the RootsWeb site, genealogy news, and sundry success stories. Send a message that says SUBSCRIBE to ROOTSWEB-REVIEW-request@rootsweb.org.

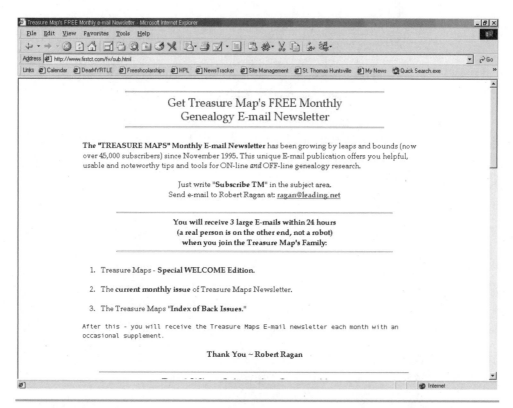

FIGURE 5-6.   *The Treasure Maps newsletter is a great tool for learning how to find your ancestors*

♦ DearMYRTLE—Has a daily column, tips, and online courses, plus much more. Her columns can be e-mailed to you. Go to http://members.aol.com/dearmyrtle/subscribe.htm and follow the instructions.

♦ JOG: The Journal of Online Genealogy—A monthly e-zine on techniques and trends, with reviews of books, programs, and other materials pertinent to the genealogist. Log onto it on the 15th of each month at www.onlinegenealogy.com.

♦ Missing Links—A weekly online newsletter for genealogists presented by Myra Vanderpool Gormley and Julia M. Case. To subscribe, send an e-mail message that says SUBSCRIBE to MISSING-LINKS-L-request.rootsweb.org.

- Somebody's Links—A newsletter of genealogical treasures discovered by its readers. To subscribe or unsubscribe, send an e-mail with the sole word SUBSCRIBE (or UNSUBSCRIBE) in the body of the message to: Somebodys-Links-Newsletter-L-request@rootsweb.org.

- Ancestry's Daily News—A daily update on the Ancestry.com site's newest offerings. To subscribe, visit the Web page http://www.ancestry.com/ and fill in your e-mail address above the button that says "Sign up free!"

- Everton's Family History Newsline—Constitutes a daily tip, news item, or historical fact from one of the major genealogical publishers in America. To subscribe, send a message to lists@everton.com with the single-line message SUBSCRIBE HISTORY.

Finding More Mailing Lists

Even though that may seem like more mail lists than you can shake a stick at, there are many more. To find more mail lists, first check out RootsWeb's World Wide Web site for their ever-growing list. If you point your Web browser to http://www.rootsweb.org/ ~ maillist/, you'll have access to the hundreds of mailing lists hosted by RootsWeb.

John Fuller and Christine Gaunt maintain a categorized directory of genealogy mail lists at http://www.rootsweb.org/ ~ jfuller/gen_mail.html (see Figure 5-7).

Another good site to keep up on the latest in mail lists and newsletters is Cyndi's List, http://www.CyndisList.com/magazine.htm.

Finally, you can search a database of publicly accessible mailing lists at the Publicly Accessible Mailing List site, http://paml.net. You can search this database by keyword, or browse the index of hundreds of mailing lists.

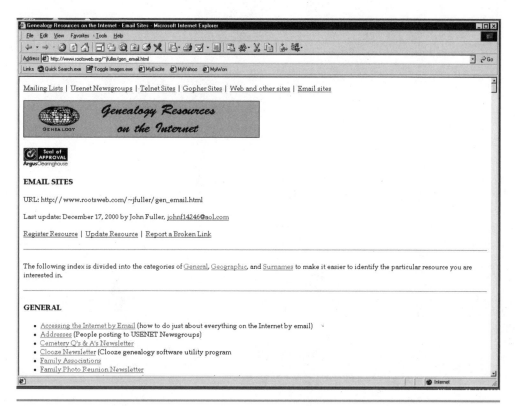

FIGURE 5-7. *Fuller and Gaunt's page on genealogy mail lists categorizes by topic*

Chapter 6

The World Wide Web

In addition to everything else it can do, the Web is a great resource for online genealogists. As you might imagine, any place on the Internet that combines ease of use regarding genealogical tools, lots of excitement, and lots of new people is a place genealogists will want to be. Hundreds of Web sites of interest to genealogists have popped up, and in this chapter, you'll find short profiles of 86 good ones for you to start with. The more major sites have been allocated their own chapters later in the book.

True Story: The Web Helps a Mobility-Challenged Genealogist

Being mobility challenged and on a very limited income, I have to depend on the Internet mostly at this time and have had some success.

I had a query on the Irsch surname board for my great-grandfather and the fact he had married a Pitts in Noxubee, MS in 1860. Just happened to decide to go to the Pitts surname board and posted the same query for a Lucretia Emmaline Pitts who had married a Frank Irsch.

I received a tentative confirmation from someone whose great-grandfather had a sister who had married an Irsch about that time frame. A few back and forths later we thought we might have a connection; I asked if she had ever heard the names Aunt Em and Uncle Henry Hill. I had heard my grandmother speak of them but didn't know if they were blood relatives.

We both knew we had established the connection. "Aunt Em" was the sister of her great-great-great-grandfather, Lafayette Newton Pitts, and another sister, Lucretia, had married Frank Irsch. Their father's name was James W. Pitts and their mother's name was Mary. We still have not discovered her maiden name.

She had a picture of some of the Irsch family that Lizzie Eaton/Bennett had identified for them as her brother and family and Grandma Pitts. She wasn't sure if the older woman was her grandma Pitts or not, but didn't think so. Lizzie Eaton/Bennett was MY grandmother, and if she identified the older woman as Grandma Pitts it would have been her grandmother. Mary ?-? Pitts. I remember my mother telling me of Aunt Annie Irsch and Grandma Pitts sending Christmas gifts when she was little.

Now we proudly know we have a picture of our shared great-great-great-grandmother. We are working on other shared lines but I would call this a wonderful tale of success from the Internet!

--- Louise McDonald

Note

Getting a browser is easy. America Online's software comes with a version of Microsoft Internet Explorer as its Web browser, as do CompuServe and Prodigy. Other Internet Service Providers may supply you with Netscape Navigator, Opera, or some other browser.

Browser Tips and Tricks

There are several ways to use your browser to better surf the World Wide Web. The following are a few helpful tips:

♦ Versions of Microsoft Internet Explorer and Netscape Navigator above 3.0 will input the http:// prefix if you type in the unique part of the address. For example, type www.genhomepage.com and the browser will change it to http:// www.genhomepage.com for you.

♦ Microsoft Internet Explorer and Netscape Navigator versions 4 and above will also run a search for you. When you input your search terms, place a question mark before them in the address box, and the program will try to find related pages for you.

♦ Type in an address that begins with the letters FTP— ftp.symantec.com, for example—and the browser will insert the necessary ftp://. An FTP site is a collection of files for public download (covered later in this chapter).

♦ If you need to copy a URL to your clipboard, you can just click in the Address box, press CTRL+C, and you have a copy of the URL that's ready to be pasted elsewhere. This can be useful if you want to reference it in another program.

♦ You can change your browser's opening page. To do this in Microsoft Internet Explorer, choose View | Internet Options. On the General tab, in the Home Page section of the tab, click Use Current. This will make IE treat the current page as your home page. You can click Use Default on the same tabbed sheet to restore Microsoft's home page as your browser home page. In Netscape Navigator, use Edit | Preferences and click Use Current to set it to the current page. In both browsers, you can browse your disk and set your bookmark.htm file as your home page.

♦ Click the down arrow in the address box to see a list of the URLs you've visited recently. This comes in very handy if you can't remember how to get back to a particularly neat site.

♦ If you forgot to bookmark a site, and the URL list in the Address box doesn't help, you can take a look in your History folder. Netscape Navigator and Microsoft Internet Explorer (MIE) both keep a history of all the sites and pages you've visited recently. You can go to the History folder and rummage around if you think seeing the name of the Web site will get you on the right track. Here's how you do it in MIE:

1. Using Windows Explorer, find the History folder in the Windows directory.

2. Double-click the History folder. You'll see a collection of Calendar folders.

3. Double-click a Calendar folder. Inside the folder you'll see Site folders.

4. Double-click a Site folder to see links to all the pages you've visited recently at that Web site.

5. Double-click a link to go to that Web page.

In Netscape Navigator, it's much easier. With Netscape Navigator running, press CONTROL+H. You can then search that list by depressing CONTROL+F and typing in the word or words you're looking for. See Figure 6-1.

♦ All browsers save copies of the text, pictures, and other files you see in your Web browser window. They use these stored files the next time you visit the site for a faster display, loading the ones on your disk that are identical to those at the remote site. If you are running low on disk space on your PC, however, you can delete these files. Web pages may take a little longer to load, but you'll free a ton of space on your hard drive. On Microsoft Internet Explorer, in the View | Internet Options window, on the

General tab, click Delete Files. In Netscape Navigator, in the Edit |
Preferences window, under Advances, click the button that says
Clear Disk Cache.

♦   If the server you want to access is too busy, repeatedly try until
you hit that moment when someone has just logged off. Another
trick: figure out which time zone the remote site is in and access
it during local mealtimes, rush hours, or times when they'll be
sleeping. A server in the UK, for instance, will be easier to access
at 4 PM UK time when school children are on their way home
and many businesses are winding up for the day. Granted, the
Internet is international in nature, but a computer tied to a given
university or organization will have peak usage at predictable
times—use that to your advantage.

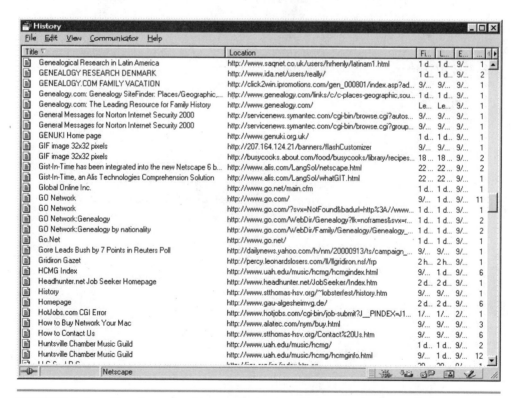

FIGURE 6-1.   *Your browsing history can be searched in Netscape Navigator*

FTP

FTP stands for File Transfer Protocol. It's a way of getting files from here to there—from another computer to yours or from yours to another computer—via the Internet.

Browsers can receive files with FTP, and in versions 5 of Microsoft Internet Explorer and Netscape Navigator, send files as well. Furthermore, many HTML editors now have a built-in FTP engine to submit your finished product to the server, so should you have a Web page and wish to share it with the world, FTP will transmit your files to the Internet server. If you want to retrieve a shareware program or large text file, again FTP is your best choice.

WS_FTP32 for PCs and Fetch for Macintosh are good choices, and relatively cheap. They both have features I enjoy: the ability to read text files, saving the addresses of FTP sites you visit, and batch send and receive. Every FTP program is different, so when you get one, poke around its Help file or manual to discover particular tricks. Some let you store the settings for several different FTP sites, or let you set a default FTP site. Many programs that store sites also let you set the initial directory to search, such as /PUB.

Note

If you are using FTP to get files from a public site, you log in with the username "anonymous" and give your e-mail address as your password. If "anonymous" doesn't work as a login name, try "ftp".

Using the command CD to change directories and LIST to look at file names, you can send and receive files, usually by clicking an arrow (as in WS_FTP), but if you have a text-based client, you simply use GET and SEND.

In FTP, case, spelling, and punctuation count. If you try to get to FOOBAR.some.edu by typing foobar.some.edu, it probably won't work. If you try to get a file called FAMILY.LOCLIST.README.html you must follow that punctuation and capitalization exactly, or you'll get a "file not found" error message.

Many Web browsers have an FTP program built-in. If you want to jump to an FTP site, just enter the address by prefacing it with FTP://.

FTP Conventions

Before using FTP, you need to know some conventions. Files that end in .zip, .lzh, .exe, .arj, .arc, and .com are binary and should be transferred in binary mode. Files that end in anything else are probably text files and should be transferred in ASCII mode. If you are transferring files to a UNIX system, binary mode is generally the best for all transfers. The programs for uncompressing files can be downloaded from several software sites such as www.shareware.coma and www.tucows.com.

Binaries will usually be in Zip format with a file extension of .zip. A self-extracting copy of PKware's shareware programs is in the DOS file pkz204g.exe. Zip files can also be read with the DOS program unz50p1.exe.

Some files are also compressed with lharc, having the ending .lzh. The software to unpack those files can be found in the self-extracting DOS archive lha213.exe. Files that end with .arj may be uncompressed with unarj.exe which is in the Zip file unarj230.zip. .arc files may be decompressed with a program in pk361.exe. There are also several files that end with .exe. These are generally either self-extracting DOS archives or DOS programs.

Files ending in .Z have been compressed with UNIX "compress." Files ending in .gz have been compressed with gzip.

Be prepared for some unsuccessful attempts to connect to an FTP site, however. Addresses are always changing. The Internet is dynamic, so expect a few detours along the way.

Four Score and Seven Sites to See

Since the first publication of this book, the number of genealogy-related Web pages has gone from a handful to literally thousands. And with the rate at which things appear, disappear, and change location on the Internet, you'll never be able to see them all. So, how do you find genealogy sites that are worth seeing? The following is a list of some that I have found useful.

The sites were included according to these factors:

- Timeliness—how often it is updated and kept accurate

- Usefulness—how well it matches the needs of genealogists

- Uniqueness—information content (how rare the information is and/or the unique manner in which it's presented)

- Organization—how easy it is to find and retrieve the information there

In the manner of Web sites everywhere, these sites will all lead you to other sites, where (it's hoped) you'll find the information you need. Realize that this isn't even close to an exhaustive list; for that, see Cyndi's List and Genealogy Resources on the Internet, shown next. In the list that follows, the sites are catalogued alphabetically, not ranked.

Note

All of these links were active when I wrote this, but considering how quickly things change on the Web, it's likely some of the links listed will already be gone.

About.com Genealogy (http://genealogy.about.com/hobbies/genealogy/) has tips, discussion groups, and weekly articles on genealogy.

Acadian Genealogy Homepage (http://www.acadian.org/) contains information about French Acadian and French Canadian genealogy, and includes ordering information for a CD-ROM covering over half a million people of almost exclusively French Acadian/French Canadian ancestry.

Adoptee Search Center (http://www.adopteesearchcenter.org/) offers links to resources for adoptees, search help, and state-specific information.

African-American Genealogical Society of Northern California, (http://www.aagsnc.org/) has transcribed records, regular columnists and collected news stories about African-American history; not just for Californians.

African-American Web Ring (http://afamgenealogy.ourfamily.com/) will start your journey on the Web with its member Web pages dedicated to African-American history and genealogy.

AfriGeneas Home Page (http://www.afrigeneas.com) is the starting place for African-American family history. Don't miss the in-depth profile of this site later in the chapter.

Alabama Department of Archives and History (http://www.archives.state.al.us/) has a specific genealogy page, with links to what records are available. The site accepts credit cards for reference requests, and is shown in Figure 6-2.

Allen County, Indiana Public Library Historical Genealogy Department (http://www.acpl.lib.in.us/genealogy/genealogy.html) has over 220,000 printed volumes, 251,000 microfilms and microfiches, and 38,000 volumes of compiled genealogies in their collection. They also have census data going back to the 1700s, city directories, passenger lists, military records, Native American and African-American

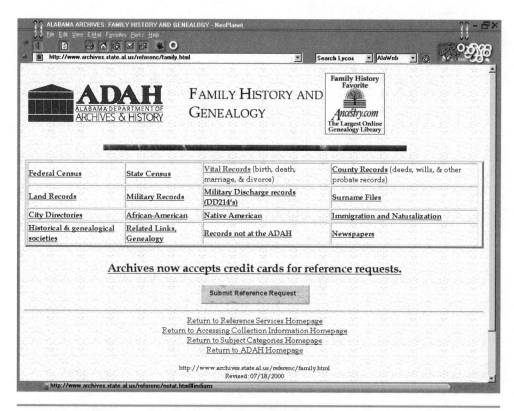

FIGURE 6-2. *The Alabama Archives has a page just for genealogists*

records and many other types. If you ever want to do a genealogy road trip, consider putting this library on your itinerary.

American Civil War Home Page (http://sunsite.utk.edu/civil-war/) has links to fantastic online documents from many sources, including those of two academics who've made the Civil War their career.

Ancient Faces (http://www.ancientfaces.com/cgi-bin/index.cfm) adds a personal touch to genealogy research by including photographs, documents, stories, recipes and more—all located under individual surnames.

AOL Hispanic Genealogy Special Interest Group (http://users.aol.com/mrosado007/) is the gathering place for a group of Hispanic genealogists on America Online. Links include a newsletter, heraldry information, a surname list and more.

Branching Out Online (http://www.didian.com/branch/) Many other sites use "Branching Out" in their title, but this one is special: It's a tutorial on learning about online techniques and genealogy sites. Great for beginners.

The British Heraldic Archive (http://www.kwtelecom.com/heraldry/) is dedicated to increasing interest in heraldry, genealogy, chivalry, and related topics.

The Bureau of Land Management Land Patent Records (http://www.glorecords.blm.gov/) is a searchable database. Invaluable especially for the western states when they were territories, and when local records were scarce. See Figure 6-3.

Byzantine.net (http://www.byzantines.net/genealogy/INDEX.HTM) is for persons of Ruthenian—Carpatho-Rusyn—ancestry and those of the Byzantine Catholic/Orthodox faiths who came from the former Austro-Hungarian Empire.

Calendars Through the Ages (http://www.webexhibits.org/calendars/) explores the fascinating history of how man has tried to organize our lives in accordance with the sun and stars.

Canadian Heritage Information Network (http://www.chin.gc.ca/) is a bilingual—French or English—guide to museums, galleries, and other heritage-oriented resources in Canada. See Figure 6-4.

Cemetery Junction: The Cemetery Trail (http://www.daddezio.com/cemetery/trail/index.html) has monthly articles on cemetery research and preservation.

Census Bureau Home Page (http://www.census.gov/) has a list of Frequently Occurring Names in the U.S. for 1990, Spanish surname list

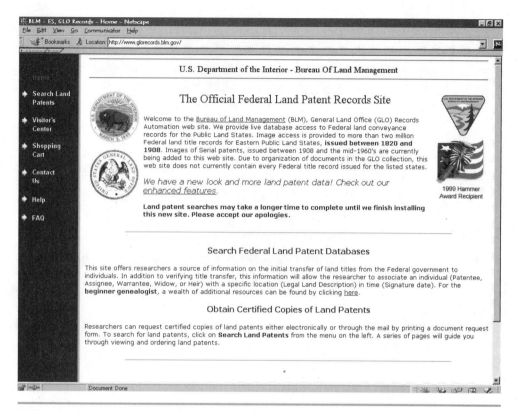

FIGURE 6-3. *The Bureau of Land Management has a database of land patents you can search from the Web*

for 1990, age search service, and a Frequently Asked Questions—FAQ—file on genealogy.

Christine's Genealogy Website (http://ccharity.com/) is an excellent site about African-American history and genealogy.

Cybertree Genealogy Database (http://www.kuhnslagoon.net/cybertree/howto/index.html) has a list of some words and phrases whose early meanings were different than today's. It also contains obscure nicknames and abbreviations, as well as certain genealogical tools that may seem mysterious at first.

Cyndi's List of Genealogy Sites on the Internet (http://www.cyndislist.com/) is the best-organized and annotated list of WWW genealogy sites on the Internet. A must see!

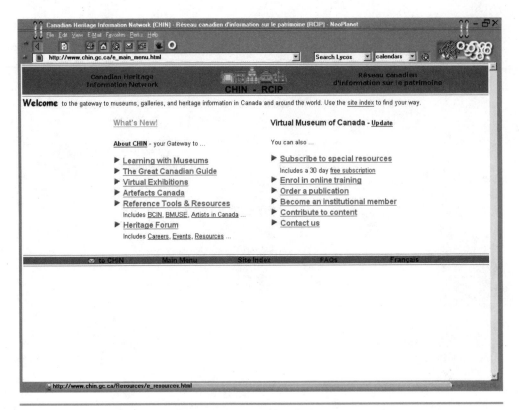

FIGURE 6-4. *The Canadian Heritage page leads you through museums, galleries, and other resources*

David Eppstein's home page (http://www.ics.uci.edu/~eppstein/gene/) has information on his shareware program Gene for the Macintosh.

Directory of Royal Genealogical Data (http://www.dcs.hull.ac.uk/public/genealogy/royal/catalog.html) is a database containing the genealogy of the British Royal family, and many other ruling families of the Western world—they all seem to be interrelated somehow. Contains over 18,000 names.

Eastman's Online Genealogy Newsletter (http://www.ancestry.com/home/eastarch.htm) is a weekly all-text newsletter on genealogy topics. A typical issue will cover reviews of genealogy computer programs, news items of note to genealogists, a list of Web sites to visit, reviews of books, CD-ROMs, TV programs, and more.

Everton's Guide to Genealogy on the World Wide Web
(http://www.everton.com/) includes an online version of the venerable
Helper. Has links to online resources and a tutorial for genealogy
beginners. Test drive their genealogical database On-Line Search.

Family Chronicle (http://www.familychronicle.com/) is the Web site
for this magazine, which is dedicated to families researching their roots.
Check out their offerings and request a free sample of the magazine.

Family History, How Do I Begin (http://www.lds.org/library/display/
0,4945,34-1-18-1,FF.html) is the Church of Jesus Christ of Latter-day
Saints' basic tutorial (see Figure 6-5).

Family Tree Finders at SodaMail Archives (http://gt.sodamail.com/
cgi-bin/gt/archives.html?&nl_master = 1) is a daily e-mail column on
genealogy topics.

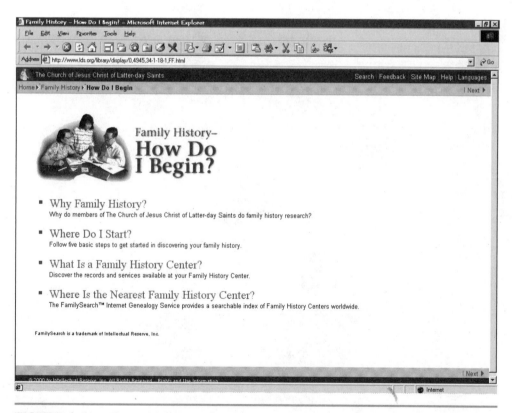

FIGURE 6-5. *The LDS site has an excellent tutorial for the beginning genealogist*

Family TreeMaker Online (http://www.familytreemaker.com/) boasts the FamilyFinder Index, which has genealogy data from users of their programs. Includes 153 million names you can search, the Internet FamilyFinder, and the Genealogy How-To—a 1200 page guide to genealogy. This site is by Borderland Software, the publishers of Family Tree Maker.

FreeBMD (http://FreeBMD.rootsweb.org/) FreeBMD stands for Free Births, Marriages, and Deaths. The FreeBMD Project is made up of volunteers transcribing the Civil Registration index information for England and Wales from the years 1837 to 1898 onto the Internet. Progress is sporadic; volunteer if you can.

Gathering of the Clans Home Page (http://www.tartans.com/) described as a reference for people researching the Scottish clans. Includes information on 65 clans, as well as certain genealogical resources (specifically Scottish). See Figure 6-6.

FIGURE 6-6.   *If you are of Scottish descent, you should check this site out*

GENDEX (http://www.gendex.com/) is the home site of the GENDEX and GED 2HTML software. When you use GED2HTML to post your genealogy on the Web, you can register to be part of the worldwide GENDEX, a search engine for all such genealogy sites.

Genealogy Dictionary (http://home.att.net/ ~ dottsr/ diction.html#DICT0) is for all those confusing terms such as "cordwainer" and "primogeniture."

Genealogy for Teachers (http://www.execpc.com/ ~ dboals/ geneo.html) lists resources, organizations, guides, and tutorials. Aimed at educators, it should help any beginner.

Genealogy Home Page (http://www.genhomepage.com/) is a wide-ranging index of genealogy resources on the Internet. It includes links to maps, libraries, software, and societies. This site, which is sponsored by Family Tree Maker Online, is examined in detail later in this chapter.

Genealogy Links.Net (http://www.genealogylinks.net/) has over 7,000 links, most of them to online searchable databases, such as ships' passenger lists, church records, cemetery transcriptions, and censuses for England, Scotland, Wales, Ireland, Europe, USA, Canada, Australia, and New Zealand.

Genealogy of the Royal Family of the Netherlands (http://www. xs4all.nl/ ~ kvenjb/gennl.htm) is a detailed genealogical history of the House of Orange-Nassau. Covers from Heinrich the rich of Nassau (born 1180) to Juliana Guillermo (born 1981).

Genealogy on the Web Ring (http://www.geocities.com/Heartland/ Plains/5270/webring.html) is a group of genealogy Web pages and sites, all connected one to the other in a giant ring. From this page, you can explore the ring's sites in sequence or select random jumps to put some serendipity — wonderful surprises — into your research.

Genealogy Pages (http://www.genealogypages.com/) is a collection of links to free Genealogical services, as well as to over 29,000 online resources.

Genealogy Resources on the Internet (http://www.rootsweb.org/ ~ jfuller/internet.html) is a site that provides you with a quality-sorted list for finding the exact genealogical information you are looking for.

Genealogy Today (http://www.genealogytoday.com) announces and rates genealogy sites, has news updates, links to databases, allows readers to vote for their favorite sites, etc.

GENUKI (http://midas.ac.uk/genuki/) all about Genealogy in the UK and Ireland.

GenWeb Database Index (http://www.gentree.com/) has links to all known genealogical databases searchable through the Web. Now includes GenDex, an index of name databases with over two million entries.

Global: Everything for the Family Historian (http://www.globalgenealogy.com/) is the Global Genealogy Supply Web site. Shop online for genealogy supplies — maps, forms, software, etc. — and subscribe to the Global Gazette, a free e-mail newsletter covering Canadian genealogy and heritage.

Hauser-Hooser-Hoosier Theory: The Truth about Hoosier (http://www.geocities.com/Heartland/Flats/7822/) explains how genealogy solved the mystery of "What is a Hoosier?"

Headstone Hunter (http://www.headstonehunter.com/) is all about cemetery research. People volunteer to find headstones for each other.

HIR—Hungarian Information Resources Genealogy Page (http://mineral.umd.edu/hir/) is a good place to start if your research leads you to Hungary. Primarily links to other sites with Hungary-specific genealogical information.

HistorySeek! History Search Engine & Historical Information (http://www.historyseek.com) is a directory search engine specifically made for historians, genealogists, scholars, and history enthusiasts. See Figure 6-7.

How to Get Past Genealogy Road Blocks (http://www.firstct.com/fv/stone.html) is a quick refresher on what to do when you are just plain stuck, and can't get past, over, around, or through that brick wall.

Internet Tourbus (http://www.tourbus.com/) is Patrick Douglas Crispen's e-mail course on how to use every part of the Internet. It taught my mom everything she knows about the Net.

Janyce's Root Digging Dept. (http://www.janyce.com/gene/rootdig.html) is yet another good place for beginners to start their online genealogical research.

JewishGen (http://www.jewishgen.org/) is a comprehensive resource for researchers of Jewish genealogy worldwide. Among other things, it includes the JewishGen Family Finder, a database of towns and surnames being researched by Jewish genealogists worldwide, and can be searched on the WWW, or via e-mail (e-mail the server commands, and results are e-mailed back to you).

Library of Congress (http://www.loc.gov/) is the Web connection to the U.S. government's vast collection of historical documents and other

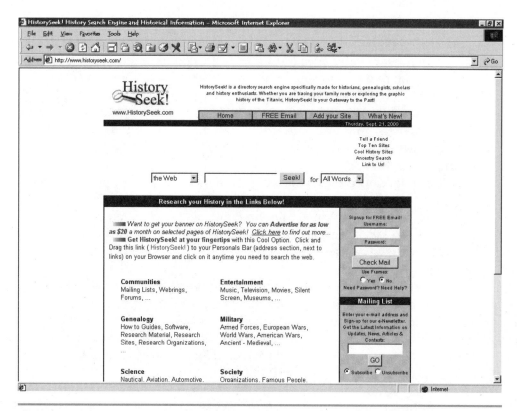

FIGURE 6-7. *HistorySeek! is a targeted search engine*

resources. There's plenty of information on how to tap into this monstrous resource later in Chapter 13.

Library of Virginia Digital Collections (http://image.vtls.com/) is a starting point where you can search Virginia colonial records as well as bible records, newspapers, court records, and state documents.

Lineages, Inc. (http://www.lineages.com/default.asp) is the Web site for a group of professional genealogical researchers who'll help you find your roots, for a fee. In addition, their site includes some free information, such as "First Steps for Beginners," a free genealogical queries page, and more.

Marston Manor (http://www.geocities.com/Heartland/Plains/1638/) is a site that offers numerous useful items for online genealogists, including a chart for calculating family relationships, and a detailed discussion of the terms proof and evidence as they relate to genealogy.

Mayflower **Web Pages** (http://users.aol.com/calebj/mayflower.html) contain the passenger lists of the *Mayflower*, *Fortune*, and *Anne*, plus many related documents.

Medal of Honor Citations (http://www.army.mil/cmh-pg/moh1.htm) contains the names and text of the citations for the more than 3,400 people who have been awarded the Congressional Medal of Honor since 1861.

National Genealogical Society (http://www.ngsgenealogy.org) is the granddaddy of all genealogical societies. Here, you'll find announcements of NGS seminars, workshops and programs, information on their home study course, youth resources, and other NGS activities. This is an excellent site for learning genealogy standards and methods. An in-depth profile comes later in this chapter.

Native American Genealogy (http://members.aol.com/bbbenge/front.html) is an AOL-based site that tries to keep up with the latest in sites and resources for Native Americans.

New England Historic Genealogical Society (http://www.nehgs.org/) is designed to be a center for family and local history research in New England. The Society owns 200,000 genealogy books and documents. If you are a New England genealogist, you should check them out.

Online Genealogy Classes (http://www.conted.bcc.ctc.edu/users/marends/geneal2/gen2home.htm) at Bellevue Community College include topics such as Beginning Genealogy, Land Records, Using Online Genealogical Databases.

Oregon History & Genealogy Resources (http://www.rootsweb.org/~genepool/oregon.htm) is a collection of genealogy information for Oregon, with links to the wider world of genealogy sites as well.

Our Spanish Heritage: History and Genealogy of South Texas and Northeast Mexico (http://www.geocities.com/Heartland/Ranch/5442/) is an interesting source if you're looking for relatives from the South Texas/Northeast Mexico area. The database has over 11,000 names, all interrelated as lineages.

Pitcairn Island Web Site (http://www.lareau.org/genweb.html) is the place to find information about the current inhabitants of Pitcairn Island. But more importantly for genealogists, this is the place to go to get information on over 7500 descendants of the crew of the H.M.S. Bounty, of *Mutiny on the Bounty* fame. See Figure 6-8.

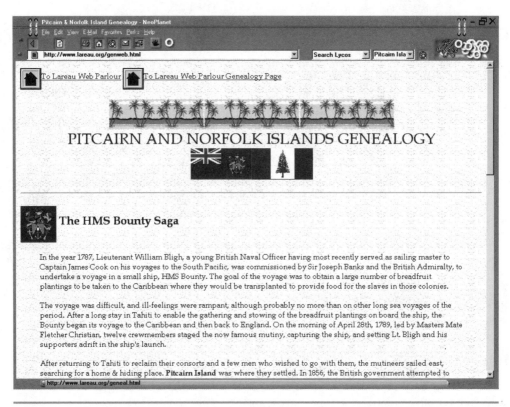

FIGURE 6-8. *Even if you are not descended from the survivors of the Bounty, this site is fascinating*

Poland Worldgenweb (http://www.rootsweb.org/ ~ polwgw/polandgen.html) has maps and other information on Polish provinces, as well as a surname search. You can also adopt a province, becoming the provider of information about it.

Quick Guide to Genealogy in Ireland (http://www.bess.tcd.ie/roots/prototyp/qguide.htm) is a beginner's guide to Irish genealogical resources.

Repositories of Primary Sources (http://www.uidaho.edu/special-collections/Other.Repositories.html) is a listing of over 2500 Web sites describing holdings of manuscripts, archives, rare books, historical photographs, and other primary sources. It's worth a look.

RootsComputing (http://www.rootscomputing.com/) is a categorized guide to genealogy on the WWW. It's CompuServe's genealogy forum's presence on the Web, and worth a look.

RootsWeb E-zines (http://www.rootsweb.org/ ~ review/e-zine.html) is the home page of the ROOTS-L e-mail newsletters. There's a link to search past issues of each newsletter.

SBt Genealogy Resources (http://www.cswnet.com/ ~ sbooks/genealogy/index.htm) is a collection of articles, links and graphics for the genealogist. Especially interesting is the article, "Comparison of Four Search Engines for Online Genealogy Research."

South Carolina Library (http://www.sc.edu/library/socar/books.html) is an online card catalog for the South Carolina Library, which houses an extensive collection of genealogy holdings.

Spanish Heritage home page (http://members.aol.com/shhar/) an AOL-based site, this is the home of the Society of Hispanic Historical and Ancestral Research.

StateGenSites (http://www.stategensites.com/) has monthly and weekly columnists on all aspects of genealogy. Uncle Hiram's weekly column is especially good! See Figure 6-9.

Surnames.com (http://www.surnames.com/) discusses general genealogy, with some focus on the Arizona area. It includes a surname search and a map of genealogical organizations in the United States. The site also has a useful beginner's section.

Surnames: What's in a Name? (http://clanhuston.com/name/name.htm) is a large collection of surnames and their meanings. The site describes the list as "fairly extensive, but it certainly isn't all-inclusive." There is also a brief history of surnames, with references.

Swiss Genealogy Project (http://www.mindspring.com/ ~ philipp/che.html) is a set of pages for researching Swiss genealogy, maintained by a group of volunteers. It includes several maps with detailed information on each district.

Traveller Southern Families (http://www.traveller.com/genealogy/) is dedicated to the genealogy of Southern Families (see Figure 6-10), with information about Civil War Pages, Government Web Servers, Genealogy Software Companies, Family Societies and/or Associations Pages, Books for Sale, and Genealogy Newsgroups.

Treasure Maps, the How-to Genealogy Site (http://www.firstct.com/fv/tmapmenu.html) is one of the best sites on the Web for novices. It is

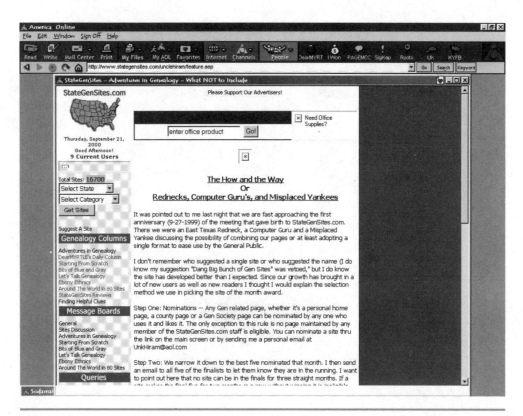

FIGURE 6-9.   *The monthly and weekly columnists at StateGenSites are interesting reading*

aimed at providing hands-on, how-to information to help you actually do research online; includes tutorials on writing queries, using the U. S. Census, and more. To keep track of the latest news on Treasure Maps, you might want to subscribe to their monthly newsletter.

Tuffsearch's Ancestor's Attic (http://members.aol.com/ Tuffsearch/Genealogylinks.html) has tips, tools, charts, forms, vital records, newspapers, maps, libraries, and more for beginners and experienced genealogists.

U. S. Gazetteer (http://www.census.gov/cgi-bin/gazetteer/) Just type in a city and/or state, and a map will appear showing the location. This service is run by the U.S. Census Bureau, and uses information from the 1990 Census.

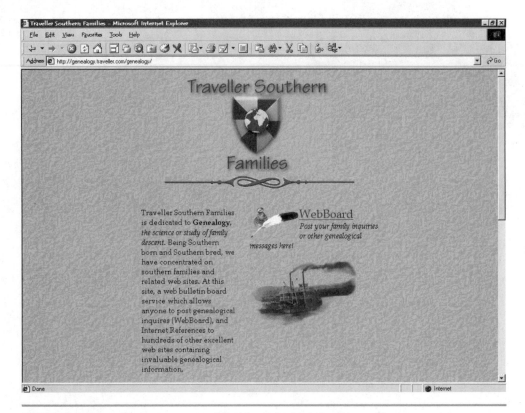

FIGURE 6-10.   *If you are researching the American South, you'll want to visit Traveller Southern Families*

United States Civil War Center (http://www.cwc.lsu.edu/) has book reviews, research tips, and articles about studying the War Between the States.

The USGenWeb Project (http://www.usgenweb.com) is a non-commercial project with the goal of providing Web sites for genealogical research in every county and every state of the United States. There is much more information on this project later in the chapter.

Utah State Archives (http://www.archives.state.ut.us/) Click the Research Center for the Archives' public services; includes research, places where questions can be answered, and where records can be ordered. Not everything here is free, but it's very convenient!

Xerox Map Server (http://pubweb.parc.xerox.com/map) offers interactive maps for finding any place in the world.

Yahoo Genealogy Page (http://www.yahoo.com/Arts/Humanities/History/Genealogy/) is a huge collection of links to guides, resources, and personal genealogies on Web sites. It includes links to related resources as well.

In-depth Explorations of Major Genealogical Web Sites

While one of the most exciting things about genealogy and Web browsing is the joy of discovery, some sites deserve a guided tour. These sites are particularly interesting or useful to online genealogists, and each one has something special to offer. However, if you want to discover everything yourself, you have more than enough information to spend years researching online. Just skip past the rest of this section and be on your way.

AfriGeneas

AfriGeneas is a site for researching families of African ancestry (see Figure 6-11). The AfriGeneas Web site (http://www.afrigeneas.com) is associated with a mailing list, and gathers and presents information about families of African ancestry, as well as a central point for pointers to genealogical resources around the world. Members of the mailing list are invited to contribute information and resources, sometimes going as far as taking responsibility for information for a certain area.

AfriGeneas provides leadership, promotion, and advocacy for genealogy resources devoted to researching African-related ancestry. It maintains a searchable database of surnames (in addition to slave data) from descendants of slaveholding families, as well as from other sources both public and private. Tips and topics to help people in their search for family history are distributed through mailing lists, chats, newsletters and the Internet. All of this is done by volunteers, who extract, compile, and publish all related public records with any genealogical value. The site also maintains an impressive set of links to other Internet resources to help African-Americans in their research.

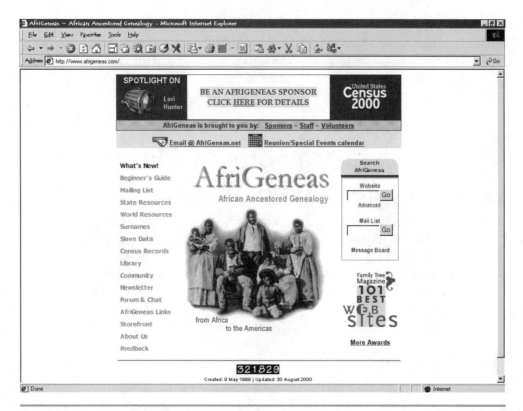

FIGURE 6-11. *The AfriGeneas Web site*

The sections of the site are listed in the navigation bar to the left of the home page, and are arranged in the best order of approach.

Beginner's Guide This slide show-like presentation steps you through online genealogy. It's a no-nonsense approach, showing what can and can't be done online; also includes some success stories.

Mailing List This is the discussion list. You'll find the rules, the archives, and information about how to subscribe and unsubscribe to the mailing list.

State Resources With a clickable map, this page links to sites for each state in the U.S. with history, links to state resources, and queries.

World Resources This is along the same lines as State Resources, but only the United States and the Bahamas are up as of this writing. Volunteers are actively sought for other countries.

Surnames This is a set of queries with names, dates, and places of known ancestors. You can search the ones that are there, as well as post your own.

Slave Data This is designed to help you find a path to the last slaveholder or suspected last slaveholder. Records kept by the slave owner are frequently the only clue to African-American ancestors, particularly during the period 1619-1869.

The site is also designed to assist descendants of slaveholders and other researchers, as well as share information they find containing any references to slaves, including wills, deeds, and other documents (see Figure 6-12). Also houses a search engine, and a form for submitting any data you may have.

FIGURE 6-12. *Wills, deeds, slave manifests and Bible records are just a few of the sources available at the Slave Database*

To use the database, click the first letter of the surname you are interested in. This takes you to a list of text files with surnames beginning with that letter. Now click a particular file name. The text file may be transcribed from a Deed book, or a will, or some other document. The name and e-mail address of the submitter will be included and you can write to that person for more information if you need to.

Census Records These are transcribed census records. As a file is submitted, it is listed at the top of the What's New list on this page. Not all states have volunteers transcribing right now, so you can only click on those states that show up as a live link.

Library This contains guides, articles, chat transcripts, and images for you to look at online or download to your computer. Among the titles are "Researching in Southwest Louisiana" and "Cherokee Freedmen in Indian Territory."

Community This page shows how you can get involved, where and how to sign up as a volunteer, and testimonials as to how much AfriGeneas has helped the people who use it.

Newsletter The monthly newsletter looks at genealogy news from the African American perspective.

Forum and Chat Topics chats meet on a scheduled basis; open discussions are usually available 24 hours a day. The forum is a Web-based list of messages sorted by date, with the most recent at the top.

AfriGeneas Links Hundreds of fascinating links, sorted by topic, from good starting points like Christine's Genealogy Web site (see earlier listing) to WPA Slave Narratives to Canadian Black History.

Other sections The Storefront sells books and forms for genealogy. The About Us page gives a short history and a list of those who have helped develop AfriGeneas. The Feedback link launches your mail client so you can tell the staff what you think.

AfriGeneas has come a long way from its beginnings as a mail list, and keeps getting better and better.

DearMYRTLE

For the beginning to intermediate genealogist, there is no better spot than DearMYRTLE's Place (www.dearmyrtle.com). DearMYRTLE has helped hundreds of genealogists with her daily columns, weekly chats, newsletters, and online courses. Her site will help you learn and grow as a genealogist.

Note

AOL Members, keep in mind that DearMYRTLE has her own keyword: MYRTLE, and that her columns are archived on AOL back to 1995. The Web site includes columns beginning in 1999.

The first page of DearMYRTLE's site (see Figure 6-13) will have announcements, links to features on the site, and often a seasonal greeting.

There are two sets of links worth following here. The first is shown at the top of the opening screen in Figure 6-13: the links leading to Chat, Books, Events, Lessons, Message Board, Topics, and so on. The second is near the bottom of the illustration. Here you can find a short

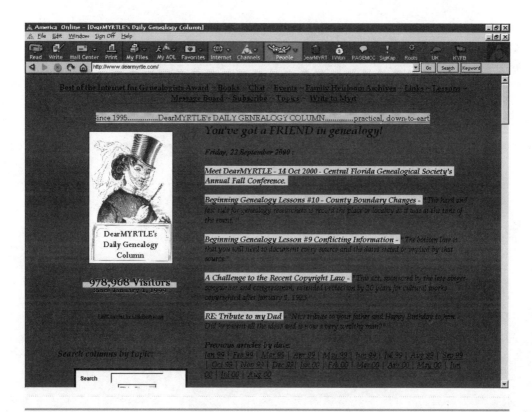

FIGURE 6-13. *DearMYRTLE's site on the Web has a great deal to offer a browsing genealogist*

list of links to her daily columns, sorted by most recent date. Topics include: Books, Lessons, Heirlooms, Index of All Articles (alphabetically listed), Internet Sites, and Sites for AOL Members.

One of the exciting things going on at DearMYRTLE's site is her Family Heirlooms Archive project. (See Figure 6-14.)

It began as the result of a DearMYRTLE column which described a photo quilt made for her father's 80th birthday in August 1998. In response, readers started sending her photos or scanned images of their quilts. More readers then wrote asking to open this up to other artifacts, and so the Family Heirlooms Archive Project was born. If you would like to participate, e-mail to DearMYRTLE@aol.com a scanned image of your ancestor's quilt, watch, rocking chair, writing table, bible, reading lenses, dinner plate, hair comb, etc., for this special memorial

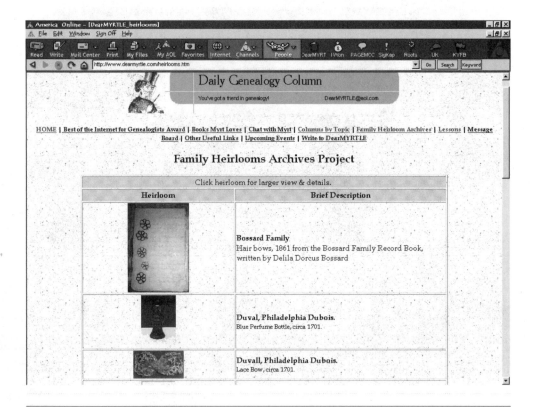

FIGURE 6-14. *DearMYRTLE is collecting images of heirloom quilts and other items on her site*

collection. Be sure to include the name of your ancestor and the time period he lived.

A quick look at other parts of DearMYRTLE's site:

Chat leads you to Myrtle's scheduled chats. You need an IRC program such as mIRC or Microsoft Chat (see Chapter 7) to connect. Set your IRC chat software to: Description: rootsweb; Server: irc.rootsweb.org; Port: 6667; channel: #DearMYRTLE. Her regular Monday night chats have scheduled topics (see Figure 6-15). Topics have included getting organized, using LDS resources, land records, and finding things on the Internet.

Best on the Internet for Genealogists is DearMYRTLE's running series on the most useful sites she has found. Links is a page of pointers to other good sites. Books is the link to a page of book reviews by DearMYRTLE.

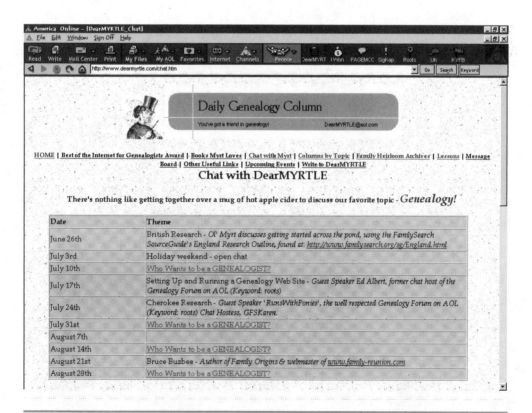

FIGURE 6-15. *DearMYRTLE schedules topics for her moderated Monday night chats*

Subscribe is the page which describes how you can get each DearMYRTLE daily column (in Digest form) via e-mail. Lessons include DearMYRTLE's free tutorials on genealogy research. If you subscribe to the List or Digest, you will get the lessons by e-mail. You can read past lessons online, and look at the topics coming up. The text of a new lesson is added each week.

Topics is a collection of links to all her past columns, sorted by topic. Let the whole page load, then use your browser's "search" or "find" function to look for your topic on the page—for example: "France" or "Internet Resources."

Bookmark DearMYRTLE's site. You'll be coming back often!

Genealogy Home Page

The Genealogy Home Page (http://genhomepage.com/) is a wide-ranging index of genealogy resources on the Internet. It includes links to maps, libraries, software, and societies. Right from the start, you can tell this site is more of a guide to genealogy resources available on the Web than a direct source of genealogical information. The home page (shown in Figure 6-16) starts off with two links to new, or newly discovered, genealogy sites. There is a URL Suggestion Form at http://www.genhomepage.com/mail.html that allows you to submit a URL for inclusion on the Genealogy Home Page. If you decide to create your own genealogy Web site, this is one way to announce it to the world.

One of the most useful sections of the Genealogy Home Page is its collection of links under the heading Genealogy Help and Guides (http://www.genhomepage.com/help.html). As I was writing this, there were several specific resources listed. Here are just a few:

♦ Jeffery Johnson gives Genealogy Instruction for Beginners, Teenagers, and Kids

♦ Maura Petzolt's Helpful Hints for Successful Searching has a variety of good tips for both beginner and expert

♦ Serendipity will give you a lift when the amount of researching work involved feels overwhelming. It is a collection of stories describing "serendipitous" genealogical discoveries others have made.

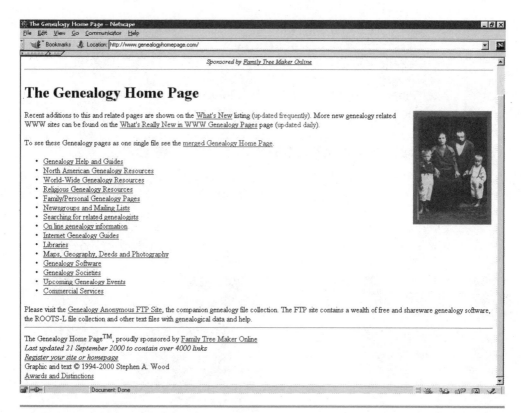

FIGURE 6-16.   *The Genealogy Home Page is a guide to genealogy information on the Web*

Another set of useful links from the Genealogy Home Page is on the Genealogy Societies page at http://www.genhomepage.com/societies.html. Here you'll find direct links to more than 30 genealogical societies, divided into three categories:

◆ Umbrella Organizations are groups like the Federation of Genealogical Societies.

◆ Geographic, National, Ethnic, ...-based Societies covers groups like the American-French Genealogical Society, and The Computer Genealogy Society of San Diego.

◆ Family-based Societies are organizations dedicated to research on specific surnames, like the Brown Family Genealogical Society or the Pelletier Family Association.

The Genealogy Home Page is the oldest effort at collecting worthwhile genealogy links together, and is still one of the most useful.

National Genealogical Society

The National Genealogical Society (http://www.ngsgenealogy.org) is one of the best umbrella organizations for family history. Their workshops, meetings and publications are invaluable.

On the opening page (see Figure 6-17), you'll find links to the newest and most relevant items on the site. This includes upcoming meetings,

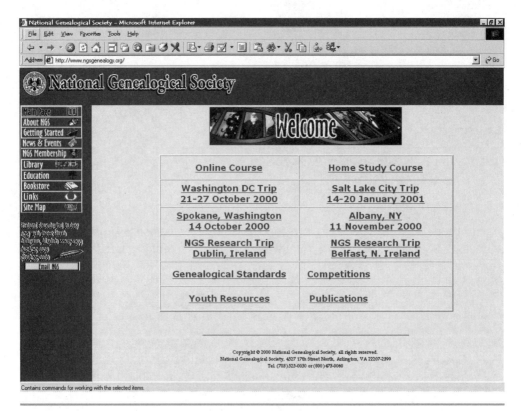

FIGURE 6-17. *Don't try to get here by just typing www.ngs.org. You'll get the National Geographic Society, who nabbed up the address first*

trips, courses, and competitions. On every page of the site is a navigation bar at the left, leading to different sections. At the bottom of the navigation bar, the Site Map link lists every page on the site, along with the section you'll find it in.

About NGS These pages describe the missions and objectives of the society, how the organization is set up and the many interesting committees of the NGS.

Getting Started This section has tips for beginners, an FAQ about genealogy, suggested reading, and NGS' Introduction to Genealogy.

News and Events News about the organization and its members, news from the world of genealogy, articles from recent genealogy conferences, press releases from other organizations, and queries are in this section.

NGS Membership Membership forms can be found here. Yearly membership types are Individual ($40), Family ($50), Institutional ($30), and Student ($25). Life memberships range from $300 to $1200 depending on your age. Membership includes three magazines, access to the NGS Library, discounts at the NGS bookstore, and the opportunity to serve on the committees.

Library The NGS has a circulating library available to members. Reference, records, and members' ancestral charts are among the holdings available online.

Education The NGS runs two courses online: *Introduction to Genealogy* and *American Genealogy*. This section also has some forms and research aids to help you in your quest.

Bookstore This has general and specific volumes on genealogy, a resource list for students and their teachers, and some specialty items.

Links As with any worthwhile genealogy site, the NGS site has links to other places on the Web that can help you. The list is searchable and sorted by topics.

USGenWeb

The USGenWeb Project (http://www.usgenweb.com/) is a group of volunteers working to provide non-commercial genealogy Web sites in every county of every state in the United States. These sites are freely accessible to everyone—no memberships or fees required. The online center of this effort is the USGenWeb Project Home Page at (http://www.usgenweb.com), see Figure 6-18.

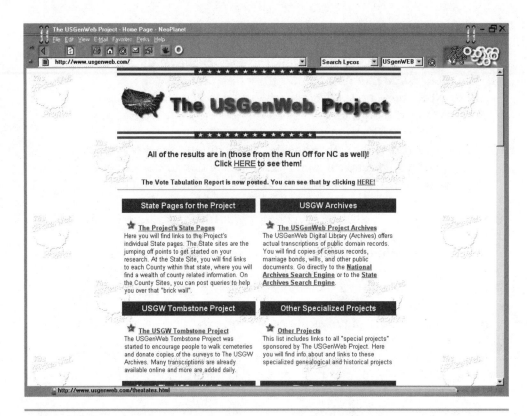

FIGURE 6-18. *The USGenWeb Project Home Page is the place to start for county-by-county genealogical information*

Originally, GENWEB was envisioned as a single entry point for all counties in Kentucky, where collected databases could be stored. The databases would be indexed and cross-linked, so even if an individual were found in more than one county, he or she could be located. In the end, this initial concept snowballed far beyond its Kentucky home, growing so popular that today—mid-2000—it contains links to every state in the union, including the District of Columbia. Each state site is unique, with its own look and feel, and serves as your gateway to the counties within the states. GENWEB's state sites are also the best place for activities like unknown county queries, family reunion bulletins, state history research, and county maps. Some state sites are even working on special projects such as transcribing Civil War troop records, or reuniting families.

You'll see lots of variety at the county level. Every page or database is created by a volunteer, and the resources they provide can be as individualistic as the people themselves. At a minimum, each county site provides links to post queries and access state archives. To put it simply, USGenWeb is an impressive accomplishment, and its volunteers deserve the thanks of every genealogist in the United States, both amateur and expert alike.

Note

If you have a lot of genealogical information about a particular county, check the listing on that county in the USGenWeb Project. Maybe you should join the volunteers who make this project possible. If you're interested, click the Information for Current and Prospective Volunteers link. This takes you to the Volunteers page (http://www.usgenweb.org/volunteers/volunteers.html) where you can learn about being a volunteer.

While the main objective today for USGenWeb is the creation of county-by-county sites, there are also several special projects underway. You can find out about them on the USGenWeb Special Projects page (http://www.usgenweb.org/projects/projects.html). Some of the special projects underway at this writing are:

♦ Archives Project—USGenWeb was originally designed to provide information county by county. Unfortunately, some genealogical information can't be organized this way. Because of this, the Archive Project aims to put non-county public domain information onto the Web. This project has several subprojects, including the Tombstone Project (http://www.rootsweb.org/~cemetery/) shown in Figure 6-19. In this subproject, volunteers travel to cemeteries around the country where they transcribe tombstone inscriptions. These inscriptions are then made accessible through this Web page.

♦ Lineage Project—For people who want to track down a particular ancestor, this project provides a place to list information about the ancestor, with contact information—an e-mail address or Web page—for the researcher.

FIGURE 6-19. *The Tombstone Project is just one facet of USGenWeb's Archive Project*

◆ National and International Links Project—This is a collection of links from USGenWeb to sites of general genealogical interest around the world.

Returning to the USGenWeb home page, click the link to Information for Researchers (http://www.usgenweb.org/researchers/ researcher.html). Here you'll find a page chock full of helpful research tips, plus an interesting section on preserving relics such as old books, photos, and newspaper articles.

USGenWeb is one of the most important online genealogy sites, in my opinion. I hope you agree.

Chapter 7

Chat: Hail Thy Fellow on the Net!

Sometimes you need to talk to someone to get beyond a genealogical problem. The online world can help you there, too, with "chat." Chat has two versions: Internet presence and Internet Relay Chat (IRC).

Introduction

Chat has been around for a long time. From the earliest days of The Source and CompuServe to the era of AOL and the Web, chat has been a staple of online communications. It's useful whether you're collaborating on a genealogy project, sending digital reunion memos to your extended family, or discussing your hobby with a large crowd.

Note

Throughout this chapter you'll find references to newsgroups, mail lists, and Web sites. This is just an example of how interconnected the genealogy resources on the Internet can be. You will learn everything you need to know about newsgroups and Web sites in other chapters.

Internet Relay Chat, better known as IRC, is the most popular form of chat. Although it can support one-to-one, one-to-many, and many-to-many messages, usually IRC is a lot of people on a "channel" typing messages back and forth in many-to-many format. IRC uses a system of clients and servers that allows people all over the world to communicate in real time by typing on their computers. So, folks in Australia, France, Hong Kong, Kenya, British Columbia, and Vermont can all sit at their computers at the same time, log into the same server, connect to the same "channel," and type messages interactively, each seeing what all the others are saying.

A group of people chatting on a channel are said to be in a "chat room." You can create private, invitation-only chat rooms, or join in on a public one.

If you just wander into any old chat room, you may be dismayed at the level and tone of the conversation. Everyday chat conversations tend to be overly mundane, or else racy. You need to search the chat server for rooms devoted to the subjects of family history and/or genealogy.

Even when you do get into a genealogy chat, the conversations overlap. This makes it hard to keep track of who's saying what. Unmoderated, general chat rooms (sometimes called *drop-ins*) are like strolling by the corner coffee shop. You don't know who you'll find there, and whether anyone inside will be of help to you. Typically, a lot of what's going on will be totally irrelevant to your search.

A moderated or hosted chat, however, is more like attending a class or a genealogy club meeting. There is usually a specific topic being discussed, an expert or two available, and a system for asking and answering questions so that the conversations are at least a little easier to follow.

A one-on-one chat, between yourself and a buddy can be even more productive. If you can set up a specific time and channel to discuss a problem or a great find, you can get a lot done this way.

Another, more controlled type of chat is called "Internet presence" or "instant message," which grows in popularity day by day, thanks in large part to America Online's Instant Messenger program. In this form of chat, a select, invited list of people (from two to a whole "room"), exchange typed messages in real time. This feature has become so popular that instant messaging is used 180 million times a day, according to AOL. Another example: ICQ ("I-seek-you"), a different Internet presence program, gets hundreds of new users a day. Microsoft's Microsoft Chat, works just great, both as an IRC client and a one-to-one client. And there are newer programs, such as Microsoft Meeting, which can be used as an intranet/Internet collaboration tool.

Note

You might ask, why not just use e-mail instead? Live chat can be more efficient, especially if you're collaborating on a project. You can create a channel where the only people allowed to participate are the ones you invite. Internet presence programs can tell you who's online now and hook you up for a conversation on the spot. Best of all, many chat clients discussed here are free. And so far, most aren't bombarding you with ads or asking for much demographic data.

Important Warnings About Chat

In Chapter 2, I discussed unsolicited bulk e-mail (UBE) in detail. Those who send UBE, especially the pornographic kind, have special programs that spy on chat rooms and report the e-mail addresses of everyone who logs on, regardless of the topic of the chat room. They are especially vigilant about chat rooms on AOL. Within minutes of participating in an AOL chat on genealogy, you will be bombarded by unsolicited e-mail about porn sites.

How do you prevent this? Simple: you must wear a disguise.

On AOL, CompuServe and Prodigy, you can create screen names under your primary account. You should create one just for chat, and encourage everyone in the family to use this screen name only for chat purposes. Then, on AOL, you can block all e-mail to that screen name. However, on a system that provided you with POP e-mail, such as Mindspring, Earthlink, or Prodigy, as of this writing, you'll just have to set up mail filters (see Chapter 2) that delete any messages sent to the chat account.

If you use Ding!, AOL Instant Messenger, ICQ or a similar program, you are hidden from the unsolicited bulk e-mailers because these programs use secure, private chat servers. So, thankfully, here you can use your real e-mail address. These programs use their own private, secure servers, and everyone on them has agreed to a Terms Of Service statement that forbids sending unsolicited e-mail to members. Furthermore, they give you the ability to filter out specific people. Thus, you don't have to worry that your chats will result in a flood of UBE.

If you avail yourself of other chat clients that use open, public chat servers (such as Microsoft Chat or mIRC), you could enter false information in the "e-mail address" portion of the setup screens in order to hide from unsolicited bulk e-mail. You could also enter your e-mail address as something like LIBBIC@nospam.prodigy.net. Most people will know to take out the "nospam" part to get your real e-mail address, but the unsolicited bulk e-mailer's automatic programs won't. However, what I usually do is enter the following as my e-mail address: available@polite.request. If someone wants my address, they have to give me theirs first.

All the clients mentioned here have security features: you can block others from adding you to their buddy list until you give permission; block people from sending you messages until you give permission, and so forth. Each program has its own way of handling twit filters and all are constantly trying to improve their privacy features. You'll have to try each out to see what's new with them.

Some chat is based on Java, meaning you don't need a chat client to use them. Several personal and commercial genealogy sites have Java-based chats that require only a browser capable of dealing with Java (Microsoft Internet Explorer or Netscape Navigator 4.0 or newer are examples). However, if your e-mail address is recorded in your browser's settings, UBE senders might get hold of it.

How It Works

How do chat services and programs work? You use the client program to log onto a chat server.

Where are the servers? I'll profile a few devoted to genealogy in the following paragraphs, but you can also look at the chat sections on Yahoo!, Excite, MSN, or any other portal (or just look at the home page of your IRC Client of choice). Most IRC programs also come with a list of public chat servers.

If it's an open, public chat server (IRC), you can use a program like mIRC or Microsoft Chat. You log on, and search for a channel that suits your interests. If there isn't one at the moment, you can create one (calling it #genealogy, perhaps) and wait for interested people to come chat with you. Once the chat gets going, it's a lot like citizen's band radio, but in print.

Other programs like AOL Instant Messenger are set up so that only people using the same program can contact you. With such a program, you can usually indicate your status (gone, accepting calls, connected but away from your desk, and so on) and keep a list of people you want to contact (often called a "buddy list" or "address book"), as well as those who are allowed to contact *you*. (Alas, you can't import a buddy list from your e-mail address book—you usually have to ask permission to add someone to your list!) To find people to add to your list, you can look them up by e-mail address, or e-mail them an invitation to use the same program you are, and then exchange ID names.

When someone hails you, a sound or small message window (or both) will alert you. Chatting typically takes place in two panes of one window: one for your outgoing messages and one for incoming ones.

If you're worried about security or just want to be left alone, fret not. Most of these programs let you shield your presence from specific people or from the world at large, as suits your mood. You can also let yourself be "seen" but not heard with an online "I'm-busy-now" indicator.

On all these systems you can choose a "handle" or nickname for your login id. This is the name by which people will know you on IRC (everyone in a channel must have a unique nickname). Remember, there are hundreds of thousands of people on IRC, so it's possible someone might already be using the nickname you've chosen. If that's the case, simply choose another one. Some programs record your preferred nickname in the setup screen, and allow you to choose an alternative if someone is using your first choice in a certain channel.

Also, be sure to make use of the chat program's help files. They'll help you get the most out of your chat time.

Security Risks in IRC

When you use the IRC type of chat, you are open to some security risks.

For example, while you are logged on to an IRC server, bad guys can look up your dynamic IP settings and bombard you with packets, clogging up your TCP/IP connection until you disconnect and reconnect.

Microsoft's security page at http://www.microsoft.com/security contains information on these security threats as well as links to fixes.

Another important caution: If someone you don't know tells you to type an unfamiliar key sequence, phrase or command in chat, don't do it! You may be opening the chat room or even your own computer to hackers.

Chat Flavors

Different programs can allow you to have one-on-one and multi-person conversations with people. Some require you to sign onto a chat server, where the program you use doesn't matter. Others only let you chat with people using the same program, who have allowed you to put them on their buddy list. The former lets you connect with more people; the latter gives you more security. A few, as noted, will let you do both.

AOL Instant Messenger

Some features of AOL Instant Messenger are:

+ www.aim.com

+ free

+ Internet Presence

The most widely used Internet presence program is AOL's Instant Messenger (AIM) program (which is separate from the Instant Message facility on the AOL service). The Instant Messenger software gives Internet users the ability to send instant messages and create chat rooms with other AIM users, whether they use AOL or not (see Figure 7-1). While easy to use, it doesn't have all the features of ICQ or Ding! (covered in the next few sections). The program is available as a Navigator or Eudora plug-in and comes in the Windows 9x, NT, and CE versions as well as with Macintosh. There is also an all-Java version called Quick Buddy that runs in your browser. No download is required, but it's very slow if you don't, so I recommend you download your own version.

AIM installs quickly and loads by default whenever you connect with the Internet. If you're not an AOL subscriber, you must register with the AOL Instant Messenger service at the Web site (www.aim.com) and supply a name and password. Then you can create your own buddy list, which you can organize into various categories. The program has Buddies, Family, and Coworkers folders already in place.

When you log onto the AIM service, the AIM window tells you who among your list of buddies is also logged on at that moment. Then, when

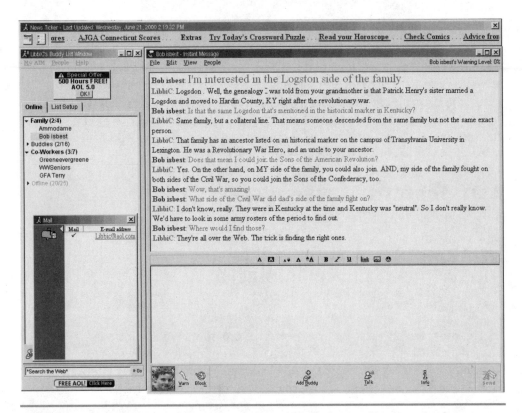

FIGURE 7-1. *AOL Instant Messenger has one window to keep track of your buddies and another to carry on your chats*

you reach out and buzz someone, you can control what personal information appears and which type size, font, and background color is used in your messages. Type or drag a URL from your browser's bookmark file or a Web page into an instant message, and the program converts it into a live link.

AIM has good privacy features. You can list which people can and can't send you messages, much like AOL's mail controls. If you step away from your PC, you can leave a custom message for anyone trying to reach you, such as "Gone for a moment. Be back soon."

In short, AIM works just like AOL's built-in instant message/buddy lists feature, with one notable exception: now you can communicate with, and track people, who aren't members of AOL. Note, too, that all Instant Messenger traffic goes through AOL's servers. Given AOL's history with online traffic jams, don't be surprised if you experience occasional delays and failures.

The newest AIM, version 4, has several enhancements: you can use your computer's sound card and microphone to chat by voice; associate pictures with buddies so the chat window displays the icon as you converse; set up a stock and news ticker to show you the latest breaking news; send pictures and sounds faster than before; and have AOL alert you when new mail arrives.

AOL chat on the service itself is a whole other kettle of fish. At least it doesn't require a separate program, as it's included in the AOL software.

I'll cover chats on AOL in Chapter 15.

ICQ

Some features of ICQ are:

+ www.icq.com

+ free

+ Internet presence

ICQ is a one-to-one or multiple person chat in the "Internet presence" model. When you are online, it registers your presence with the secure ICQ server so that other ICQ users can "see" you. You can keep a buddy list and be informed when your buddies log on. You can send messages and files, even talk by voice or send live video. All the while, the program runs in the background, taking up a minimum amount of memory and Net resources, so you can continue to surf the Web or run your genealogy program.

Launching an Internet phone or video call involves just a click of a button, instantly connecting you and a friend (or friends). This can be done with two or more users at a time. All these functions are organized in one easy-to-use interface that sits on your desktop.

ICQ2000, the beta version as of this writing, has an option to connect to IRC servers, as well as to only ICQ servers. If you are using the ICQ servers to chat, it works like AIM: you and your chat partners must all be using the same software. ICQ also has a wide range of privacy options.

When you register with ICQ, you can include hobbies, such as genealogy (see Figure 7-2), and choose to be in the ICQ White Pages so other ICQ members can find you. While trying the program out, I found about 10 other people I could have invited to chat with me who had put "genealogy" in their profile.

You can also right-click the ICQ icon on your computer to set ICQ to be "open" to a chat with anyone on a specific subject. Or you can go to the ICQ Guide and look for an open chat room by topic (look under "Family – Genealogy"). You can elect to keep a chat room open all the time, just join a user's group on genealogy for occasional chat invitations, or participate in a message forum, where the messages aren't in real time.

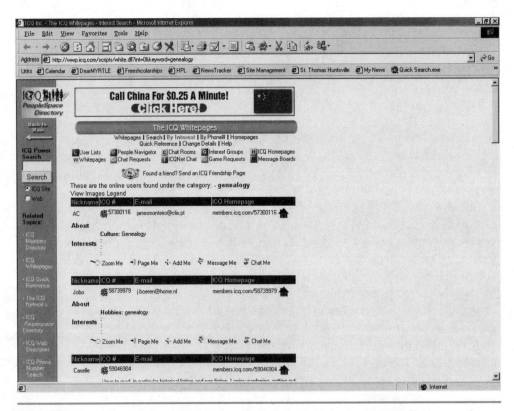

FIGURE 7-2.   *To join a genealogy group or chat, visit the ICQ Web page and look for "genealogy"*

Probably the best way to use ICQ, though, is to set up specific times and rooms with your friends who also use ICQ. People have told me about holding online family reunions this way!

MSN Messenger Service 2.2

Some features of MSN Messenger Service 2.2 are:

♦ www.windowsupdate.com

♦ free

♦ Internet presence

Of all the services I've covered here, this one is the hardest to set up (see Figure 7-3). The program sends you to a non-existent page for the sign

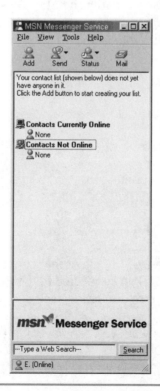

FIGURE 7-3. *MSN Messenger Service is like AIM in use, but not as convenient to sign up for*

up routine; skip the "sign up" button and just go to www.hotmail.com and get a hotmail address. You don't have to use hotmail for e-mail except to use MSN Messenger Service; but you do have to sign on now and then to keep the hotmail account active.

Another reason I did not like this particular program is that during registration you have to turn over an alarming amount of information, including address, exact date of birth, and occupation, in order to sign up. It will all be used for marketing, of course, but hotmail has been hacked in the past, so it made me nervous; I lied on several of the questions.

Once you are signed up, for your hotmail account to remain active, you must sign in at least once within the next ten days. Then, after the initial ten day period, you must sign in at least once every 60 days to keep your account active. If your hotmail account isn't active, your MSN Messenger Service won't be either.

After sign-up, you can search the MSN Messenger Service for people you know by first name, last name, and location, to see who can communicate with you. Or, send e-mail invitations to friends to join. When you start to chat, it works very much like AIM, but all in all, I didn't find this service as useful as AIM.

Microsoft Chat

Some features of Microsoft chat are:

♦ www.windowsupdate.com

♦ free

♦ IRC

Microsoft Chat is a free IRC client that connects to the open, public chat channels. In Figure 7-4, I've connected to the RootsWeb chat room for site administrators, and we're discussing access to the RootsWeb pages. In this view, I've chosen the option to have the people shown as characters. You don't have to chat this way: you can have the traditional text interface, too,

FIGURE 7-4. *Microsoft Chat gives you an option for a cartoon character layout, as opposed to strictly text. It connects to open public chat servers*

but when you choose a different face for each person, you can more easily track the several conversations going on at once.

There are commands to go to a private chat with someone, look up their logon information (name, Internet service provider, etc.), and save the entire conversation to a file. Microsoft Chat has lots of powerful features, a good Help file, and it's free (see Figure 7-5). I recommend it as a first chat program until you get used to the way chat works.

Microsoft Chat does not, however, track the online presence of a list of buddies as AOL IM, Ding!, and ICQ do.

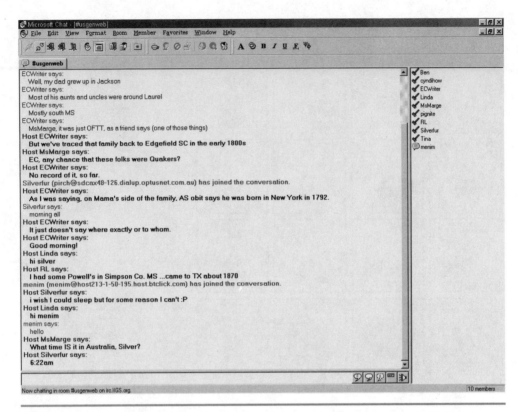

FIGURE 7-5. *Microsoft Chat in text mode is much like any other IRC client*

mIRC

Some features of mIRC are:

♦ www.mirc.co.uk/get.html

♦ $20

♦ IRC

mIRC may not have a "comic" mode like Microsoft Chat, but it has all its other features, plus more (see Figure 7-6). A very popular IRC program, mIRC is shareware, so you can try it for a while before you send the author $20 for it.

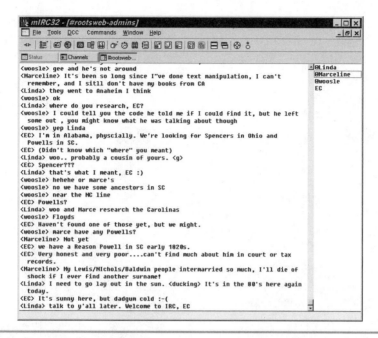

FIGURE 7-6. *mIRC has a traditional IRC text display and can connect to all IRC servers*

As in Microsoft Chat, you can set your own text and background colors, and send a sound file with a chat message. In addition, you can customize the toolbar for the commands you use most often, and change your nickname on the fly. A really neat feature is the channel filter: if you log onto a public IRC that has 19,000 channels going, you can simply filter the channel names for "genealogy" or "family" and see if there's a chat you want to join. You can also hide or even totally block channels that you dislike, too.

How to Chat

IRC and Internet presence programs work slightly differently, but have many of the same functions. Let me urge you again to read the Help file of your program; most of the time the Help file is a mini-manual that will tell you how to best use the client.

Many modern IRC chat programs type your commands for you; you just choose what you want to do from a menu. Still, you should learn a few commands anyway (see the following box if you wish to type commands directly).

Some Common IRC Commands

IRC servers may vary, but you will generally find these commands available on most IRC channels. (Note: these won't work in Internet presence programs; you'll have to use the menu commands to do the same things.)

- /ACCEPT - accepts an invitation to join a chat room

- /ACTION - sends virtual hugs, etc. For example, you could type /ACTION ECWriter hands DearMYRTLE the "Best Chatter Award!" It will appear in special fonts or colors to the rest of the group. /THOUGHT is a similar command.

- /AWAY - tells others that you are still connected to the server, but had to step away from the computer for a moment. Some servers use /BUSY.

- /EXIT - logs off chat

- /GNAME - changes the group name or inquires about the group

- /JOIN - puts you in a chat room, or leaves the current group and enters another

- /LIST - shows a list of active channels. You'll usually want to use the Menu version of this; some IRC servers have tens of thousands of channels going at once! Most IRC clients can let you filter or sort the display of the list.

- /MODE - can be used to set properties for chat rooms as well as for individuals. Can generally only be used by the moderator(s) of the room.

- ◆ /NAME - declares your nickname or handle. Also checks status

- ◆ /PAGE < someone's handle > - asks a member to join

- ◆ /PASS - sets password for admittance into password protected chat room

- ◆ /RNAME - shows the "real name" of a member

- ◆ /SEND - sends a one-line private message to any member logged into the chat room, like: /SEND MARY This is a private message!

- ◆ /SQUELCH < someone's handle > - ignores another member. Some IRC servers may use /KICK or /IGNORE.

There are other commands for moderators (the person who started the group, and anyone that person designates as a moderator with the /Mode command.)

When you join an IRC chat room, the server will send you the Message of the Day or MOTD. Some IRC programs show you this in a side window, some in the main window. If it flies by too fast for you to see it, send the command /MOTD. Just type that into the same place you would a message. (Anything preceded by a / is a command in an IRC chat room.)

Most IRC clients will log you into the default channel, usually called "Lobby," while you search for a channel or room you want. Once you find one, lurk for a moment, reading the messages. If this is a room you want to join, send a polite greeting (like "hello, everyone!") You may find some rooms so friendly that the moment you log on, someone sends you a greeting. Politely acknowledge it.

Besides /JOIN and /MOTD the most important IRC command for you to know is /IGNORE (or whatever is the equivalent for that server). When someone is offending, bothering or flaming you, typing **/IGNORE < badguy's handle >** will keep that person's messages from appearing on your screen.

If the chat is moderated, you often have to send a line with a question mark, wait for the moderator to recognize you, then send your question or comment.

Internet presence programs such as AOL Instant Messenger allow you to block people from paging you or chatting with you.

Where to Chat

Okay, let's say you have Microsoft Chat, mIRC, or some other program that uses public, open chat servers. Where do you go to chat?

Several Genealogy sites have both scheduled and impromptu chats. RootsWeb, (point your chat client to irc.rootsweb.com, port 6667, alternative 7000) is just about the best place for genealogy chats.

Note

If you want to keep on top of the genealogy IRC scene, subscribe to GEN-IRC-L (GEN-IRC-D-digest mode). Send an e-mail message to GEN-IRC-L-request@rootsweb.com (or -D if you want Digest mode) with just the single word SUBSCRIBE in the body of the message. This mailing list covers mainly the IRC genealogy channels on NewNet, but other networks are also discussed. The main purposes of this list are to enable a genealogist to communicate and set times for live discussions on IRC with other genealogists, post problems or ask questions relating to genealogy and IRC, and announce new channels or topics of channels in genealogy and IRC. See Chapter 5 for a discussion of mail lists.

The chat server is hosted in conjunction with the International Internet Genealogy Society, http://www.iigs.org/. If you point your IRC chat client to irc.IIGS.org, it will send you on to irc.rootsweb.com in a couple of seconds. There's usually an impromptu open chat going on among the people who manage genealogy Web sites. However, among the most wonderful resources on the whole Net are the moderated, as opposed to the impromptu, RootsWeb/IIGS chats. The scheduled ones are listed at http://www.iigs.org/cgi/ircthemes/ircthemes. The topics range from very general, such as the Dear MYRTLE help chat for beginners, to very specific, such as Estill County, Kentucky genealogy. DearMYRTLE is online many nights for just casual chats, as well. Check out her page at http://www.dearmyrtle.com for the scheduled topics.

Besides the wonderful experts and helpful people, the niftiest thing about this IRC server is the translation bot. This is a program on the server that allows you to log onto a chat channel and have the conversations translated to another language. DearMYRTLE told me of a recent chat where people speaking German, Spanish, and Norwegian were all able to ask her questions (which were translated into English for her) and receive her answers (translated back to their respective languages).

Still in testing as I write this, the translation bot runs a parallel window for the translation so you can follow the conversation in the original window as well as in the translation. It works automatically, all you have to do is join the original chat, and then join the translation channel for your language of choice. I think this is one of the most exciting developments in online genealogy in this decade!

Another good source of scheduled chats is the About.com set of pages; specifically, About.Genealogy. The page http://genealogy.about.com/ hobbies/genealogy/mpchat.htm has a list of the scheduled genealogy chats (see Figure 7-7).

Note

Often, IRC programs like Microsoft Chat come with a list of chat servers. Just let your IRC client connect to one and look for rooms with "genealogy" in them, trying all those listed under dalnet, undernet, and newnet. Another popular server is irc.scscorp.net.

In particular, look for these channels on these servers as noted below:

Server (what you type into your IRC client)	Channels
irc.chat.org:6667	#FTMCC (Family Tree Maker Chat), #genealogy
irc.IIGS.org:6667 or irc.IIGS.org:7000	#Australia, #Benelux, #Canadian-Gen, #cert, #Cogenweb, #CZER-Group, #DEUgen, #genealogie.fr, #Ger-Rus, #htmlhelp, #IIGS-Ontario, #IIGS-Ukgen, #IIGS-UK-IRE, #IIGS-UnivHelp, #Ireland-gen, #KY-Estill, #NewEngland, #SE-USA, #SHANNON

irc.dal.net:7000	#Canadian GEN #Fianna (Irish Genealogy), #genealogy-events, #genealogy-help, #Genealogy_IRC, #Gen_Family_Tree, #Gentrace, #lunie-links (Lunenburg Co., NS, Canada)
irc.another.net:6667	#genealogy
irc.afternet.org	#GenealogyForum, #Genealogy-n-UK
irc.rootsweb.com	#DearMYRTLE, #IIGS-UnivHelp, #htmlhelp
irc.newnet.net:6667	#family_history, #genealogy, #genealogy101
irc.rootsweb.com:6667 or irc.rootsweb.com:7000	#MSGenWeb
irc.scscorp.net:6667	#genealogy
irc.superchat.org:6660	#Genealogy
irc.webmaster.com	#TMG (the Master Genealogist software discussion)

Chat Without a Chat Program!

Some chat sites don't require you to have any sort of extra program besides your browser. Many surname-specific chat rooms set up browser chats. The Gen Forum, http://chat.genforum.com/ and Genealogy Online (http://genealogy.emcee.com/) Web sites have browser-based chat as well.

In addition, many "portal" sites have developed communities where people exchange messages. Many of these sites have browser-based chats, and the genealogy ones are often the most popular. See the table for how to go about it.

Site

URL

Click

You'll need

Excite

http://www.excite.com/communities/

Chat > Interests > and then scroll through the list to see if a room is discussing Genealogy.

Java-enabled browser.

Go through the member sign up procedure.

Yahoo!

http://chat.yahoo.com

Sign in. When chat starts, you'll see "Tools" in the bottom frame. Click Change Room, choose Hobbies and Interests, then choose Genealogy.

Go through the member sign up procedure. Has Java and HTML chat.

Infoseek/GO

http://www.go.com

Click Chat. Scroll down to look for a genealogy chat room.

Go through the member sign up procedure. Has Java and HTML chat.

Snap

http://www.snap.com

Click Chat, then sign in. In the side frame, click Change Room. If there are no genealogy rooms going, click Create Room and start one.

Go through the member sign up procedure. Get the Ichat plug-in (free) for Netscape; allow ActiveX control for Microsoft Internet Explorer.

Chat Etiquette

Generally, you are going to find helpful, polite people in genealogy chat rooms in IRC. Of course, if you have one of the Internet presence programs, you will be chatting with people you have at least contacted before. Nevertheless, in both scenarios, there are certain etiquette standards to meet in chat.

All the etiquette covered in earlier chapters applies to chat: capital letters, except to mention the surnames you are researching, will be considered shouting. Flames are useless and annoying; show respect for everyone. IRC servers and the Internet presence programs track your connection; many require you to input an e-mail address.

When you choose a nickname or "handle" to join a chat or use the Internet presence program, as a security measure, you may want to avoid using one that reveals your real name or gender, where you live, etc. Of course, never use offensive handles or nicknames. Chat is very public, so be careful about what you reveal in chat rooms.

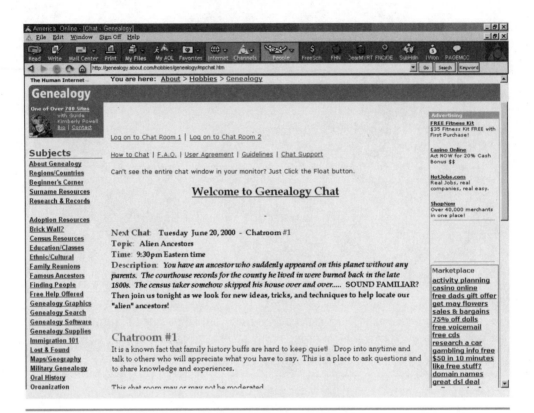

FIGURE 7-7.   *About.Genealogy has regularly scheduled topics for chats*

Stay on topic, or if you get sidetracked, create a separate room to follow your tangent.

Lurk before you leap into sending messages: check out the room and see if the topic is what you are looking for.

Obscenity, cursing and the like, are forbidden on such systems as AOL; you can report people for using them. You can also use the /IGNORE command in IRC to block all messages from someone who is annoying you. If it's persistent, read the MOTD to find out the name of the system administrator and report that person's handle.

You can send your e-mail address by private message, but don't post it in the IRC channel. If someone refuses to give you theirs, don't be insulted; it's probably just a security measure.

If you want a particular person's attention (for example, to ask or answer a question), precede your message with his or her handle or an abbreviation of it. Someone with the handle RootsNewbie might send: "ECWriter: where can I buy your book?" I could reply, "RN: it's a mass market paperback, so it should be in most bookstores! :-)"

Smileys will be common, as will all sorts of acronyms; see the following section, Chat Shorthand, for some of the more common ones.

Many IRC servers, and most of the Internet presence programs, allow you to send sound files, pictures, even programs over the chat room. Be wary of this feature for two reasons: first, it obviously represents a security risk to receive files from someone you don't know very well; second, it adds to the traffic on the server, and will slow down everyone's interaction, not just the sender's and receiver's.

Chat programs have some limit to the number of characters that can be sent in one chunk. If you find your thoughts running longer, type the message in parts, each ending in an ellipsis (. . .) until you are done. Don't be surprised to find that as you do this, other messages are "walking on your lines" so to speak. Those paying attention will be able to better follow your train of thought if you have taken advantage of a feature of many programs: the ability to send your text in a specific color and/or typeface.

Don't ignore people who are asking polite questions (such as "How are you?"). If someone is being rude, you can use the command /ignore < person's nickname > .

Note: Several Web sites have tons of information about Chat. Check Cyndi's List page: http://www.CyndisList.com/chat.html for the latest!

Chat can be a very useful Internet tool, especially when moderated and when a specific subject is chosen. But it can also be addictive, and if you're not careful, you may find yourself doing more chatting than researching. Just remember, I warned you!

Chat Shorthand

If you see: The chatter meant...

Y: why
U: you
C: see
BRB: Be right back
< g >: grin
< bg >: big grin
< vbg >: very big grin
BTW: by the way
CWYL: chat with you later
FWIW: for what it's worth
GIWIST: Gee, I wish I'd said that!
HHOK: Ha, ha! Only kidding!
HTH: Hope this helps
HTHBE: Hope this has been enlightening
IMHO: In my humble opinion
IMNSHO: In my not so humble opinion
IOW: In other words...
IRL: In real life
ITRW: In the real world
JK: Just kidding
LOL: Laughing out loud
OTP: On the phone
OTF: On the floor
OIC: Oh! I see!
OTOH: On the other hand
POV: Point of view
RL: Real Life
ROTFL: Rolling on the floor laughing
RTFM: Read the fine manual [or help file]
TTFN: Ta ta for now
TTYL: Talk to you later
WRT: With regard to

Chapter 8

Using Search Sites for Genealogy

Throughout this book, I've tried to point you to the best genealogy newsgroups and Web sites. Nevertheless, there are plenty of incentives to search the Internet for yourself.

For example, the rate of change on the Internet is incredible. Web sites disappear, or move to a new server, which changes the URLs. Great new newsgroups and Web sites pop up all the time. Besides, as a genealogist, you know the thrill of discovering things for yourself. It can be quite a kick to find a Web site or newsgroup none of your friends know about.

So, what you need is a way to find genealogical resources on the Internet on your own. You could use sites that link to other sites, but a better way is to search for what you want yourself. That's where search sites come in.

Defining Terms

"Search engine" is an all-purpose label used to describe anything that will let you search for terms in a group of data. That data could be on a single site, such as DearMYRTLE.com, or on the entire Internet, or some subset in-between the two. Just about anything that lets you search gets called a "search engine." However, there are some other terms that are more accurate for specific sites.

A *spider* is a program that looks for information on the Internet, creates a database of what it finds, and lets you use a Web browser to run a search engine on that database for specific information. As noted, this can mean millions of pages, or just the pages on one site. A *search site* may have one or more search engines and may claim to search "the whole Web," but in reality probably covers about 15% of it at any given time. This is because pages appear and disappear rapidly on the Web.

A search site called a *directory* or *catalog* uses a search engine to let you hunt through an edited list of Internet sites for specific information. The value of these sites is that in a directory or catalog, the newsgroups and Web sites are sorted, categorized, and sometimes rated.

Yahoo! (http://www.yahoo.com) is one of the first Web catalogs or directories; it is also a good example of a search engine of the Web, which offers other services. When a search site proffers chat, news, forums and other services, it becomes a *portal*. A portal is a little bit of everything: a search engine for the Web at large, a catalog of sites the owners recommend, and usually a group of other features, including stock prices and so on.

A *metasearch engine* submits your query to several different search sites, portals and catalogs, at the same time. You may get more results, and you will usually be able to compare how each one responded to the query. These searches may take longer, however.

Searching with Savoir Faire

The following sections describe various search engines, portals, and directories. While the content in them overlaps a great deal, each one uses slightly different methods to search Web sites and rate how well your terms were matched. This means you may find what you are looking for with one search engine or directory, but not another. First though, some general search tips.

Use phrases instead of single words in your searches. Type several words that are relevant to your search. `Spencer genealogy Ohio` will narrow a search well.

Enclose phrases in quotes. Searching with the phrase `Spencer family history` without quotes will match all pages that have any of those three words included somewhere on the page, in any order, and not necessarily adjacent. Searching with the phrase `"Spencer family history"` will return only those pages that have those three words together. The order of the words, however, may or may not be flexible depending on the specific search engine.

The more specific you are, the better. Searching for `Irish genealogy databases` will give you fewer, but closer matches than searching for `Irish genealogy`.

Use + and - in your searches. A word preceded by a plus sign (+) must appear on the page to be considered a match. A word preceded by a minus sign (-) must not appear on the page to be considered a match. There can be no spaces between the plus or minus signs and the words they apply to. For example: entering `+Spencer -royal genealogy` would ask the search engine to find pages that definitely used the word Spencer, but didn't use the word royal, with genealogy preferred but optional. Most search engines would get some Spencer genealogy pages, but leave out those that include Lady Diana, Princess of Wales. More about this type of search is in the sidebar about Boolean searches.

Narrow your searches if you get too many matches. Sometimes the page with your search results will have an input box to narrow or broaden the search. This may mean adding terms or deleting terms and running the search again only on the results from the first search.

Using Boolean Terms

Searching the Internet is no simple matter. With literally hundreds of thousands of sites, millions of documents, and more words than imaginable, finding exactly the right needle in all that hay can be daunting. The key, of course, is crafting a precise query.

Handy tools for honing searches are Boolean operators. Coined for George Boole, the 19th century mathematician who dreamed up symbolic logic, Boolean operators represent the relationships among things using terms such as AND, OR, and NOT. When applied to information retrieval, they can expand or narrow a search to uncover as many citations or "hits" as you want.

The Boolean OR   When you search for two or more terms joined with an OR operator, you'll get back hits that contain any one of your terms. Thus the query `Powell OR genealogy` will retrieve documents holding "Powell" or "genealogy," but not necessarily both. You should realize that almost all search pages default to OR, that is, they assume you want any page with any one of your terms in it.

You can see it makes good sense to use OR when searching for synonyms or closely related terms, for example, if you are looking for variations on a name search for `SPENCER SPENCE SPENSER`. The average search engine will assume the OR operator and find any page with any one of those terms.

The Boolean AND   In the Boolean boogie, joining search terms with AND means all terms must be found in a document, but not necessarily together. The query `George AND Washington` will result in a list of documents that have both "George" and "Washington" somewhere within. Use AND when you have dissimilar terms and need to narrow a search. Usually to get AND in a search, you type a + mark, or put the term AND between the words and enclose it all within parentheses: `(Spencer AND genealogy)`.

Just remember that a simple AND doesn't guarantee the words will be next to each other. Your search for George Washington could turn up documents about George Benson and Grover Washington.

The Boolean NOT   When you use NOT, search results must exclude certain terms. Many search engines don't have this; often, when you can use it, the syntax is to put a - in front of the unwanted term.

The query `Powell NOT Colin` will return all citations containing the term "Powell," but none including the word "Colin," whether "Powell" is there or not. Use NOT when you want to exclude possible second meanings. Banks can be found on genealogy surname pages, or on pages associated with finance or with rivers. Searching for `banks AND genealogy NOT river` increases the chances of finding documents relating to banks who are people, not sides of rivers. In some search engines, the minus (-) sign often takes the place of NOT.

The fun part is combining Boolean operators to create a very precise search. Let's say you want to find documents about the city of Dallas. If you simply search for "Dallas," you could get irrelevant hits about Dallas County in Alabama, which may not be the Dallas you want. To avoid that, you would use AND, NOT, and OR in this fashion:

- `(Dallas AND Texas) NOT (Selma OR Alabama)`

- `(Powell AND genealogy) NOT`
  `(Colin AND Powell)`

Beyond AND/OR/NOT   In most Web search engines, unless a phrase option is specifically offered, the capitalization or order of the terms isn't important: a Venetian blind is the same as a blind Venetian. Some search engines allow you to fine tune a search further. The WITH operator, for example, searches for terms much nearer each other. How "near" is defined depends on the engine.

Some would look at `George WITH Washington` and deliver documents only containing the words "George Washington" next to each other. Others might consider words in the same sentence or paragraph to be near enough.

Check the search engine's help files to see if it uses wildcards or word stemming (for finding all variations of a word such as ancestry, ancestral, ancestor, ancestors).

Using these techniques, you can search the Web much more efficiently, finding just the right document on George Washington Carver or a genealogy site on the right set of Powells. Learn the steps to the Boolean boogie, and you'll soon be Web dancing wherever you please!

Search Sites

There are lots of search sites out there, some more useful to genealogists than others. General search sites, White Pages directories for finding living people, and sites that search newsgroups will be used most often; rarely will you use a site to search for files.

AltaVista (http://www.altavista.com)

A portal, AltaVista can search the whole Web or the edited catalog, called the AltaVista Directory. Turn the Family Filter on (the link is to the left of the page near the top) to exclude pornography sites.

The best bet for genealogists is the Advanced Search (see Figure 8-1), which you can get to by clicking the link at the top of the AltaVista page on what looks like a file folder tab. You can use an asterisk as a wild card (for geneal* for example) on the Advanced Search tab, and you can use Boolean operators AND, OR, NOT, and WITH. The "Advanced Search Cheat Sheet" link shows you a printable guide to the syntax for these operators; it's worth your time to use it.

Also, on the advanced search, you can limit the dates of the pages you find (to retrieve only the newest ones, for example).

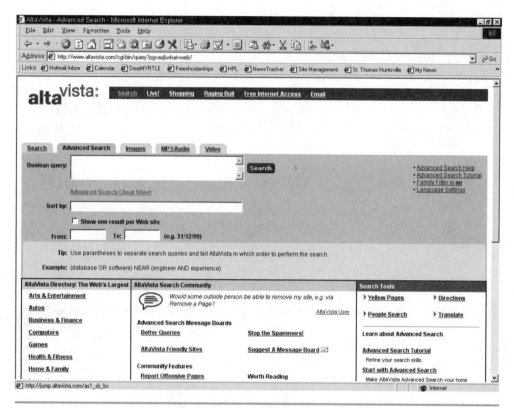

FIGURE 8-1. *AltaVista's advanced search lets you fine-tune a query*

Ancestry - GenPage Finder (http://www.ancestry.com)

A free service from Ancestry.com, GenPage Finder looks at 2,000,000 genealogical sites and is updated every week. It can use the Boolean WITH; select the proximity from the drop-down box beneath the query space. The full URL address is: http://www.ancestry.com/search/rectype/directories/gpf/main.htm

Enter your keywords, choose the Boolean limiters, and click Search. Adding or deleting keywords will fine-tune the number of search results.

The more keywords you enter, the more specific your search will be and the fewer search results will return. Some of the pages GenPageFinder will turn up are quite large. If your keywords are not immediately visible on the page GenPageFinder finds for you, try pressing CTRL+F and entering your keywords again. This should take you to the spot on the page where your keywords appear. Whatever your research interests and whatever searching you've already done, chances are that a search on GenPageFinder will yield fruitful new sources.

AOL NetFind (http://search.aol.com)

AOL NetFind is a portal. To reach AOL NetFind from within America Online, you can go to the Internet window and click the NetFind button, or you can go directly there by entering keyword: NetFind. In either case, you'll get to the AOL NetFind home page, shown in Figure 8-2.

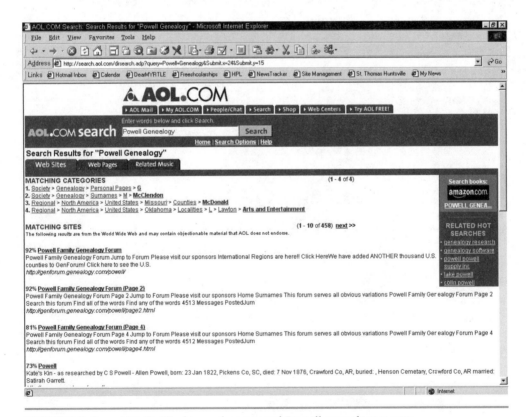

FIGURE 8-2. *AOL NetFind turned up several Powell genealogy pages*

AOL NetFind uses + , -, and quotation marks to give you AND, NOT, and WITH Boolean searches.

AskJeeves (http://www.askjeeves.com)

A "natural language" metasearch engine, AskJeeves is fast, if a bit flaky. You are supposed to be able to put in "Where can I find Powell genealogies" and get reasonably accurate results. In practice, it really zeroes in on the nouns, and presents the results in three parts:

♦ First, rephrasing the question with emphasis on different nouns such as "Where can I find information on tracing my genealogy?" and "Where can I find Powell's Bookstore?"

♦ Second, a listing of actual pages, sorted in order of relevancy to the query

♦ Third, a listing of results from other search engines such as AltaVista.

It is fairly useful, but not as accurate as some others, and doesn't find pages newer than the last month or so.

Biography Guide (http://bioguide.congress.gov)

Was any ancestor of yours a member of Congress? Search for biographies of members by last name, first name, position, and state at this site. Fascinating, this site can add a new dimension to your family history, if your ancestors are in the database. The full URL is: http://bioguide.congress.gov/biosearch/biosearch.asp.

C|Net Search (http://www.search.com)

A metasearch site, where many search sites are asked to reply to your query at once, C|Net's search site is also a directory, where you can browse to a subject and look at the edited selections. The results come back quickly, sorted by how relevant the search engine judged the sites to be in relation to the terms you put in.

To use C|Net Search for genealogy, click on Search People, then Genealogy. This page will serve as a metasearch page, and you can choose which of six Web catalogs to include: American Memory from the Library of Congress, GenForum, RootsWeb, Family Search,

GenSource, and Yahoo! Genealogy. You can check any or all of them, and record your choice for later searches.

Be aware that the default is OR. You can enclose a phrase in quotes and add + or -, but not all the search sites will use them. I found the results slow to come back and often close, but not exactly, to what I wanted.

Excite (http://www.excite.com)

Excite was one of the first search engines; it soon developed the ability to "personalize" the Excite page with your favorite links, news headlines that match your keywords, and local information such as TV and movie schedules. Now a portal like Yahoo! and Infoseek/GO, it offers chats, e-mail, forums and other services. There is a genealogy section, at http://my.excite.com/lifestyle/hobbies_interests/genealogy/. Here you'll find a "Genealogy Book of the Day" reviewed, pointers to new sites, and a browseable index of 50,000 genealogy sites. That should keep you busy for a while!

Excite uses +, -, and quotation marks, and its search algorithm gets very good results. In fact, its search results are so good, many other search sites use Excite's search software, simply tweaking it to look for their specialties.

FastSearch (http://www.alltheweb.com)

FastSearch, like AltaVista, has an advanced page, which is the best bet for finely tuned searches. Here you can choose whether up to three terms or phrases should be on the page, must be on the page, or must not be on the page. This is equivalent to OR, AND, and NOT, respectively. You can also designate where your term should appear—in the text is the default, but you can choose title, link, or URL, as well. It lives up to its name: the results are always fast, and the results page will have the most relevant hits at the top; just to warn you, though, it does return many, many hits.

GO/Infoseek (http://www.go.com/WebDir)

This is my favorite search engine. Infoseek/GO is an Internet portal similar to Yahoo!, with a set of reviewed sites called "guides." The Genealogy Guide is at http://www.go.com/WebDir/Family/Genealogy.

Like Lycos, Infoseek has a filter that will keep all the pornography sites out of your results. You have to click the tiny GOGuardian link at the top to turn it on. Click the "How to Search" link next to it for information on how to use Boolean searches. In brief, quotation marks make it look for a specific phrase; a + means a term must appear and a - means it must not.

When doing searches on InfoSeek, capitalization counts, so you can search for surnames such as "Weeks" and "Fox," without getting so many irrelevant matches. In addition, InfoSeek doesn't ignore common words like "the" and "new," so you can efficiently search for terms such as New Hampshire. The pipe symbol, |, means "with" as in "William Reason Powell" | genealogy.

If you don't want to use all that punctuation, you can use the Search Options page, where all these operators are represented by fill-in boxes (see Figure 8-3).

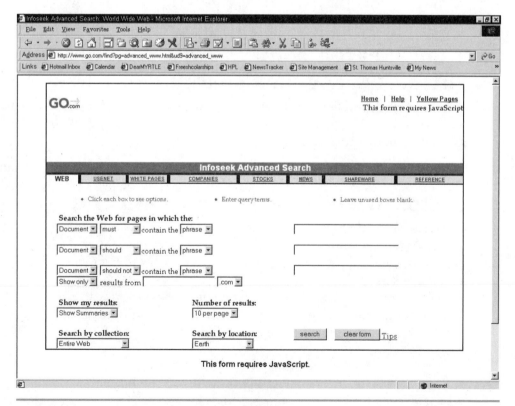

FIGURE 8-3. *Infoseek's Search Options page*

The folks who created Infoseek were bought out by Disney/ABC, and now the whole thing is very family-oriented. You can browse the InfoSeek channels (categories) or you can run a search on the contents of the InfoSeek databases.

Genealogy Pages (http://www.genealogypages.com)

A collected catalog of genealogy sites, this site also offers you a free e-mail box and a browser-based chat site, so it qualifies as a "portal."

You can browse the collection of links by category, or search the entire collection. Because it's all about genealogy, you don't have to put that term in the search box. A search for "South Carolina Powell" in the regular search box turned up nothing, and even though in the Advanced Search, I was able to choose between AND (the default) and OR, and whether it would be recognized as a phrase, I couldn't get a match on all three. Searching on "South Carolina" got good results, however, as did searching on "Powell."

GeneaSearch.com (http://www.genealsearch.com)

This is another portal along the lines of Genealogy Page. There are several options, but searching by surname is your best bet. Its results were very similar to that of Genealogy Page.

GenealogyPortal.com (http://www.genealogyportal.com)

A joint venture of Steve Wood, who founded the original Genealogy Home Page, and Matthew Helm of Genealogy Tool Box, this is a site that uses one form for eight separate search engines to help you efficiently search the Web.

The GenealogyPortal.com search engines provide you with five options when conducting searches. Three of the options are under the MATCH drop-down box and two options are under the FORMAT drop-down box.

Under the MATCH drop-down box, you can choose the ALL option (Boolean AND), the ANY option (Boolean OR), or the BOOLEAN option, which lets you insert the operators AND, OR, and NOT into the search terms yourself, using parentheses for nesting to further refine your search by creating sets. For example, a search for (A or B) and (C or D) finds all pages that contain either A or B AND either C or D.

The FORMAT drop-box contains two options—DETAIL which will include a brief description of the web page, and SHORT which will only show a link to the Web page (no description).

The site also includes a short edited catalog of sites under headings such as Archives and Libraries, Primary Records, and Guides to Research. You can browse the catalog by clicking the links to these categories from the front page of the site.

GenGateway (http://www.gengateway.com)

Another version of a catalog of Web sites organized into categories for genealogists, this site by Steve Lacy indexes thousands of Web pages and sources. Choose the category to search, such as surname or obituary, and you'll get well-sorted results.

To navigate the site, use one of the many useful "gateways" listed in the navigation bar to the left of the opening page. If you are new to the site, first try the "Beginners Gateway," or the "Search Pages."

For example, the "Beginner's Gateway" will give you links to general guides such as "20 Ways to Avoid Genealogical Grief" (http://www.smartlink.net/~leverich/20ways.html). The "Search Pages" link is a metasearch engine that uses several sites, such as Infoseek, Magellan, Excite, and Yahoo, with limiters. It also searches specialized sites such as Irish on the Net for surnames.

You might also notice the search field at the top. With the drop box you can select to search just surname listings, site listings, or the entire database. If your main interest is surnames, use the search field or the A-Z search to help you find what you are looking for. The online Guides to the left will also lead you to their interactive message boards where you can ask and answer questions. A search for Powell on this box turned up six good pages.

GenServ (http://www.genserv.com/)

An all-volunteer effort, GenServ is a collection of donated GEDCOMS with a very sophisticated set of search commands. (Remember that this is all secondary source material; when you seem to have a match, you need to contact the submitter to find out what primary source material he or she might have.) The database has over 19,000,000 individuals in more than 14, 000 databases. All this family history data is online and available by search and reports to subscribers.

GenServ has been online since 1991 and on the Web since early 1994. To access the system you have to at least submit your own GEDCOM, but by paying optional yearly fees, you can perform many more searches per day than the free access allows.

The ability to do complex searches on the databases means there is a real learning curve; furthermore, only the "surname count" search can be done from the Web; all the rest are done via e-mail messages. This has the advantage of letting you input your terms, and then surf onto other sites. The results, meanwhile, come back by e-mail (and very quickly, too).

It's worth the time to upload your data and learn how to query this set of databases.

GenSource (http://www.gensource.com)

This specialized genealogy directory site provides the online genealogist with three databases to assist with research online.

The first database is called Search Common Threads. You use this to find other genealogists researching your family name. If you are at a "dead end" finding information on an ancestor, add an entry to Common Threads so other family members can find you.

Search I Found It! to locate genealogy sites on the Internet. You may use the I Found It! search engine to locate pages on: surnames, one name studies, ship passenger lists, genealogical societies and associations, researchers, software, books, family mailing lists, online records of churches, census data, cemeteries, and more.

Search the I Found It! archives for sites containing actual historical records. Many individuals have taken the time to transcribe records and place them on the Net for your use, all of which are indexed for research purposes.

GenealogySearch.com (http://genealogysearch.com)

Like Genealogy Source, this site has databases for you to search, specific to their site. All the information is uploaded by volunteers.

Google (http://www.google.com)

Google is both a site and a search engine. In fact, the search engine part now powers Yahoo! Searching with Google is simple: Put in the terms and click Google search. If you click "I'm feeling lucky," it will take you straight to the best match for your search, instead of presenting you with a list sorted by relevance. Google also has a directory, which you can browse by subject. The Genealogy listing is at http:/ /directory.google.com/ Top/Society/Genealogy/.

Search tips for Google: first, the search engine does no stemming or guessing; it matches on your terms exactly, including misspellings. The default operator in Google is AND, never OR, as in many search engines, so the top matches are always those with all your terms. It can use NOT if you place a - in front of unwanted terms. Searches are never case-sensitive, so a search for surnames that are common nouns (Banks, Rivers, Green) should always include some form of "genealogy" as well to take advantage of the AND feature. Quotation marks will make Google search for a phrase. The plus sign in Google is for commonly ignored terms such as numerals, and single letters. To search for George I, you would have to put a plus sign in front of the Roman numeral: George +I.

HotBot (http://hotbot.lycos.com)

Many Internet experts consider HotBot the best search site. The Boolean operators are used with drop-down boxes, or you can combine them in parentheses as you can with Lycos and GO/Infoseek. Lycos and HotBot merged a while back, but most feel the HotBot site still comes up with the best hits.

LookSmart (http://www.looksmart.com/)

LookSmart positions itself as a Web directory. The technology of the search engine, however, is licensed by many other portal sites. If you do a search on Iwon.com, FreeScholarships, and many others, you'll really be using LookSmart.

The thing about LookSmart is that "sponsors" (those who have paid LookSmart advertising money) float to the top of any relevant search, so the results aren't as reliable.

Lycos (http://www.lycos.com/)

Lycos is named for a spider that hunts at night and is very, very fast. Like its namesake, Lycos uses a program called a "spider" to hunt for new Internet files every night. It's one of the best search engines on the Web.

Lycos Web Search works very much like AOL NetFind, but may return different results for the same search. Lycos does have some special plusses, however. The search engine includes separate databases for pictures, sounds, programs, and other categories of information.

Lycos is also a portal: it has chat, news headlines, and other services. Worth a look is the Lycos Top 5% (http://point.lycos.com/categories/), a catalog or directory to what Lycos feels are the best 5% of all Web sites.

You can also search within the results (see Figure 8-4); for example, if you've gotten back over 16,000 sites for the search "Powell genealogy," you can search within those results for "William Reason."

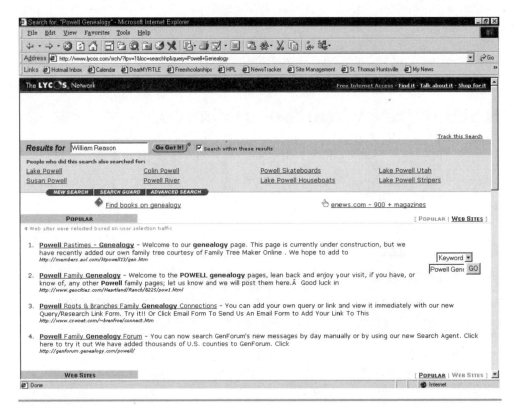

FIGURE 8-4. *Lycos can let you search within a set of results to narrow down the hits*

Lycos reviewers have to hear of a site, visit it, review it, and post it (assuming the site makes the top 5%) so this isn't a good place to look for a brand new site. But if you are looking for sites that someone else has reviewed and rated for you, this is a great resource.

MetaCrawler (http://www.metacrawler.com/ index_power.html)

The Power Search of this metasearch site contains is the page you want. Here you can choose which search sites to use, choose "any," "all," or "phrase" for your terms and determine the sort of results you receive. It's fast, it's powerful, but the results can be overwhelming.

Northern Light (www.northernlight.com)

Another one of my favorite sites, this one not only searches Web sites, but also documents on the Web such things as magazines, newspaper articles, and so forth. It sorts the results into folders, as in Figure 8-5.

In the Power Search, you can determine what sites are searched, and what sort of documents, define the dates to be searched, and more. However, some of the results may cost money to see, if they are copyrighted magazine or newspaper articles. This is a great site for the latest news on genealogy, and I also found good hits on "Powell genealogy."

Northern Light also offers a notification option; you can tell it to look for specific keywords in new documents and e-mail you as they appear in the database. This is a good way to keep track of new genealogy pages.

Obituary Search Pages

There are several pages that allow you to search recent and older obituaries.

- ♦ Legacy.com, http://www.legacy.com/NewspaperMap.asp has a page called "ObitFinder," which searches recent obituaries by name, keyword, and location.

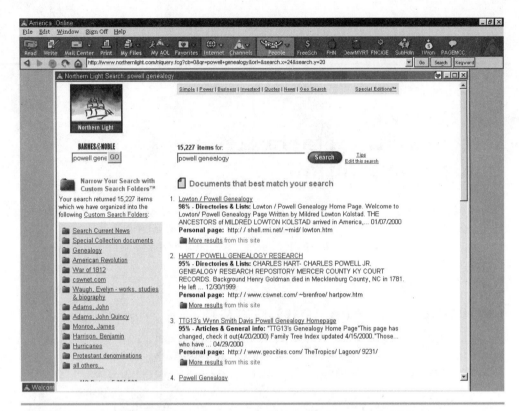

FIGURE 8-5. *Northern Light sorts the results into custom search folders*

- ◆ Obituary Links, http://www.geocities.com/ ~ cribbswh/obit/, searches cemetery records, obituaries, and other pages from sites such as Ancestry.com, RootsWeb, and so on. It's a metasearch engine that focuses on death records.

- ◆ 4Obituaries, http://4obituaries.4anything.com/, has a list of links to modern obit pages.

Surname Web (http://other.surnameweb.org/search/)

This site has a database of names submitted by users, as well as pages from other Web sites. Simply input the surname.

SurnameSite (http://surnamesite.org)

Note that there is no www at the beginning of this URL. This site lets you search an ancestor archive with over 45 pages of wills, obituaries, birth records, and other documents posted by visitors. You can also search a directory of over 1,000 genealogy and historical sites with ancestor names, or post and view queries about your ancestors on the message board.

Snap (http://www.snap.com/)

Snap is a portal owned by NBC and Microsoft. Its Power Search page allows Boolean searches, date limitation, as well as domain and language specifications. It's fast and its results are comparable to the other major search sites. The full URL address is: http://www.snap.com/search/power/form/0,179,home-0,00.html?st.sn.srch.0.pwr.

World Connect (http://worldconnect.rootsweb.com/)

A part of RootsWeb, this search engine's motto is "Connecting the world, one GEDCOM at a time." People are free to upload to and search in this collection of GEDCOM databases. All you need to do is fill out the form with name, place of birth and death, and dates of birth and death. You can choose an exact search if you are sure of your facts, or a range of 2 to 20 years for dates and soundex searches for names and places. It's fast, but the results depend entirely on the uploaded GEDCOMS. If you have no hits, consider uploading your information for others. If you have already uploaded your information, you can exclude your own database from future searches.

Like GenServ, this is all volunteer, amateur information. You have to contact the submitter of a database to find out the sources for the data, and unlike GenServ, you can do the searches via the Web.

Yahoo! (http://www.yahoo.com)

The first Internet directory worthy of the name, Yahoo! is an edited, sorted catalog of sites. And it is big. It features about half a million sites divided into 25,000 categories. Yahoo! (Figure 8-6) is arranged in a hierarchy of categories, so you can browse through it. But with so many sites and categories, it's good to know Yahoo! has a search engine built in. Mind you, this search engine doesn't search the Web, it searches Yahoo!, looking for sites and categories within the directory.

Yahoo! gets updated frequently, with users providing most of the new sites. Each site gets visited by a Yahoo! Surfer, who decides where each site should appear within the directory. It's also a portal with chat, e-mail, forums, and other services.

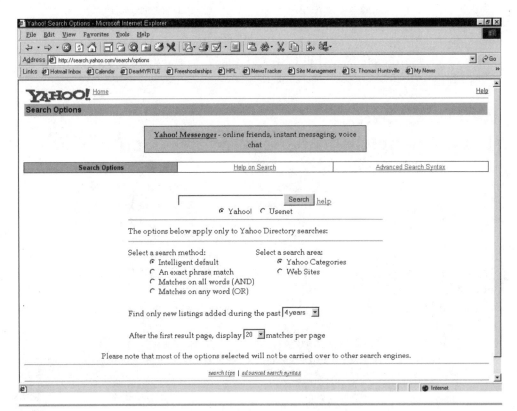

FIGURE 8-6. *Yahoo! is a huge directory containing links and information for over half a million Web sites*

People Directories

So far, you've looked at search engines and directories for finding a Web site. But what if you need to find lost, living relatives? In that case, you need people search engines, called White Page directories. Like the white pages of your phone book, these specialize in finding people, not pages. In fact, all the search engine sites mentioned previously have white page directories.

For example, AOL NetFind has http://www.aol.com/netfind/whitepages.adp and http://www.aol.com/netfind/emailfinder.adp. In the first page, White Pages, you can enter the first and last name of a person, as well as the city (optional) and state the person lives in. A successful search turns up a person's mailing address and phone number. Beside each name returned by the search are three buttons. You can send them personal greetings, flowers, or some other gift.

Note

The people you find using the Find a Person window are AOL subscribers.

The E-mail Finder lets you find the e-mail address of a person if you know their first and last name.

Switchboard (www.switchboard.com) is one of many "White Pages" services on the Web. It's free, and has the e-mail and telephone numbers of millions of people and businesses taken from public records, as well as a Web site catalog. If you register as a user (it's free), you can ensure that your listing is not only accurate, but has only the information you wish it to reveal.

BigFoot (http://www.bigfoot.com) is another such effort to catalog people, with the same general rules: input your information and you get searches that are more specific. BigFoot also has surface mail addresses in addition to e-mail and telephone information.

To search many such pages at once, look into The Ultimate White Pages at http://www.theultimates.com/white/. It also has links to reverse telephone lookups as well as map sites for finding towns. (See Figure 8-7.)

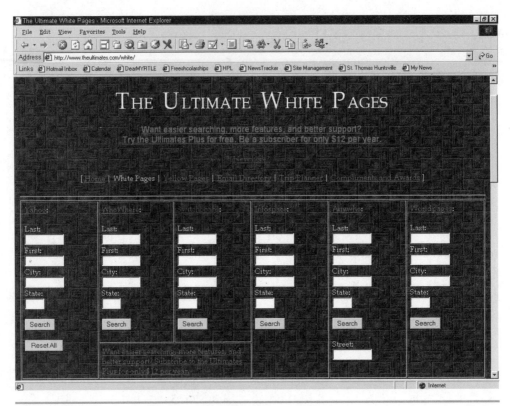

FIGURE 8-7. *The Ultimate White Pages offers a quick way to do many searches*

File Search Sites

Sometimes what the online genealogist needs isn't a site, or a person—it's a program. To find the most recent programs, such as new Web browsers or genealogy programs, you can go to several sites that keep track of software and where the latest versions are. I've listed a few in the following paragraphs.

FileMine (http://www.filemine.com) is a vast collection of software, most uploaded by the authors and offered as shareware, or rarely, freeware. FileMine catalogs and rates the software. In the category Home & Leisure, you'll find a Genealogy section with about 64 entries as of this writing. It contains such all-time favorites as Brother's Keeper and Family Matters. When you find a category that has files in it, you can choose to look at their edited catalogs of software. Under Jewels, you'll find software judged best in its class. Under Packs, you'll find customized collections of software around a theme (holidays, privacy, etc.). Digs, on the other hand, gives you a list of software that compete head to head (Web browsers, etc.). New will have the newest files.

The Ultimate Collection of Winsock Software, TUCOWS (http://www.tucows.com) is a site that tracks more than Windows, despite the name, and has a capsule profile and a rating for each program. TUCOWS has mirror sites all over the world, so you can choose a site close to you for faster downloads. My search for "genealogy" turned up 30 titles.

Shareware.com (http://www.shareware.com) is a premier software search site. Updated weekly, the search engine lets you choose your operating system, choose a keyword, and even choose a date for the newest software, or the oldest! Shareware.com then lets you see where the file can be found, and rates the reliability (how easy it is to get in and get a file) of each site. My search for genealogy turned up 15 files.

ZDNet Software Library (http://www.hotfiles.com/) has the latest software, usually rated by the staff on a 5-star system; some of it is trial versions of popular commercial software. All the ZD sites are integrated to some extent, so you can search from the ZDNet Software Library into a bunch of magazines (PC Magazine, Computer Shopper, and Yahoo! Internet Life to name a few) for site reviews as well as the latest software. A recent search turned up over 70 titles under "genealogy" (see Figure 8-8).

Searching for Information within Newsgroups

While newsgroups can be great sources of genealogy information, reading all the messages, or even the headers, can be a lot of work. Fortunately, you don't always have to read the whole newsgroup to find the information you need. There are several places where you can search newsgroups, one or several or all at a time.

InfoSeek (http://www.infoseek.com)—the search engine for this directory can search Web sites as well as newsgroups, news archives, and company listings. With regard to newsgroups, InfoSeek has the most recent two weeks of newsgroups stored in a searchable database. To search newsgroups, just enter the text you want to search for, click Newsgroups, then click Seek. To do quick and easy genealogical searches, type in the surnames you are interested in and follow them

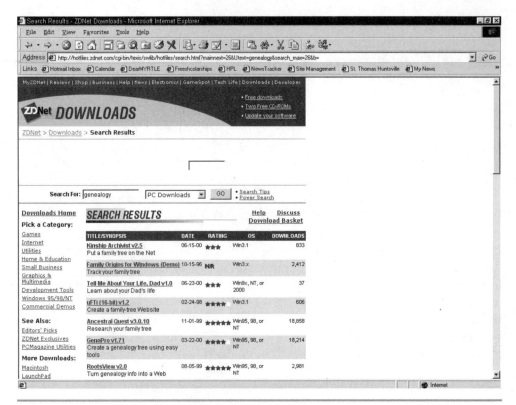

FIGURE 8-8.   *ZDNet has a large library of shareware*

with + genealogy. InfoSeek will return a list of the genealogical messages, where each message title is a link. Click it to read it.

Deja.com carries over 50,000 newsgroups, with postings going back as far as two and a half years. It makes basic searches simple, yet supports more complex ones. You can click Power Search to get fancy. Create a Query Filter by typing in the first part of the name of a group of newsgroups you want to search. For example, enter soc.genealogy.*. Now type in the surnames you're looking for and click Find. Within seconds, Deja.com will return a list of messages that are in the soc.genealogy.* group, and mention the surnames you gave it. You can also limit the date of those messages to a certain range; using this feature, a monthly search will let you know if something interesting is happening in your surname on Usenet!

Part III

The "Must See" Online Resources

Chapter 9

RootsWeb

How would you like a place where you can search dozens of databases of genealogical material, hundreds of genealogical Web pages, and subscribe to thousands of mail lists? Or perhaps publish your own page, upload your own data, and create your own mail list?

Welcome to Online Genealogy Heaven! The place is called RootsWeb, http://www.rootsweb.com. It started out as a site for a group of people working at RAND who dabbled in genealogy on the side. Once upon a time, they had a little mail list, hosted by the University of Minnesota, and a little database on the RAND server. That was 11 years ago. Today it is the largest all-volunteer genealogy site on the Web. Note that the main page of RootsWeb has this statement: The RootsWeb project has two missions:

1. To make large volumes of data available to the online genealogical community at minimal cost.

2. To provide support services to online genealogical activities such as USENET newsgroup moderation, mailing list maintenance, surname list generation, etc.

A quick guided tour of the site only scratches the surface of all the wonderful things at RootsWeb. Still, let's give it a try.

True Story: RootsWeb Leads to a Reunion

About 3 years ago I started searching for my Powell (on my father's side) ancestors, but about the only thing I knew how to do was search the surname and message boards.

One night, after having not done anything in about 2 months, I decided to get online and read the [RootsWeb] surname message boards. On a whim, I went into the Hubbard message boards (my mother's side). The first message I read was about someone searching for descendants of my grandmother's parents.

When my grandmother was about 3 or 4, her mother passed away and she went to live with an aunt and uncle. Eventually she lost contact with her brothers. She did see the oldest brother once when she was about 15, but never saw or heard from him again. That night I found him, a person she had not seen in over 70 years.

We flew to Washington State and met all kinds of new cousins, aunts, and uncles. Over the next two years, she spoke with her brother many times. Unfortunately, he passed away last summer, but at least she got to see him twice and was able to speak with him on numerous occasions.

We figured out that the message I responded to had only been posted for about a minute before I discovered it. The surname message boards are a wonderful tool in searching for the ancestors and relatives you never knew you had, or had but didn't know who they were.

---Jennifer Powell Lyons

Searching for Surnames

On the first page, you'll find a search template to input a surname, first name, or any keywords (Figure 9-1). Then click a button to search the databases and text files, the World Connect GEDCOMs, the RootsWeb Surname list, or the Social Security Death Index. If you choose a keyword,

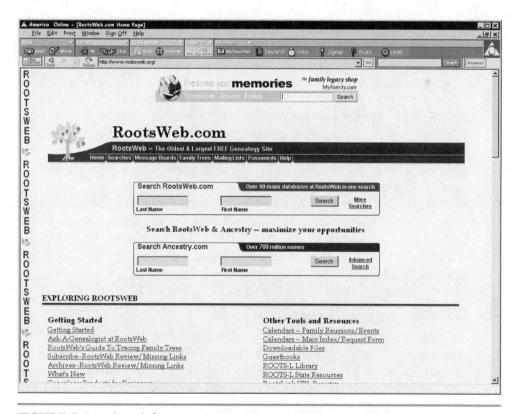

FIGURE 9-1. *Search for your surnames on RootsWeb on your first visit*

you can choose to search the major text files or the GenSeeker database of uploaded documents.

Let's look at each of these resources.

RootsWeb Surname List

The RootsWeb Surname List (RSL) is a registry of who is searching for whom, and in what times and places. The listings include contact information for each entry; if you find someone looking for the same name, in the same area, and in about the same time period, you may be able to help each other. That's the intent of the list. To submit your own data or to search for data is free.

To search the list, you can use the form on the opening page, or go to the page http://rsl.rootsweb.com/cgi-bin/rslsql.cgi.

On the RSL page, you type in the surname you want to search for. If you want, also input a location, using the abbreviations you'll find at the link below the location box. Use the radio buttons to choose whether your search is "surname" (exactly as you spelled it) or "Soundex" or "Metaphone" (sounds like it, but spelled differently). In future attempts, you can limit the search to new submissions within the last week, month, or two months. The list is updated once a month.

The "Migration" field shows you the path the family took. SC > GA, for example, shows migration from South Carolina to Georgia.

You can also send e-mail search commands to the RSL database: simply send a message with the surname you want to rsl-search@ rootsweb.com. The results will be e-mailed back to you, just as they would be displayed on the Web page.

In the blink of an eye, you'll get a chart that shows the surname, date range and locations that match, as well as a link to the person who submitted the data, showing how to contact him or her (see Figure 9-2). You can use the information to contact that person explaining what you have on that surname, and what you need.

World Connect Project

As explained in Chapter 8, the World Connect Project is one of several GEDCOM databases searchable through the Web. Searching it from the RootsWeb home page, you can only input first and last names; the results page will have another input form at the bottom allowing you to fine tune the search by adding places and dates.

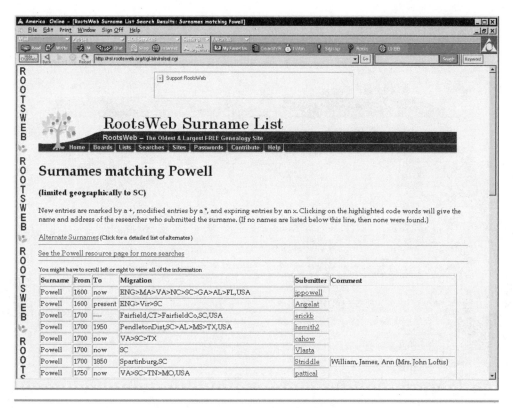

FIGURE 9-2. *When I searched for Powell in South Carolina, I got several hits*

If you go to the World Connect page at http://worldconnect. rootsweb.com/, you can find links to tips and hints for using World Connect. Remember, all the data here is uploaded by volunteers, so there may be errors!

Automated Surname Search

Clicking this button from the search form on the RootsWeb home page will search various text and database files on RootsWeb. You will get a results page for hits within the Obit Times, World Connect, RSL, SSDI, and many other records on RootsWeb. Essentially, this is a meta-search on the RootsWeb site—a sort of RootsWeb's Greatest Hits! See Figure 9-3 for a sample output.

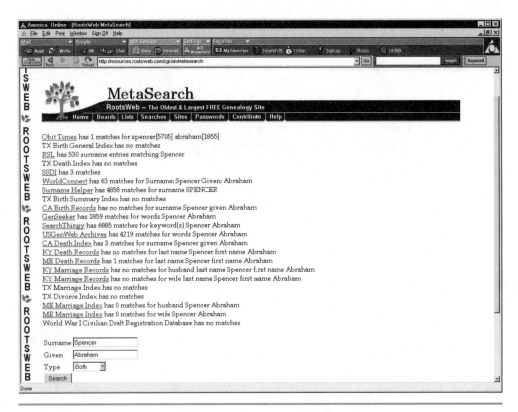

FIGURE 9-3. *MetaSearch gets results from several different sites*

SSDI

The Social Security Death Index searches the Federal records of deaths. Anyone who died before Social Security began in the 1930s will not be in this database.

Searching from the RootsWeb home page, all you can input is the first and last name. However, the results page will let you link to the Advanced Search page. Here you can narrow the search by location and date. This is an excellent tool for researching 20th century ancestors.

Automated Keyword Search and GenSeeker

These two options from the RootsWeb home page search input are meta-search engines which will look at text files and databases uploaded to RootsWeb such as obituaries, wills, deeds, and so on.

Surname searches will work using this, but so will searches for place names or keywords such as "census." Combine the two and you can get some very good hits.

Other Search Engines

These searches can be very helpful in your research, but they assume you are a rank beginner with no more than a name or a place to launch your inquiries. Perhaps you know for sure you're looking for a land record in Alabama or a cemetery in Iowa. RootsWeb has several searchable resources for items such as these. You'll find the search engines for the RSL and the other databases at http://searches.rootsweb.com/ (see Figure 9-4).

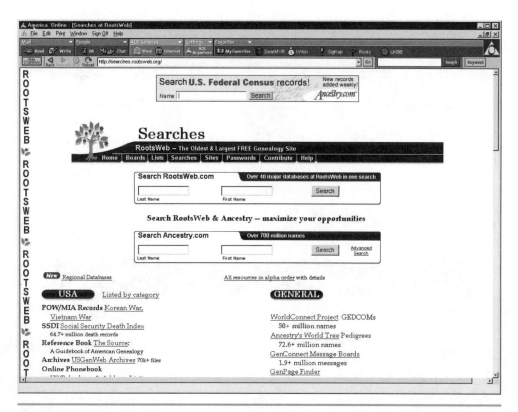

FIGURE 9-4.   *From this page, you can reach dozens of specific searchable databases on RootsWeb*

GenConnect

GenConnect is the collection of message boards on RootsWeb. A message board is a place where messages are read, sent, and answered on the Web, using a browser to read them. A mail list is where messages are e-mailed to and from the members, whereas a mail client is used to read them. Both the message boards and the mail lists are archived and searchable on RootsWeb.

You will also see "suites" of GenConnect message boards. A surname may have a variety of boards, for queries, obituaries, wills, etc. A Spencer Query board is shown in Figure 9-5.

Perhaps the easiest way to understand GenConnect boards is to visit their site at http://genconnect.rootsweb.com. Someday, you may want to administer a GenConnect board, or even a suite of boards. If so,

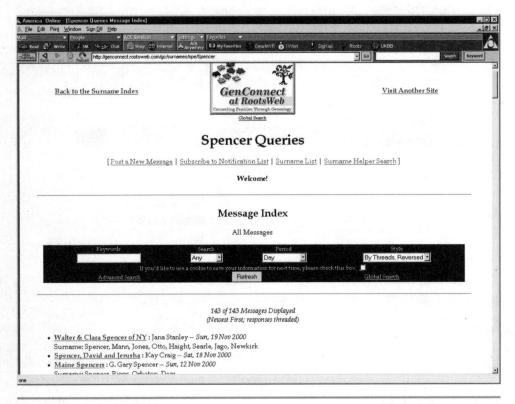

FIGURE 9-5. *On GenConnect, the surname Spencer has message boards pertaining to queries, Bibles, biographies, deeds, obituaries, pension files, and wills*

you'll find information on how to request a board(s) at http://resources.
rootsweb.com/adopt/.

Web Sites

RootsWeb hosts thousands of genealogy Web sites. Some, like Cyndi's
List at http://cyndislist.com/ or the USGenWeb Project's main site http://
www.usgenweb.com/, you have already read about in this book. RootsWeb
also hosts the WorldGenWeb Project http://www.worldgenweb.org/ and
a majority of the country sites. Most of the RootsWeb-hosted boards can
be found on the index at http://www.rootsweb.com/~websites/. It won't
include all the Web sites at RootsWeb, because the listing is voluntary
(and because more Web sites come online every month), but announcements of the newest ones appear in the e-mail newsletter, RootsWeb
Review (see below).

State Resource Pages

One of the main areas of RootsWeb is its State Resource pages (http://
www.rootsweb.com/roots-l/usa.html) which offer a wealth of information
(for those researching in the United States). Just the upper portion of
one page appears in Figure 9-6, listing articles on federal censuses, old
ports, and all the counties in the Unites States. This is a great place to
begin your search for records within a certain geographic area.

The HelpDesk

The HelpDesk maintains a page at http://helpdesk.rootsweb.com/ where
you will find a FAQ file about RootsWeb and its services. Check there
first if you have a question or problem. If you can't find an answer
there, you can follow the links from that site to the message board
where you can post a question for the HelpDesk team to answer.

Newsletters

RootsWeb has several e-mail newsletters, all of which are worth reading.

RootsWeb Review

RootsWeb is always growing and you can't depend on luck to find
out about the latest and greatest sites! For help in this area, use the
RootsWeb Review, a free weekly newsletter sent to contributors and

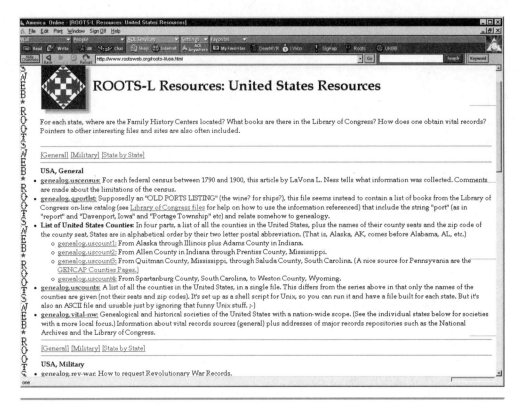

FIGURE 9-6. *Learn about resources for your research at Roots-L Resources*

users via e-mail. You'll find announcements of programs and services for RootsWeb users, new mailing lists, GenConnect boards, and Web sites, plus success stories from other cybergenealogists.

If you are interested in reading through previous issues, go to ftp://ftp.rootsweb.com/pub/review/. You can subscribe by sending an e-mail to RootsWeb-Review-L-request@ rootsweb.org with only the word "subscribe" (without the quote marks) in the subject line and message area.

Missing Links

Missing Links is a weekly compilation of articles about genealogical research methods and sources from all parts of the world. You will also find delightful, amazing, and otherwise wonderful tales of genealogical research at *Successful Links*, as well as articles acknowledging the efforts of particularly helpful librarians, archivists, town or county clerks, and other unsung heroes, in an appreciative digest titled *Virtual Bouquets*. You can contribute your own stories by e-mailing your submissions as plain text messages (not as attachments) to rwr-editors@rootsweb.com. To subscribe, send a message to rootsweb-review-subscribe@rootsweb.com.

Somebody's Links

Somebody's Links is a monthly collection of uncovered genealogical treasures, such as photographs, diaries, letters, and family Bibles. The contributors describe each item as accurately as possible, hoping someone out there is looking for it. Back issues of the newsletter are available as plain text files at ftp://ftp.rootsweb.com/pub/somebody/. Files are named according to the date of the issue (e.g., 19991201.txt).

All back issues of RootsWeb Review and Missing Links are searchable at http://search-rwr.rootsweb.com/.

Mailing Lists

Besides Roots-L, RootsWeb hosts literally thousands of mailing lists. As mentioned in Chapter 6, you can find lists for surnames or family names, regions or topics being researched. The index at http://www.rootsweb.com/ ~ maillist/ has thousands of lists you can join, along with instructions explaining how to subscribe. It won't include all the mailing lists at RootsWeb, however, because it's a voluntary listing and not all listowners have chosen to be featured.

A good rule of thumb: be choosy in joining lists! Take on only a few at a time. Read them for a while, sign off if they don't prove useful, and try some others. Some lists are very active, indeed overwhelmingly so. One RootsWeb user who signed up for every possible mailing list for the United Kingdom had 9,000 e-mails in his in-box within 24 hours! Be careful what you wish for…

And remember that some lists are archived, so you don't have to subscribe to see if that list is talking about subjects that interest you. Just search the archive for your keywords and save those messages that are important.

Someday you may even want to start a mailing list of your own, which contributors can do. You can learn more about what is required of a listowner by following the link titled "Information for Listowners and Potential Listowners" at the main page for Mailing Lists.

The Merger

In June 2000, Ancestry.com and RootsWeb merged. In other words, the largest commercial genealogy site and the largest volunteer site were joining forces. (Use of RootsWeb remained free, contributions being completely voluntary.)

This meant several things. First, people were no longer asked to contribute $25 a year to RootsWeb. Second, Ancestry.com would now subsidize the hardware and software to keep RootsWeb up and running

In the months immediately following the merger, many were concerned that RootsWeb's privacy and fair use policies would change, but so far they have not. To date, if you submit data to RootsWeb, it won't be slapped onto a CD-ROM and sold (of course, you still need to be sure that data on living people isn't included in your submissions). So, for the user, little has really changed.

More and More

This quick tour is just enough to whet your appetite. Spend some time getting to know RootsWeb. Then get acquainted with Ancestry.com, the subject of the next chapter.

Chapter 10

The Ancestry.com Family of Sites

Ancestry.com, a company based in Salt Lake City, publishes books, magazines, and other genealogy materials. The online service is less than five years old, but it has grown rapidly. Ancestry.com's online services include a research site, an interactive site and a community site. All the sites are designed to help the amateur family historian in a variety of ways.

Ancestry.com

This site, the original Ancestry.com Web site, is designed to help you exchange information with other genealogists, and learn new techniques for family history. The features include:

♦ A large on-line genealogy library, searchable from the Web. These include such records as land, birth, marriage, death, census, and immigration records; the PERiodical Source Index (PERSI); Daughters of the American Revolution Lineage Books; the 1790 Census Collection; and the Early American Marriages Collection, to name just a few.

♦ Name databases, which are updated frequently, so that future searches may turn up what today's did not.

♦ Regular genealogy columns written by: George G. Morgan, Dick Eastman, Kip Sperry, Juliana Smith, Elizabeth Kelley Kerstens, and Drew Smith—all available for free.

There are three levels of membership to Ancestry.com: free, Preferred ($60 a year), and Gold ($100 a year). The Preferred and Gold levels include a year of access to all the databases of the site, EasyTree genealogy software, and a CD-ROM of Ancestry.com publications, such as back issues of their magazine. The Gold plan also includes a very good book on how to do genealogy called *The Source*, a year's subscription to the Ancestry.com magazine, and 15% off on purchases at the online store.

Even if you don't sign up for a subscription, you can find lots of useful information in the free areas on Ancestry.com. Every workday, Ancestry.com adds a new database such as Andersonville Prisoners of War or New York City wills, and when a new database is added, it's free for a few days.

The most popular part of the site, without doubt, is their searchable database of the Social Security Death Index. If you are looking for someone who died after the 1930s, this is a good place to start.

Another popular free area is the Ancestry.com World Tree database. Visitors to the site are welcome to submit what data they have for this database, the largest collection of its kind on the Internet. It's all-volunteer, and Ancestry.com has pledged to keep the searches free. Be aware, however, that Ancestry.com doesn't check the data submitted, so it all must be considered secondary material at best. Nevertheless, it can give you some good clues.

To use it, simply enter a name, with birth and death dates if you have them. The matches in the databases are presented in a table, as in Figure 10-1.

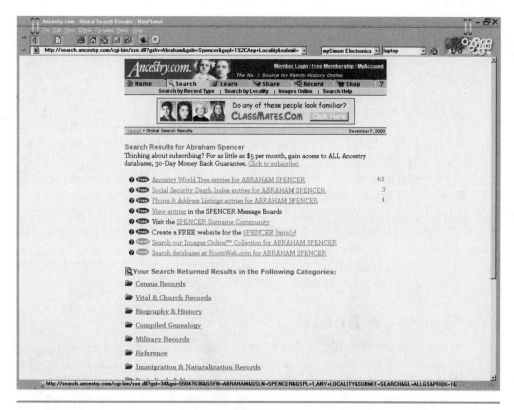

FIGURE 10-1. *In the Ancestry.com World Tree, you can find information from other genealogists. You can download the GEDCOM or contact the submitter*

You can click on the links in the far right to view the person's pedigree, look at data for that individual, e-mail the submitter, or download the GEDCOM.

Other good links in the free area include the regular columnists (Dick Eastman, DearMYRTLE, and others), genealogy lessons, phone and address searches, Juliana's Links, a searchable database of Web sites, and maps and gazetteers. In addition, it's always worth looking at the daily news page (http://www.ancestry.com/library/view/news/articles/d_p_1_archive.asp).

The site also features a chat area, bookstore, and sample articles from Ancestry Magazine, the print version.

FamilyHistory.com

Message boards, uploaded GEDCOM databases for exchange, and Society Hall add up to a genealogy community. This part of the Ancestry.com empire is an online community, along the lines of RootsWeb and GenealogyForum.com. The main sections are the Message Boards, the World Tree and the Society Hall. The mission of FamilyHistory.com is to give everyone interested in family history a community to swap information and improve their research by working together. The opening page is shown in Figure 10-2. Note that the message boards are the starting place.

FamilyHistory.com's policy is to keep all messages in place unless they break the rules of the community (flames, obscenity, copyright laws, etc.) or the author requests them to be removed (new data, change of plans, etc.). The message boards are completely free and your e-mail address is protected from unsolicited bulk e-mail. The goal is to have a place where you can give and get help, post and find data, and find organizations pursuing the same genealogical ends you are.

Message Boards

In the message boards, hundreds of thousands of topics are being discussed all the time. As noted in Chapter 5, message boards are different from mail lists in that you have to go to the site to get the messages, as well as go to the site to post messages. In a mail list, the same sorts of discussions go on, but the messages are sent and received

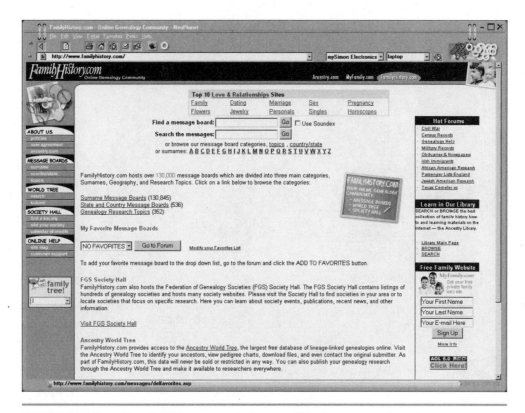

FIGURE 10-2. *FamilyHistory.com starts you off in the message boards*

in your e-mail program. Except for the method of posting and retrieving, they are basically the same thing: one-to-many communication, and many-to-many communication.

The message boards are divided into three broad categories: surnames, geography, and research. You can search all the message boards with the form on the Message Boards page, and use Soundex to get close matches (Spencer, Spenser, Spence, for example). You can also browse an alphabetical list of the board topics.

When you find a board discussing a surname, place, or technique you feel you need to keep up with, click "Add this forum to my favorites list" (see Figure 10-3). Then the opening page will have a drop-down list of the forums you like.

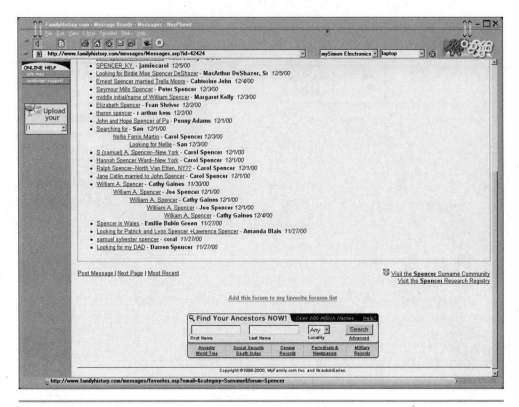

FIGURE 10-3. *Click "Add this forum to my favorites list" for the discussions you want to follow*

World Tree

From FamilyHistory.com you can get to the Ancestry World Tree, a free database of lineage-linked genealogies online. With the Ancestry World tree, you can view pedigree charts, download files, and contact the original submitter of a set of data. As part of FamilyHistory.com, this data will never be sold or restricted in any way. You can also contribute your genealogy research to the Ancestry.com World Tree so that other researchers can contact you.

Society Hall

FamilyHistory.com also hosts the Federation of Genealogy Societies (FGS) Society Hall. This set of pages has listings of hundreds of genealogy societies and hosts many society Web sites. Use the Society Hall to find organizations in your area or to locate societies that focus on specific research. The Society Hall can help you learn about genealogy society events, publications, recent news, and other information.

MyFamily.com

The free MyFamily.com site is a portal. As I've noted in Chapter 8, a portal hopes to be the first place you see when you log onto the World Wide Web, and the last place, too, by offering you so many features and activities you never want to surf anywhere else.

MyFamily.com's portal is a family history/community portal. The tools on the MyFamily.com site include a family calendar, family chat, family history features, message boards, a photo album, and more. Access to each family's site has both private password-only areas and public areas. You can use up to 75 MB of free space per site you create, giving you ample room to create a site for your family, another one for your spouse, and so on. You can store photos, sounds, and video clips in your album, and you can upload games or shareable applications to the file cabinet.

There are other features, too (which have much less to do with genealogy), but for this book, I will only cover those areas related to genealogy.

At the My Sites link (on the MyFamily.com home page), you can create a private message board, calendar, and file cabinets. You can also put together online scrapbooks of image, sound, and video files, upload your genealogy, and host private chats among those of your family you choose to invite. Once you have created the site, your MyFamily home page looks like Figure 10-4.

Creating a site is just a matter of clicks. You define a name and login, and then craft a list of relatives. You input their birthdays, anniversaries, and other important calendar dates, then invite them

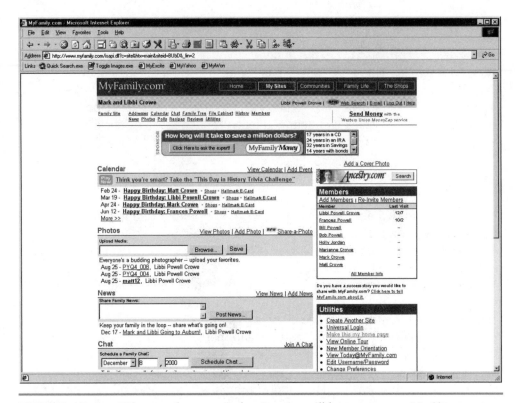

FIGURE 10-4. *When you have created a site, you will have your own My Sites page for adding messages, genealogy, and more*

to join you by creating a list of e-mail addresses. Everyone on the list is e-mailed a specific logon name and password for that site. No one can get in without those. You can also create an address book with phone numbers, etc., for you to access when you're online.

Family Tree

Now, it's time to begin constructing your online family tree. To do this, use the "Family Tree" link in the navigation bar at the top of every page on your MyFamily site. You can create it by typing in entries online, or by uploading a GEDCOM (by far the recommended method!). I uploaded a GEDCOM, and it looks like Figure 10-5.

By clicking the globe icon on the Family Tree creation page, you can make the GEDCOM available to Ancestry's World Family Tree, or click it

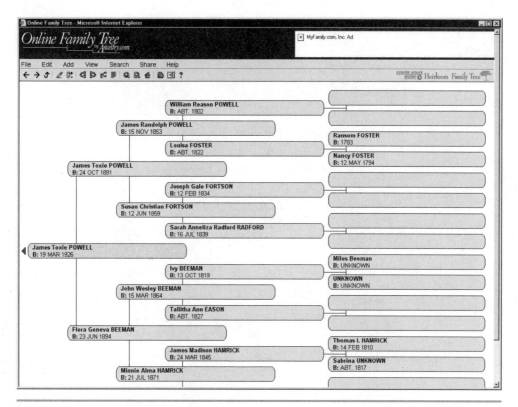

FIGURE 10-5. *The family tree on MyFamily.com can show descendant or ancestor views, as well as family groups*

again to remove it. Updates are simple: you can do them offline and then upload to overwrite the old tree, or click on any individual's name in the display in Figure 10-5 and correct data on the fly. Those who have logon privileges to your site can download the data and submit trees of their own.

History

A really nice feature is the "Our Family History" (listed as History in the navigation bar). Every family member you have invited to participate can log on, click Add History, and contribute memories of events, stories, and experiences. By clicking List History, the members can view all the contributions. When reading one, they can "Reply" and add their perspectives, ask questions, and so on. (See Figure 10-6.)

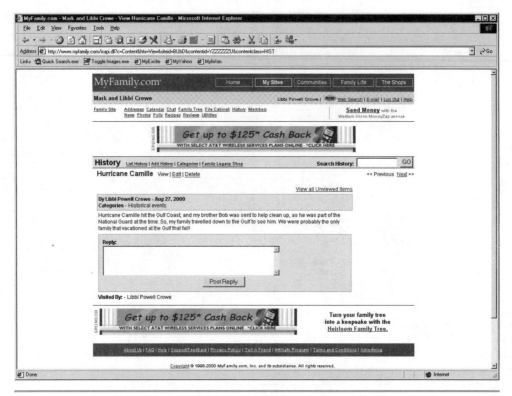

FIGURE 10-6. *Family history stories can be collected on your MyFamily site*

Remember that all this information is available only to those people you have invited to join your family site.

Chats

Whenever you like, all the members of your family site can sign on together for private, real-time chats. To do this, scroll down the first page of your site to the Chat listing and pick a day and time. Everyone who is a member of your site will then be e-mailed regarding when to sign on. This is good for planning family reunions, interviewing relatives about family history, or swapping genealogical data.

Other Features

Other features include: news (where you can post current family events); photo albums (where you can post pictures); a recipe swap area; a reviews area where you can share opinions on current movies, music, and art; and utilities for maintaining the Web site you created. Furthermore, the site offers a gift center, channels on health and parenting, contests, and so on. All of these are fun, even if they aren't related to genealogy!

A Nice Collection of Sites

The Ancestry.com collection of sites, which now includes RootsWeb, is a great place to start your genealogical quest. RootsWeb allows you more creativity in your Web site design than MyFamily, but the MyFamily sites are more interactive. Either way, both sites can be very useful in continuing and sharing your genealogy research.

Chapter 11

Everton's

One of the venerable agencies in genealogy, Everton Publishers (www.everton.com), produces books, CD-ROMs, *Everton's Genealogical Helper*, and this excellent Web site.

The Everton Web page offers several free features, although you do have to register your name, address, and e-mail to access them. Figure 11-1 shows those features available to you in the Free Guest Area.

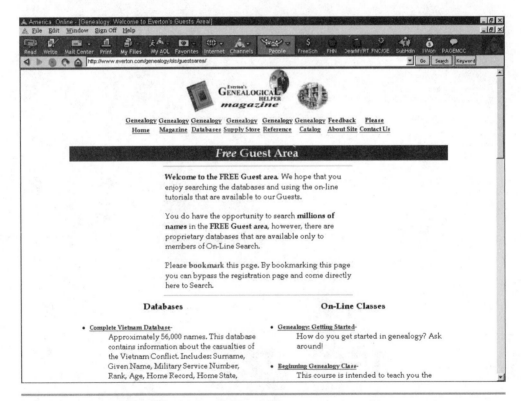

FIGURE 11-1. *Databases and online classes are some of the features in the Free Guest Area on Everton's Web site*

Databases

Like Ancestry, Everton accepts GEDCOM files from genealogists: unfortunately, the database is available for free search use only on a limited basis. Submitting your own GEDCOM files gets you one month free searching on their database. For $50 a year (which includes a subscription to *The Genealogical Helper*), you can have access to that database and many others as well. Everton also has a searchable database of the SSDI, included in the free guest databases. Other guest privileges include a searchable catalog of genealogical CDs, a photo database, and a relationship chart.

Some of the databases you can search in the free area are:

Vietnam Database   Searchable by surname, given name, military service number, rank, age, home record, home state, casualty date, and birth date, this database of 56,000 names has information regarding casualties of the Vietnam conflict.

CD-ROM Catalog   If you're wondering whether to buy a CD-ROM from Everton's Web site, check out this index. You can search over 200 of them by state, county, country, and in some cases, surname.

Surname Search   A listing of all the names Everton has on the site, including the paid member area. The results displayed are an index of surname, given name, and the database where the name can be found in the member area. See Figure 11-2.

Roots Cellar   One of the oldest and most popular features on the Everton site, this is a collaborative, volunteer collection of genealogical data. With about 1,000,000 names, this database contains information submitted by people who want to share information. You can search by surname, given name, event, year, place, location, and name and address of the submitter. Remember, as with many such sites, no one has checked the data for accuracy. However, you can still benefit from this database by finding genealogists who are searching for the same

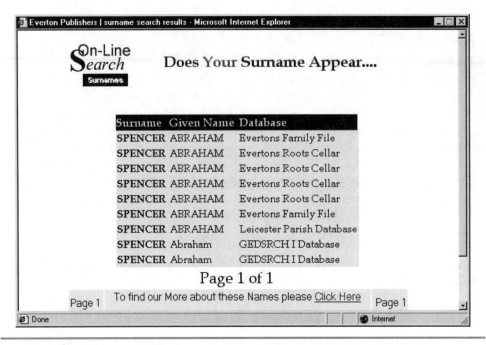

FIGURE 11-2. *In the free area, you can search the entire site for a name*

lines and people you are. To submit to the Roots Cellar costs $5 for three entries (persons). To do so, click the link from the Roots Cellar search page and fill out the form.

Internet Family File Like Roots Cellar, this has genealogical data, but in GEDCOM form. You can add your own GEDCOM for free. You can also search by surname and given name, and receive information on how to download matching GEDCOMs. Remember, no one has validated the data you find here; you have to contact the submitters to discover their sources.

Complete PhotoFind Database Tom Allison started compiling this index over 32 years ago, traveling to almost every state in the union (and several foreign countries) as he collected a wide assortment of photographs at yard sales, flea markets, estate sales, etc. Today the database houses over 11,000 records to help those searching for pictures of their ancestors. Should you find one in the collection, you can order a print of the photo.

Social Security Death Index   Commonly referred to as the SSDI, this database contains information on persons, now deceased, who once collected social security benefits.

Family History Centers   This search page helps you find Family History Center addresses and telephone numbers throughout the world.

Everton's Workshop Locations   A list of all the workshops sponsored by Everton Publishers, including location address, date, and time. Search it by state or by ZIP code.

Online Classes

Everton's online classes are a free collection of text files to help you get started in the world of genealogy, learn proper research techniques, and use various resources such as the Family History Centers. Since there is a lot of material here, you may want to download the files so you can read them later offline.

Reference Library

The Everton Reference Library page (http://www.everton.com/ resources/usa-resource.html) is worth a bookmark. See Figure 11-3. Here you'll find links to queries, the online classes, blank charts (which you can print out for your research), even links to RV-n-Genealogists, folks who camp and trace!

In the Download Area, you'll find Everton's Ancestor Research Tool program, a very simple shareware program (price tag: $15) designed to help you sort and store your information.

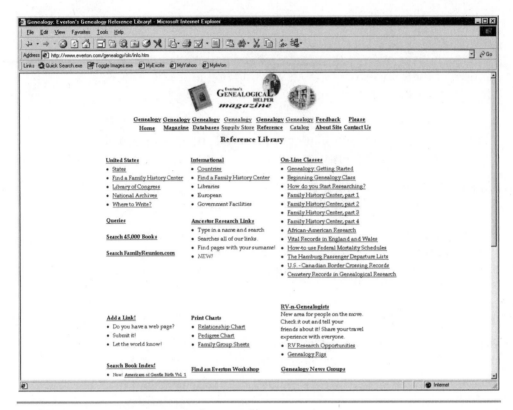

FIGURE 11-3. *The Everton Reference Library*

Subscribing

By subscribing to Everton's Web site, you gain access to more databases, magazine articles, and features.

Rates are:

- One Week Subscription: US $9.95

- One Month Subscription: US $15.00

- Six Month Subscription: US $29.50

- One Year Subscription: US $49.50

A Valuable Resource

The resources and how-to articles in the site's free area are excellent for the beginner and intermediate genealogist. Similarly, *The Genealogical Helper* is one of the most respected journals in genealogy, and worth subscribing to with or without the online access. Whatever you do, I recommend you try the site at least once; you may find many treasures to take away with you.

Chapter 12

Online Library
Card Catalogs

Despite all the wonderful things appearing online, many of your genealogical expeditions will still be in libraries. The online world can help you here, too.

One of the wonderful things about the online world is the plethora of libraries now using electronic card catalogs. This greatly speeds up your search at the library. Not only can you perform an instant search of all their holdings (even place a hold on the material), but with many terminals scattered throughout the building, you don't have to look up your subject, author, or title on one floor then repeatedly run to another to actually find the referenced material. If your local library hasn't computerized its card catalog yet, it probably will soon.

But oh, the joys of looking in the card catalog before you actually visit the library. You know immediately whether that library owns the title. With a few more keystrokes, you can find out whether the title is on the shelf, on reserve, on loan to someone, or lost without a trace. If the title in question isn't at that library or branch, you can find out whether the book is available by interlibrary loan. Some libraries are part of an online system, like the Greater Manchester Integrated Library Cooperative System at http://www.gmilcs.org/ (Figure 12-1). Such systems link groups of libraries, allowing you to search for titles across most or all of the libraries in the area. Some more advanced systems will even let you enter your library card number, in effect checking the book out to yourself, before leaving home.

There are two main ways to connect to online card catalogs. The newest and easiest way is through the World Wide Web. Here, the card catalog appears to be like any of the Web-based databases you've encountered in this book.

However, with older online library card catalogs, the connection could be by telnet. Should this be the case, you use a separate program to send commands to, and receive information from, the database. I will explain more on this later in the chapter.

A third way to connect to an online card catalog is with a hybrid Web-telnet connection. In this case, the library (or libraries) maintains a Web site with all the relevant information on how to use the card catalog. Then, when it is time to look at the card catalog database, your browser starts a telnet program to actually work with the database.

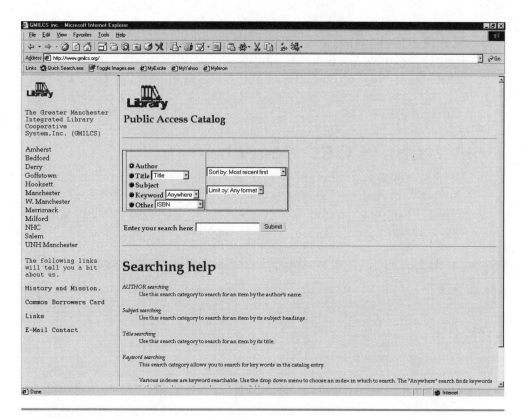

FIGURE 12-1. *Sometimes a group of libraries shares a Web site, making it easy to search all of them at once*

Connecting to Card Catalogs by Web Browser

The easiest and most visually appealing way to connect to online card catalogs is via the World Wide Web. The mechanics of how this works are irrelevant. What's important is that a Web-based interface lets you use the card catalog without having to install and load a telnet program.

A wonderful example is the University of Texas at Austin's UTNetCAT (http://dpweb1.dp.utexas.edu/lib/utnetcat/). You can use the forms that appear at this Web site to search by author, title, subject, or any combination thereof. The results of the search are links to the card catalog; click one and you get a full display of that item's record, as shown in Figure 12-2.

A Sample OCC Search

Another, slightly more complicated, example is the Web site at the University of Alabama in Huntsville. To log in, go directly to the card catalog's search page at http://library.uah.edu and click the "I'm a Guest" button.

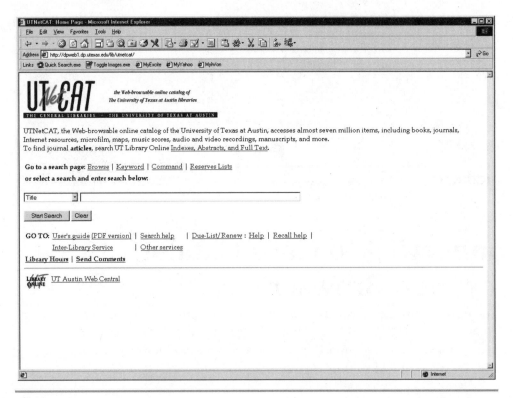

FIGURE 12-2. *The University of Texas provides a wonderful example of Web-based card catalogs*

The search screen is shown in Figure 12-3. Once in the system, you can look for items in any field that contain certain words or phrases. Even better, by using Boolean options (AND, OR), you can specify that words, author names, title words, or subject terms must have a particular relationship to each other. If you want something written by a specific person, searching by Author makes sense. If you know most of the words in the Title, a Title search can tell you if the library has the item and where it is located. If you don't know an author or title, you can search by Subject.

You'll have better luck with your searches if you narrow them as much as possible. You can choose to search on Author and Title, Subject,

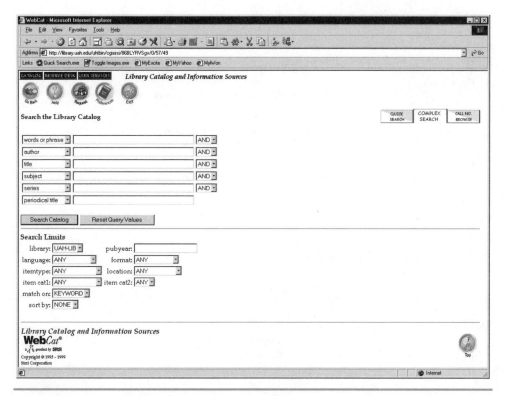

FIGURE 12-3. *The library card catalog at the University of Alabama in Huntsville lets you construct complicated queries if you select Complex Search*

and Word or Phrase, or any combination of these. Optionally, you can search recent issues of magazines using the Periodical Title option.

To show you how this works, I chose a search with *genealogy* in the general keyword field, and *Alabama* in the subject field. Figure 12-4 shows the results of that search which turned up seven cards matching the search criteria. Each card has a short synopsis that appears on the Results page. By clicking the View button next to a synopsis, you can

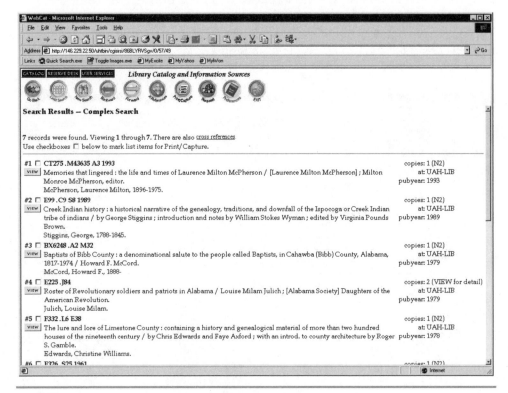

FIGURE 12-4.   *The results of a search at this site include a short synopsis*

get additional details about the book like the publication date, author, and cross-links to other relevant cards in the catalog. Then, if you like, you can print the results, or have a copy of them e-mailed to you.

The Library of Virginia is home to a similarly powerful online card catalog (located at http://eagle.vsla.edu/catalog/). Figure 12-5 shows a sample of the Bible records from their catalog.

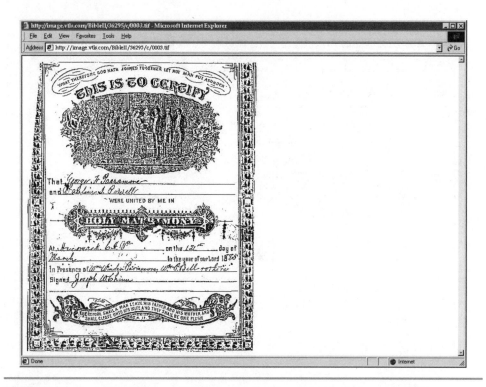

FIGURE 12-5.   *The Library of Virginia searchable catalog includes many Bible records, which you can view online*

I ran a test with *genealogy* as the general keyword, and *Powell* as the subject keyword. The results can be seen in Figure 12-6. Should I wish to refine my search further, I could also use Boolean terms such as AND, NOT, and so on.

Overall, the Library of Virginia's card catalog is very easy to understand and read, and, I might add, a real pleasure to work with.

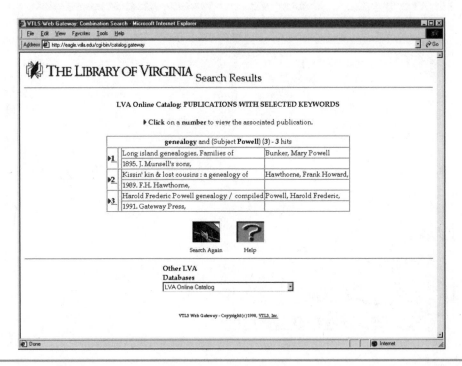

FIGURE 12-6. *Search results at the Library of Virginia often display links to the actual cards in the catalog*

Connecting to Card Catalogs by Telnet

Some card catalogs, while online, haven't been put in Web format just yet, which means you have to get at them another way. Enter telnet. Telnet is a system that lets you connect to another computer as if your PC were a terminal on that computer. Though telnet is an older Internet service, it's still widely used for online card catalogs.

Windows comes with a basic telnet program that's activated by Microsoft Internet Explorer and Netscape Navigator whenever you try to connect to a telnet address. Just enter the address on the browser's Address line and a telnet window will pop up, ready to go.

A typical card catalog you can reach using telnet and the Internet is the South Carolina State Library card catalog (telnet://leo.scsl.state.sc.us). By entering the previous address, the Web browser automatically starts the telnet program, establishing a connection to the library. Afterward, enter the password (LION) listed in the first window (just type it in where the cursor appears) and press ENTER. You'll see the library's Main Menu (Figure 12-7).

I started by typing an *1* to get into the LION card catalog, then searched by Subject using the term *genealogy*. As a result, the catalog returned a list of cards containing my search word. I also received several references to other sections of the card catalog (see Figure 12-8).

If you've ever used the electronic card catalog at your local library, this should all look pretty familiar to you. By following the onscreen instructions, you can find out what titles are available, where they are located, in short, get all the information you would get if you were physically in the library, looking at the card catalog.

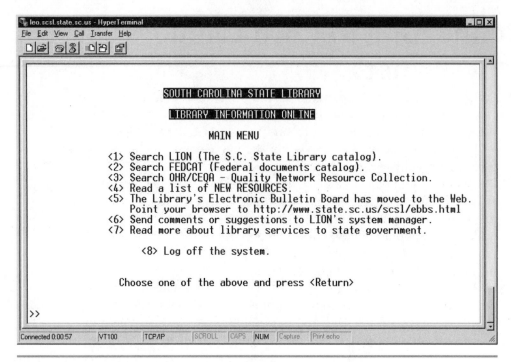

FIGURE 12-7. *The telnet LION system menu*

Where to Find More Online Card Catalogs

Once you've explored the online card catalogs shown in this chapter, it's likely you'll want to find some more. One place to look for both the Web and telnet kinds is the Genealogy Resources page at the University of Minnesota. Browse down to the Libraries and Archives

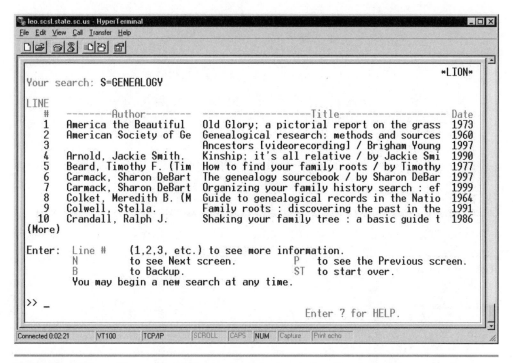

FIGURE 12-8. *The results of a search of the South Carolina State Library card catalog*

section (http://www.tc.umn.edu/~pmg/libraries.html). As Figure 12-9 shows, this section of the page includes links to both types of online card catalog.

Other places to look for online library card catalogs:

- ♦ *HYTELNET Library Catalog*   Located at http://www.lights.com/ hytelnet/, HYTELNET is a searchable catalog of telnet library sites. It has not been updated for a while, but when I tested several of them at random, I found they were still accurate.

♦ *National Union Catalog of Manuscript Collections (NUCMC)*
NUCMC can point you to not only library card catalogs, but
also archives and repositories with Web sites. You can find
it at http://lcweb.loc.gov/coll/nucmc/index.html.

♦ *USGenWeb*   When visiting this site, look under your state,
then county, to see if the library catalog is linked. You can
find it at www.usgenweb.com.

Learn to use these systems. Who knows what treasures you will find!

FIGURE 12-9.   *Here's a collection of online card catalogs you can browse via the Web or telnet*

Chapter 13

Library of Congress and NARA

Among the best of the online sites maintained by our federal government are the Library of Congress (LOC) and the National Archives and Records Administration (NARA). The LOC site is slightly more navigable than the NARA, and has more original source material available as well. Still, you'll find the NARA site useful in helping you decide what to ask for by mail or during a personal visit.

This chapter will give you a short overview of what each facility contains and how to access the resources of their two sites.

Library of Congress

The mission of the Library of Congress (http://www.loc.gov/) is to "make its resources available and useful to the Congress and the American people and to sustain and preserve a universal collection of knowledge and creativity for future generations." To that end, the Library of Congress, since its founding in 1800, has amassed more than 100 million items, and become one of the world's leading cultural institutions. The Library of Congress Web site (Figure 13-1) makes a small portion of the Library's contents available to the world through the Internet.

Three sections of the Web site are of particular use to genealogists. The American Memory section contains documents, photographs, movies, and sound recordings that tell some of America's story. The Research Tools section of the site offers many online databases, and connections to resources at other sites. The American Treasures section of the site is of interest more for the wonderful historical artifacts found there, than for any specific genealogical information.

American Memory

Click the American Memory link to begin your exploration of the Library of Congress site. The subtitle for this page is "Historical Collections for the National Digital Library." This project is a public-private partnership that is designed to create a digital library of reproductions of primary source material that supports research into the history and culture of the United States of America. Since this is an ongoing project, you can expect that the resources here will continue to grow for the foreseeable future.

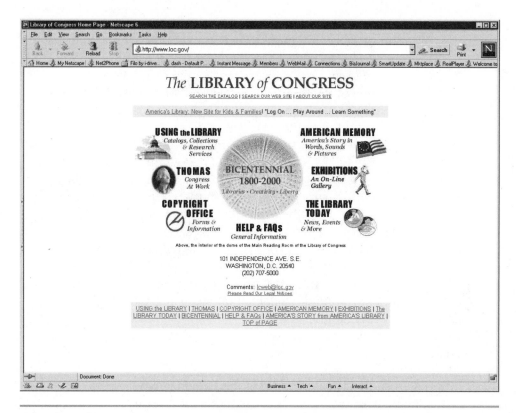

FIGURE 13-1.   *The Library of Congress Web site is a vast general information source, with some significant genealogical resources*

If you are researching African-American roots, you'll want to look at the African-American Odyssey page at http://memory.loc.gov/ammem/ aaohtml/aohome.html. This exhibition examines the African-American quest for full citizenship, and contains primary source material, as well as links to other African-American materials at the Library.

Going back to the American Memory home page, you can click Collection Finder to explore other primary source material. The best way to find specific things in American Memory will often be to first find collections that interest you the most. Each collection has its own distinct character and subject matter, as well as narrative information to describe the content of the collection. While searching all the collections at once will probably leave items of interest to you "buried" in a long list, visiting a collection's home page and reading the descriptive information about the collection can give you more direction in finding what you want.

The drawback to the Collection Finder is that it's a browseable catalog; it does not always list every single item in a collection, but gives an overview of the topic. For instance, if only a few items in a collection pertain to the Broad Topic of "Agriculture," the collection may not appear under that topic. Clicking a category is like saying "I would like to see a collection that is mainly about a certain subject." The list of subjects is at http://memory.loc.gov/ammem/collections/collsubjindex1.html. Let's say that you know of an ancestor who owned a hotel in the early 20th century. In that case, the collection "Hotels 1870-1930" might help you uncover him or her.

You can search for phrases or keywords across all collections, view essays, images, and primary source material, but keep in mind you'll likely get a *lot* of hits this way. Searching for "genealogy" across all collections gave me 52 hits that included the genealogy of Pocahontas, letters written to Abraham Lincoln about genealogy (see Figure 13-2), and Memoirs of a Southern Woman Within the Lines (Civil War). Some of the items you'll find in the American Memory collection include:

♦ Almost 200 books describing the personal experiences of individuals involved in the California Gold Rush

♦ Hundreds of objects associated with the Women's Suffrage movement

♦ Significant and interesting documents from Americans both famous and obscure, as collected in the first 100 years of the Library of Congress Manuscript Division

♦ American Life Histories: Manuscripts from the Federal Writer's Project, 1936-1940

A third area of the American Memory section worth exploring is the Maps section. On the Subject page mentioned above, click on "Geography." From here, you can search collections containing hundreds of digitized maps from 1639-1988. You'll find city maps, conservation maps, exploration maps, immigration and settlement

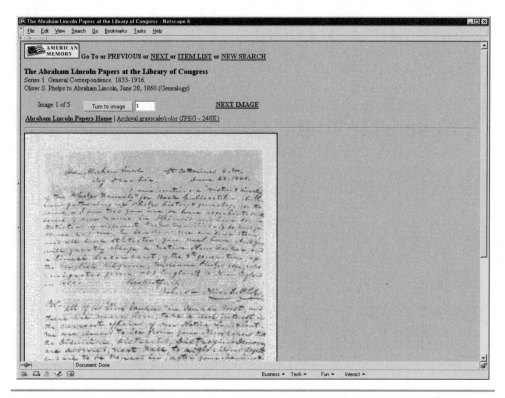

FIGURE 13-2. *Oliver Phelps wrote to Abraham Lincoln about a genealogy he was working on; the letter is in the American Memory collection "The Abraham Lincoln Papers"*

maps, military maps, and transportation maps to name a few. The amazing thing is that this wealth of maps is only a tiny part of the Library of Congress's full 4.5 million item Geography and Map Division holdings.

Using the Library of Congress

Click "Using the Library of Congress" from the home page, and you can click your way through an excellent tutorial on the ins and outs of researching the library in person. Specifically, pay attention to the Local History and Genealogy page in this section, http://lcweb.loc.gov/ rr/genealogy/. This will tell you about tours, how to prepare for a visit to the library, and links to other Internet genealogy resources.

The Library Today

This link from the home page will tell you about new exhibits, collections, and events at both the LOC and its Web site. Visit it at least once a week because anything new posted to the Web site will be announced here.

Research Tools

The Research Tools page at http://lcweb.loc.gov/rr/tools.html displays several links (on both the LOC site and elsewhere on the Web) of interest to researchers. These include online desk references, the LOC card catalog of all materials (including those not online), and special databases. One of these is the Vietnam Era Prisoner of War/Missing in Action and Task Force Russia databases (http://lcweb2.loc.gov /pow/powhome.html). This page (Figure 13-3) offers you access to a massive database of over 137,000 records pertaining to U.S. military personnel listed as unaccounted for as of December 1991. Yes, it's an ugly page, but the information there is great!

At the bottom of this page is a link to Task Force Russia (http://lcweb2.loc.gov/frd/tfrquery.html), a set of documents dealing with Americans believed to have been held in the former Soviet Union.

Exhibitions

Finally, under the Exhibitions heading on the Library of Congress home page, check out the Featured Attractions. You'll find reproductions of dozens of the most treasured objects in the Library's collection. Each featured item—from the *Whole Booke of Psalmes Faithfully Translated into English Metre, 1640* to an image of the New York Herald's story on the sinking of the Titanic to an official program from a baseball game between the Kansas City Monarchs vs. Indianapolis Clowns, 1954—has some special historical significance. You may not find any long-lost relatives when browsing this collection, but such artifacts help fill in details about the eras in which our ancestors lived.

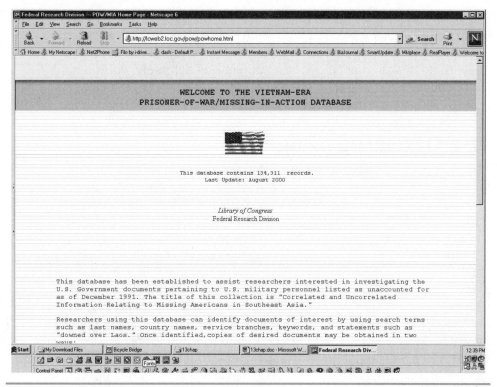

FIGURE 13-3. *POWs and MIAs from the Vietnam War era are recorded here*

NARA

While the Web site of the National Archives and Records Administration (http://www.nara.gov) is not nearly so user-friendly or professional-looking as the LOC site, it still has some useful features. Specifically, a genealogist would be interested in the NARA Web databases, such as the NAIL system to search the catalogs of NARA holdings; the genealogy column of the NARA quarterly, *Prologue*; and the Genealogy Page, which is an outline of how to research Genealogy with NARA resources.

The opening page of NARA is a bit of a mishmash, but the navigation bar at the top has a tab called "Research Room," which is an excellent place to start. Here, you'll find links to general information, such as "How to do Research at NARA," and others—all definitely worth a read. On the other hand, if you're a beginner, the quick link to "Genealogy & Family History" is an easy way to get your feet wet.

The Genealogy Page

This is a general outline of the finding aids, guides, and research tools to help you prepare before visiting one of NARA's facilities, requesting records from NARA, or using the Web to look up information. Divided into six parts, it links you to various documents and sites revolving about specific genealogical tasks.

Part 1 notes the different NARA facilities across the country and has links to pages listing hours, locations, and directions. Part 2 links you to essays and data on how to do genealogical and biographical research, with an emphasis on topics such as census records, women, and African-American research. Part 3 explains NARA's polices and plans as they affect genealogists. Part 4 directs you to free and for-fee publications of NARA that will help you with specific topics such as military service records and how to order them. Part 5 will link you to workshops and courses being offered by NARA in Washington, D.C. and around the country. Part 6 directs you to other genealogical resources on the World Wide Web, with links to the National Genealogical Society, the Association of Professional Genealogists, and Ancestry, to name just a few.

Though it hasn't been updated recently (as of this writing, the last update was July 1999) it still has a lot of useful information for both the beginning and experienced genealogist.

After touring this general help section, you are ready to tackle the specific resources on NARA.

NARA Web Databases

You can search various subsets of the NARA holdings from their Web databases (http://search.nara.gov/). Click Search in the navigation bar at the top of any page in the NARA site to get there.

On the Search page, you can input any term and search the NARA Web site (see Figure 13-4). You can also search individual databases, which may find items on other Web sites, on the NARA Web site, or at some regional NARA site.

To search the main site, simply insert a term or two in the box at the top. Typing in "Powell genealogy" got me over 900 hits. Obviously an embarrassment of riches! Note, however, that you can search the results to narrow them down, or you can exclude specific databases like the Presidential Libraries, and so on. To do this, choose Advanced Search.

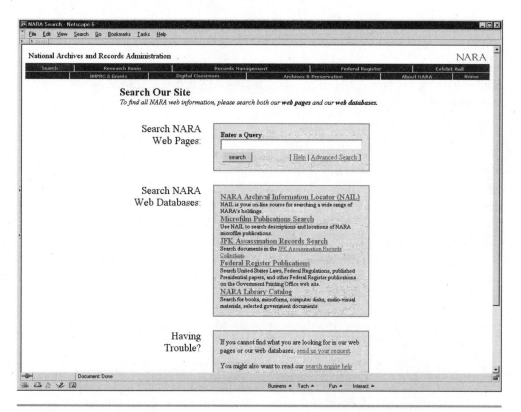

FIGURE 13-4. *The Search page is a good place to start when visiting the NARA Web site*

On the Advanced Search page, you can uncheck boxes next to the Sites you wish to omit from your search, such as Main: Full text of all Web pages; Presidential Libraries: Full text of all Web pages on Presidential Library Web sites; and a prototype collection of selected federal agency records, schedules, and manuals called ARDOR. You can also define search words in Boolean terms: must (AND), must not (NOT) and should (OR). In addition, you can limit the date of the results, as well as how many hits display on a page.

Using genealogy as a "should" term and Powell as a "must" term, I got 266 hits. When I unchecked the boxes on ARDOR and the Presidential Libraries, the result was reduced by nearly 35%, to 177 hits. Making both terms "must" cut it down to 5. You can see how the advanced search can be a powerful tool.

NAIL

NAIL is an experimental version of what is hoped to be the future online catalog for NARA. In final form, it should list the holdings in Washington, D.C., the regional records services facilities, and the Presidential libraries.

In its present form, NAIL contains more than 3,000 microfilm publications descriptions, 400,446 archival holdings descriptions, and 124,000 digital copies. However, it represents only a fraction of NARA's vast holdings. For example, not all images on the NARA Web site are described in NAIL. To find other images, you can go to the Digital Classroom, the Online Exhibit Hall, and the individual Presidential Libraries' Web sites, all linked from the NARA Research Room page.

From the NAIL main page (http://www.nara.gov/nara/nail.html), you can choose to search microfilms or archival holdings. If you choose the archival holdings, you can select from:

♦ NAIL Standard Search—this is a basic search by keyword, media type, and/or NARA unit.

♦ NAIL Expert Search—this advanced search allows you to limit your search to a specific keyword, title, media type, NARA unit, description level, control number, and/or specific description level identifier.

♦ NAIL Digital Copies Search—this page searches only for archival descriptions that link to digital copies. You can limit the searches by keyword, media type, and/or NARA unit.

♦ NAIL Physical Holdings Search—here, you search only the physical holdings information at NARA's Motion Picture, Sound, and Video Branch. Media types, specific titles or title keywords, control numbers, and/or specific description levels may be used to limit search results.

Choosing the NAIL Digital Copies Search, for example, turned up the record shown in Figure 13-5, a draft registration from World War II.

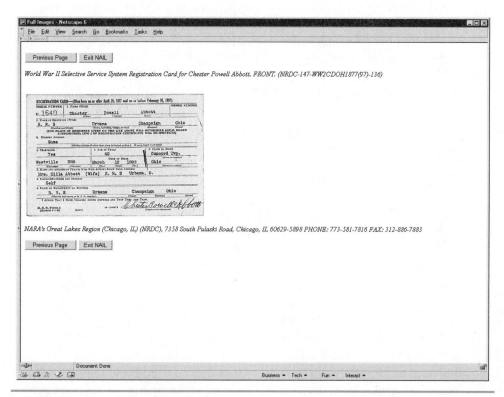

FIGURE 13-5.   *This draft registration is one of the images available from the NAIL search of NARA databases*

Microfilm Publications Search

The NAIL microfilm publications search is a basic search of up to two terms (using AND, OR, or NOT), or the Microfilm ID, or the Record Group Number. You can also choose all NARA units, or limit the search to one. The results for each individual hit will tell you which NARA locations have the microfilm for viewing, and how to order a copy from NARA.

JFK Assassination Records Collection

As the name states, this is every document the NARA has on the assassination of John F. Kennedy. A disclaimer on the site says, "**Users should be aware** this database is a compilation of entries input by the originating agencies. Although the National Archives and Records Administration provided guidelines for data entry, the master database is inconsistent in the terms used to describe records. Please keep this in mind when planning your database searches."

Federal Register Publications

The main attraction for family historians here would be the public papers of the U.S. presidents, and then only if you have a president in your genealogy.

NARA Library Catalog

If you click on the link for the NARA Library Catalog from the search page, you'll get another page that directs you to http://www.nara.gov/alic/. Some of this is available only to the archivists at NARA; you have to go to a NARA facility and ask the staff to do the search for you. Parts of it, however, are available from the Web. As I explained in Chapter 12, looking at a card catalog before you go can save you a lot of time and frustration during your visit. If what you need is available by loan or can be copied for a fee, it may save you a trip altogether.

You simply fill out the form shown in Figure 13-6 with the desired terms. The page comes back just the same as before, except the number of hits is shown in red at the top. You then have to click the button that says "Display Search Results." From that page, you can sort by Subject or Author, and see complete records for the items you select.

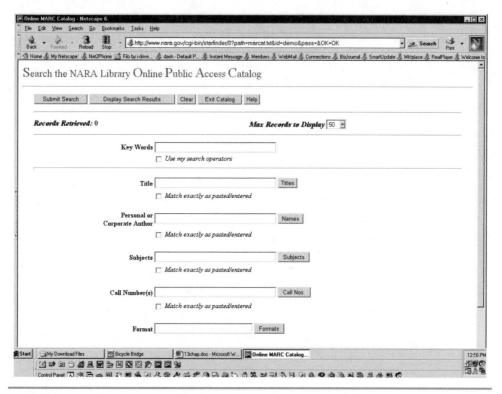

FIGURE 13-6.   *The NARA Library Online Public Access Catalog has a simple form to fill out*

As with any card catalog, you will get the call number, details on the size of the work, and links to related items on the same subject.

Prologue

On the NARA home page, there's a link to its quarterly magazine, *Prologue*. You can also reach it directly at http://www.nara.gov/ publications/prologue/prologue.html. Special issues, such as the recent *Federal Records in African-American Research* (see Figure 13-7), may be posted almost in their entirety, but usually a regular issue will have one or two features on the Web site, plus the regular column, Genealogy Notes. A list of previous columns is at http://www.nara.gov/publications/ prologue/artlist.html#genea. Definitely a site worth bookmarking.

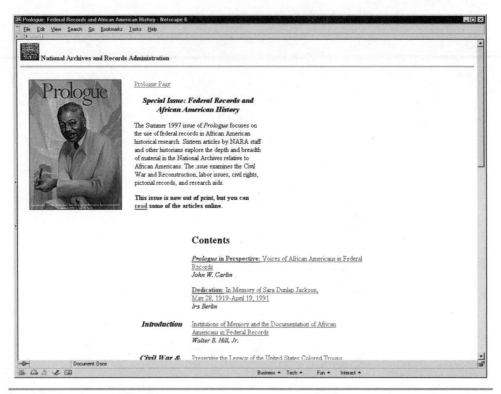

FIGURE 13-7. *Full text articles from Prologue can be found on the NARA site*

Some Experience Necessary

Much of what is available at the LOC and NARA sites is more helpful to intermediate and advanced genealogists, as they are already familiar with certain online research techniques, and often know precisely what media types they are searching for. Nevertheless, the beginner will find some elements at these sites obliging, such as the schedules of workshops on NARA and the how-to articles on the LOC.

Chapter 14

The Church of Jesus Christ of Latter-day Saints

I n May of 1999, what we've all been hoping and praying for finally came true. The Church of Jesus Christ of Latter-day Saints (often abbreviated as LDS) put up a searchable Web site of their millions of names. At this writing, access to the Web site is free, though some sort of fee in the future is possible.

> ✒ *Note* ─────────────────────────────
>
> *The information in this chapter is accurate as of this writing. Refinements, additions, and deletions are sure to be introduced as users give the Web masters their feedback. For the time being, though, consider this a general guide to the site.*

FamilySearch Internet

FamilySearch Internet (www.FamilySearch.org) has access to these databases and Web sites:

♦ Ancestral File™

♦ International Genealogical Index®

♦ FamilySearch Internet Pedigree Resource File

♦ Family History Library Catalog™

♦ Family History SourceGuide™

♦ Non-LDS genealogical Web sites from a list compiled by LDS editors, some of which have original source records

All except the last are from LDS records. FamilySearch Internet is designed to be a first step in searching for family history information. When you are searching LDS proprietary sources, the first screen doesn't give you the information itself. The search results simply tell you if the information you need is available, with links to the Web site, Family History Library Catalog citation, International Genealogical Index or Ancestral File reference, or citation in one of the CD-ROMS the LDS has for sale.

This is more helpful than it sounds, actually. Just finding a match in the Family History Library Catalog can save you hours of research.

Some FHCs are so busy that patrons are only allowed one hour per week at the computer! Searching the catalog before you go can make your trip much more productive. Finding a reference in the CD-ROMS might tell you whether it's worth the price of ordering it. Finding a reference in the IGI or AF will tell you if someone else has already found the primary record or source you're looking for, and, sometimes, how to contact the person that found it. In short, this can save you a lot of time and travel. Unfortunately, only rarely will you be able to use this resource to access primary (original record) sources.

Most of the records in FamilySearch Internet are abstracts of original records. If you find a reference to a record you want in the LDS sources, you usually can get a complete copy of it from a Family History Center (FHC). Family History Centers are located throughout the world and have many of the records found in FamilySearch Internet. You'll learn more about FHCs later in the chapter.

Another big advantage to this site is that it has more international data than most online sources. While the greatest part of the data is from English-speaking countries, you'll find something from every continent. Asian sources are the scarcest; North American and European the most abundant.

A Run-through

For many days, the site was so popular I found it hard to get through to the server. The record so far is 11 million hits in one day, according to some newspaper reports. Even after I got on, I found it difficult to maintain contact with the server. But don't give up, just keep pressing ENTER once you have www.familysearch.org entered in the address box.

The opening page of Family Search, which was redesigned in late 2000, is shown in Figure 14-1. To the left is a navigation bar with links to information on the Mormon church and genealogy in general. On the top is a navigation bar to the most-often used features of the site. It's worth your while to click on "Why Family History?" and "Where Do I Begin" on this page. These will take you to basic how-to files.

In "Search for Ancestors" (the tab "Search" in the navigation bar takes you to the same page), you can search the Ancestral File, International Genealogical Index, the Pedigree Resource File, and Web Sites. The Web Sites are from a catalog gathered by Family Search editors and submitted by Family Search users. You can click on any one of these on the left to limit your search to just one; the default is all four. The link

FIGURE 14-1. *FamilySearch's opening page gives you several choices*

above the input form, "Tips on How to Search for Your Ancestors," is worth reading. It will tell you in plain language what will work and what will not on the search page (you can't search for just a given name, for example), and how to narrow your search.

Using a pedigree chart form on this screen, you can input just a last name, or a first and last name, even the names of the person's spouse and parents if you know them. Of course, the more information you put in, the fewer matches you will get, and the easier your search will be.

I ran a search on our family's most elusive ancestor, Abraham Spencer. After 20 years of searching, Mother and I still cannot find his parents. Just about all we know was that he was born in 1792. Our results are shown in Figure 14-2.

Selecting the one that seemed the closest match, I can see no one has yet recorded parents for Abraham. Still, if I needed what information is there, I could click on "Prepare records for download" at the bottom of the page, and save it to my disk.

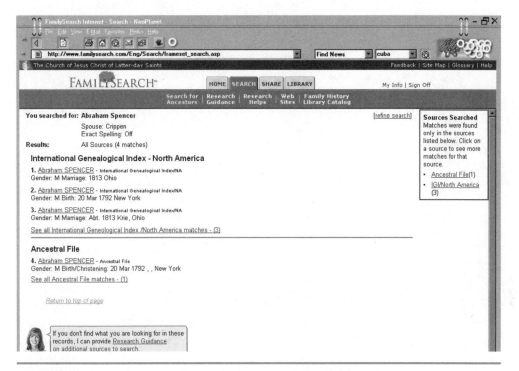

FIGURE 14-2. *Three records matched my search for Abraham Spencer*

By choosing the Ancestral File citation, I can look at pedigrees and GEDCOMS. Figure 14-3 shows the results of a search on my grandparents.

Research Guidance

Research Guidance is a tool to help you decide what records are most likely to have information about your ancestor. It lists the best records to use, recommends the order in which to search them, provides step-by-step instructions for finding information in the records, and tells you where the copies of the records may be located. Select a place where your ancestor was born, christened, married, or died. If you are not sure of the country, click on "Determining the Country Where Your Ancestor Lived" for some suggestions regarding how to figure it out. Only places that research guides have been created for are listed on the page; as more are added, they will appear. So, for example, you can find guidance for Baden, Germany, but not for Zaire.

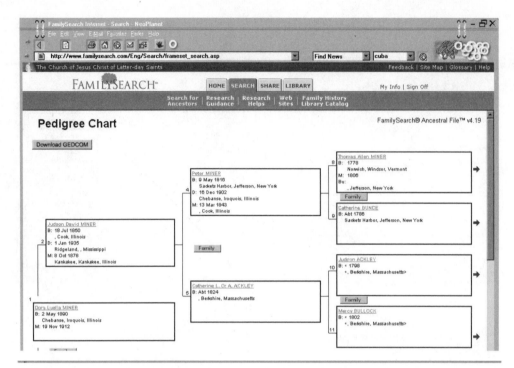

FIGURE 14-3. *The FamilySearch Ancestral File can display a pedigree submitted on a certain name*

Research Helps

This will help you find research outlines, forms, maps, historical backgrounds and information on how to find a map, name variations, and so forth. You can sort the list of links by place, title, subject or document type. As in Figure 14-4, you can sort by document type and choose helps that are forms, government publications, LDS research guides (excellent resources and they are all available online!), maps, and word lists.

Other Cool Stuff

Just as with any Web site worth its salt, FamilySearch Internet has interactive elements. You can find these under "Share" on the navigation bar tabs. Before you can enter this area, however, you need to register

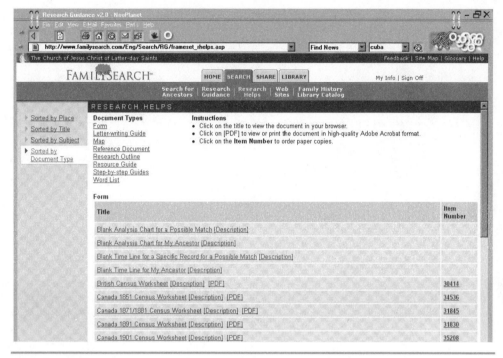

FIGURE 14-4.   *You can find Research Helps by document type*

as a user. Enter your name, address, and e-mail address, then choose
a username and password. (Keep in mind that Microsoft Internet
Explorer 5.0 will store and remember passwords for you.) When I
registered as a user, and accepted the terms of service, I searched the
mail lists, as in Figure 14-5.

In my search, I came across one e-mail list for Spencer and one for
Powell. One click on "join," and I was a member. When I clicked on the
link for the Powell list, my mail program opened up: the link is a mailto:
link. So, I sent in a query to the list. Within a day, I started receiving
messages from both lists.

Another interactive area allows you to share your research with
others on FamilySearch Internet. By clicking on Share Your Genealogy,
you get instructions on how to upload a GEDCOM for the LDS church
which it will store in its granite vaults in Utah.

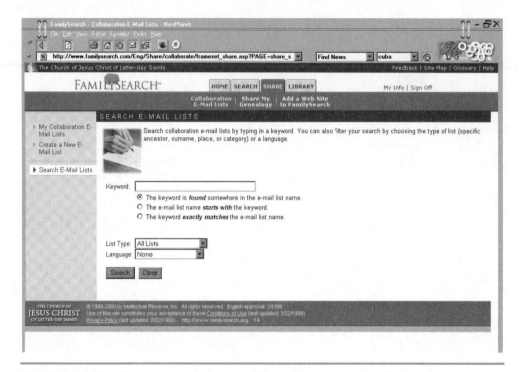

FIGURE 14-5. *You can search for e-mail lists of interest on FamilySearch*

> ## Note
>
> *Be sure of the accuracy of your data before submitting. It would be a shame to preserve for all time some mistakes and miscalculations! Also, be aware that when you submit, you must verify that you have the right to submit the information, and that you accept legal responsibility for any permitted use made of the information, by LDS or anyone using the site.*

GEDCOMS submitted to FamilySearch Internet will be preserved at the Granite Mountain Records Vault, near Salt Lake City, Utah. They also will become part of the FamilySearch Internet databases. The information will become publicly available on compact disc or at the FamilySearch Internet site. Although your genealogy may later be added to Ancestral File, if you want to be sure it is, you should follow the normal process for contributing information to it.

> ## Note
>
> *Carefully read the conditions before you upload! For example, you must get permission from all living persons named in your GEDCOM to send their information to FamilySearch Internet. By uploading, you give the LDS permission to publish your name and address as the contributor of the information you submitted. Uploading your GEDCOM gives the LDS permission to use, copy, modify, and distribute any of the information included in your submission without compensation. It also gives them permission to use information from your submission to create new databases.*

Even though you give LDS certain rights to your information, uploading it to FamilySearch Internet does not limit your right to publish, sell, or give the information you submit to others.

To upload your GEDCOM, have your genealogy program create the file. Click on the Share tab and then on Share My Genealogy. Read the information at the links "How do I submit my genealogy?" and "What will be done with my genealogy?" When you are ready, click "I am ready to submit," read the rules, and click "I agree." Fill out the form (shown in Figure 14-6) and click "Submit."

Under the listing Add A Site, you can register your genealogy site with FamilySearch Internet. The editors of the site will review it and decide whether to include it in the database of Web pages to be searched from the opening page of the site.

Library

The Library tab of the navigation bar leads to information on the Family History Library in Salt Lake City, including a search form to find a Family History Center near you, an online version of the card catalog to the Family History Library, and a list of courses and classes on the library and genealogy.

Other Resources

From the Family Search home page, the link "Order/Download Products" leads to a page that lists books, forms, CD-ROMs, and other items that you can buy from the LDS store.

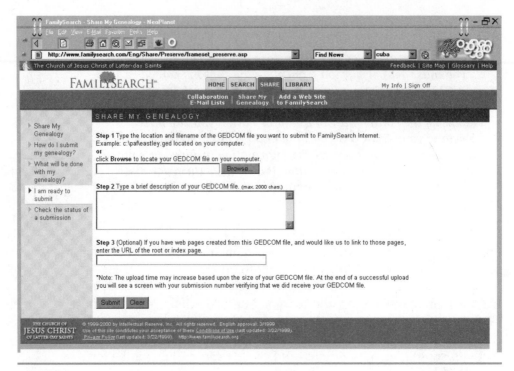

FIGURE 14-6. *Fill out this form to upload your GEDCOM to FamilySearch Internet*

How to Use Information from LDS

The LDS has scores of computerized resources. They willingly share much of the data as a public service through their Family History Centers. Their microfilms, computer programs and other sources are slowly becoming available to libraries, archives, societies, and the general public. Modern genealogical research owes a great deal to the Mormons, and it seems natural to include their publicly available resources, whether available online or not.

Information is collected from Temple work that goes into the IGI from both submissions and extractions. Other submissions, that may or may not have Temple work, go to the Ancestral File. If you have not submitted your ancestors to one of these files, and they have not been extracted as part of some other activity, they will not be included. Also, remember if they do happen to turn up in the file, you should check out the original documents to make certain they *are* your ancestors and that the submissions are correct. Keep in mind that these files, like any of the books and CDs you can purchase, are only as good as the work of the submitter or author.

Some Background

Without trying to explain the theology involved, I'll simply say that Mormons consider it a religious duty to research their family history. A detailed explanation can be found at the LDS home site, http://www.lds.org/.

The results are archived at the church's headquarters in Salt Lake City and are distributed in microfilm, microfiche, and CD-ROM to their many Family History Centers throughout the world. The data is in several forms, but the most important ones to the online genealogist are the Ancestral File and the International Genealogical Index. Both of these are updated regularly; new data are inserted in the databases, and you can search them at local Family History Centers on CD-ROM.

One of the LDS church's objectives is to build their copyrighted databases, known as the Ancestral File and the International Genealogical Index, and continually improve both the accuracy of their databases and the software used to search them. The IGI is a record of the temple work; the AF, meanwhile, offers pedigrees that the IGI doesn't.

Note

According to LDS, the IGI contains "several million names of deceased persons from throughout the world." However, that is "entries," not distinct individuals. Different people descended from the same family duplicate many entries. Furthermore, many individuals are listed with both a birth and a marriage entry.

The IGI contains two basic kinds of entries: (1) submissions by individual LDS members of data on their ancestors (which may or may not be accurate), and (2) submissions from the extraction program. This is a systematic and well-controlled volunteer program of the church. Members all over the world extract birth or Christening dates, as well as marriage dates and locations, from microfilms of original parish and civil records.

The source of the data from information provided for each entry is on the CD-ROM version of the IGI. But always remember, the IGI is only an index. You should go to the source document to verify the information.

The IGI and the AF are really unrelated, as evidenced by the fact that data entered in one file doesn't necessarily show up in the other. Each has a value of its own and both files are worth searching. The advantage of the AF is that you can get pedigrees from it; the advantage of the IGI is that there's more detailed information.

Most non-LDS genealogists see the IGI as the more valuable of the two. While errors turn up in both, the IGI is closer to the original records (data is normally entered into the IGI first) and it has excellent bits and pieces of information, especially its references as to where the information came from. Many non-LDS genealogists will always go to the IGI first, but the Ancestral File with the new 5.5 GEDCOM format allows you to find out what documentation supports the entry. Considering you can get the submitter's name and address, as well as pedigree or descendancy charts, Ancestral File is a very valuable resource, too.

The LDS apparently wants to make the AF and IGI available to more people, too. Originally, you had to visit the Family History Library in Salt Lake City, Utah to use these databases. Today, that library has their CD-ROMs on a LAN that's connected to the Joseph Smith Memorial Building next door, as well as about 200 access terminals scattered about the buildings. But there's still no remote access.

About 15 years ago, the church set up local Family History Centers around the world. In 1988, they started selling the databases on microfiche. In 1991, the church released them on CD-ROM to their local centers, then later to societies and libraries. The New England Historic Genealogical Society has a copy at their library in Boston, as does the California State Sutro Library in San Francisco. More organizations are certain to follow suit. In 1994, the LDS began testing in-home use of the CD-ROMs, but as of yet they are still not available to individuals. Discussion continues about future online access.

The pattern here is more and more access via more and more means. However, the Mormons are very cautious and they take very small steps, one at a time. The church has not worked out all the legalities of online access, and are very concerned about presenting a useful, viable program and database for its members and the rest of the world. In other words, their main concern is turning out a good product.

A Visit to an FHC

Terry Morgan, Genealogy Forum Staff Member on America Online (terryann2@aol.com), is also a volunteer at the two Family History Centers in Huntsville, Alabama. The setups there are very typical, she says, and she gave me a personal tour of the one closest to our homes.

"The best way to find one near you is to look in the white pages of the phone book for the nearest LDS church," Morgan says. "Call them and find out where the nearest FHC is, and the hours. Honestly, since the hours vary so much from place to place, the best time to call is Sunday morning around 10; everyone's at church then!" If you call any other time, she says, give the staffers lots of rings to answer the phones, which might be on the other side of the church from the FHC. Or, she says, you could write to the LDS main library at the address listed in the last section, and ask for the latest list of FHCs. There's also an excellent list of FHCs maintained by Cyndi Howells at http://www.oz.net/~cyndihow/lds.htm, and a list of the larger FHCs at the LDS home site at http://www.lds.org/Family_History/Where_is.html.

All Family History Centers are branches of the main LDS Family History Library in Salt Lake City. The typical FHC is a couple of rooms at the local Mormon church, with anywhere from one to ten computers, a similar number of microfilm and microfiche readers, and a collection of books (usually atlases), manuals, and how-to genealogy books.

The FHC I was visiting had two IBM-compatibles that shared a printer in a room with a small library of about 25 reference books. A room away, there were two film readers and two fiche readers. Users are asked to sign in and out, and a cork bulletin board holds the latest genealogical technique brochures from the Salt Lake City Family History Library.

In some FHCs, Terry told me, the computers are networked so that patrons can use the CD-ROMs in a shared environment. In the future, FHC might have a direct satellite hookup to the main FHL and the latest version of the CD-ROMs there, cutting distribution time of the member data. However, this is still in the development stage. Meanwhile, FamilySearch Internet and IGI are available at most FHCs, and usually only one person at a time can use them.

"Some centers offer training on the programs, some insist they train you before you start using the computers, and some just help if you ask," Terry says. "We offer help if you ask. We've not had much trouble installing ours here. The only tricks were it has to have expanded memory, and you can have some TSRs [terminate-and-stay-resident programs, which sometimes cause conflicts] running, but few enough to have low memory and expanded memory as well." The programs, as of this writing, won't run under Windows, but Morgan said that may change in the near future.

In the typical FHC setup, you must reserve a computer and get a certain block of time to use it. Printouts of what you find are usually a nickel a page. Some centers allow you to bring your own disk to record the information, but others insist you buy certified virus-free disks from the FHC at a nominal fee.

Before you make a trip to the FHC near you, check out FamilySearch and determine which resources you'll need. You'll save lots of time!

Chapter 15

America Online's Golden Gate Genealogy Forum

Long before general public access to the Internet, most of us got our online jollies from the major commercial online services: America Online, CompuServe and Prodigy among them.

While each online service has something that distinguishes it from the others, they have several things in common:

Proprietary Content

The commercial online services offer you content you can't get on the Internet, such as special connections to news and research services. For example, on CompuServe and AOL, you can search databases of magazine articles as well as databases of genealogy records submitted by members.

Because access to the commercial online services comes at a premium, you get a smaller group sometimes than you get on an Internet site (which can be a good thing, if it's a group of knowledgeable people), and you have somebody to enforce the rules should anyone get out of line. Should you wish, you can even search online services for other members who share the same interests you do, a useful option when it comes to chat, e-mail, and forum messages (which is often a hit and miss proposition on the Internet).

In today's Internet world, sites called "portals" are trying to compete with the commercial online services via news, Usenet searches, chat rooms, and message boards. Time will tell whether they make it.

Front End Software

Commercial online services offer you a graphical interface, complete with a Web browser, to help you connect to the service and use it. Often, after you get used to online life, you find the front end more trouble than it's worth. In all the major online services right now, that means some form of Microsoft Internet Explorer wrapped in a specialized front end that has other functions besides just browsing. The deal between AOL and Netscape may change that in the near future.

Quick Jumps

All the commercial online services have their proprietary content divided into "channels" or sections. You can browse through them, clicking perhaps "Lifestyles," then "Hobbies," then "Genealogy." However, after you get used to where the genealogy is, you'll want a short cut. On AOL, these are called "keywords," on CompuServe, "GO words." It means you can type in a single word, "Roots" and skip the three or four clicks it would take to get you there normally.

Forums

Forums are message exchanges. You leave a message, as if tacking a 3×5 card to a bulletin board. On a later visit, you'll find others have replied to your message with comments and questions of their own. Like a mailing list, the conversation does not occur in real time. Like Usenet, you have to remember to go get the new messages at some point. Unlike both, you have to join a specific service in order to participate in forums.

Mail

All commercial online services provide you with e-mail. Sometimes they even offer you a way to download your mail, sign off the service, and then read and answer the messages while offline. Occasionally you have the option of doing this with Usenet and forums, as well.

Usenet

All the commercial online services have a Usenet newsreader as part of the front end software. AOL and CompuServe allow you to filter out the porn, unsolicited advertising, and get-rich-quick messages. Both also allow you to download Usenet messages to read offline.

Files

The claim to fame on commercial online has always been files, especially patches and fixes to commercial programs. All the major software vendors have a presence on the commercial online services, where you can post questions and problems and find the latest upgrades. Genealogy software companies are no exception.

In this section, we'll take a look at commercial online services with genealogy sections. Others, such as MSN and Mindspring, have small genealogy sections without much happening on them. However, should you decide to go with a service that is not profiled here and you think it's worthwhile, e-mail me at libbi_powell_crowe@bigfoot.com. I could include it in future editions of this book.

If you live in North America, you probably got a free trial membership from America Online in the mail or with your modem. The history of America Online is nothing short of amazing. Just eight years ago, AOL wanted to be as big as CompuServe and Prodigy. Now it's bigger than those two services combined; it owns CompuServe and Netscape, as well as other software companies such as ICQ. And the genealogy forum is one of the best offerings on all of AOL.

AOL is "open" 24 hours a day, seven days a week. Their basic rate gives you unlimited use for $29.95 a month, which includes AOL's own content as well as the ability to surf the Internet with their browser, Usenet reader, and FTP programs.

A warning though: AOL sends out software with a free month's membership about three times a year. Whenever they do, getting connected to AOL and staying connected are problematic, because AOL's hardware gets overloaded. Even if you get on and stay on, the response from the system can sometimes slow to a frustrating crawl. This has caused some people to deride the service as "Almost Online."

In such a case, your best bet is to sign off the system and log back on at a time when things are less busy. Mornings are usually good—the earlier the better—as well as late afternoons. And the offerings in the AOL genealogy forum are worth trying at those times of day.

Like most commercial online services, AOL is available only through their proprietary front-end software. AOL's network has local access numbers throughout the world, but not necessarily in rural areas. The software package will find the phone number closest to you during the setup procedure, but every now and then this list is expanded. It's a good idea to go to Keyword: access to see whether you are using the best and closest connection.

Note

Keywords are quick ways to jump to different areas on AOL. Type CONTROL + K *and enter the keyword and click GO; or simply type a keyword into the URL box in the AOL toolbar. For genealogy, the keyword to remember is ROOTS.*

During the sign-up process, you choose a main screen name for your account. Choose this carefully; you cannot change it without closing the old account and starting a new one. However, you may have up to seven screen names assigned to the main account, so each family member can have a mailbox, a set of favorites, and a place to file messages and downloads. To add and delete additional screen names, use the keyword Names.

The Genealogy Forum (Keyword: ROOTS or GENEALOGY) is the center of genealogical activity on America Online. From the Beginners' Center to the Genealogy Chat rooms and the Resource Center, this forum is an incredibly rich resource. The Forum's tens of thousands of members make it the largest genealogical society in the world, online or off. Figure 15-1 shows the Golden Gate Genealogy Forum main window.

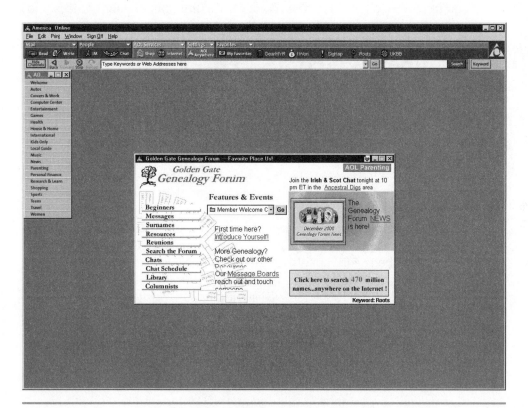

FIGURE 15-1. *The Golden Gate Genealogy Forum. Details will change from time to time, but the basic choices will remain the same*

> *Note*
>
> *In 1998, the AOL Genealogy Forum became the Golden Gate Genealogy Forum. The Golden Gate Genealogy Forum on America Online is a production of Golden Gate Services, Inc. of Franklin, MA, whose president, George Ferguson, has been the forum leader for years. (Screen name: GFL George.) Much of the AOL content, although not all, is reflected at the World Wide Web site, http://www.genealogyforum.com.*

Don't forget to add the Genealogy Forum to your list of Favorite Places. To do this, just click the heart on the top right side of the forum main window. You can also add it to the toolbar of AOL 5.0 or 6.0: click and drag the heart up to the toolbar area. A window will pop up asking you to choose a picture and a name for the link. Make your choices and there you are.

Member Welcome Center

On your first visit to the Genealogy Forum, plan to spend some time in the Member Welcome Center (Figure 15-2). You get there by double-clicking the folder labeled Member Welcome Center in the Genealogy Forum Main Menu.

In the Member Welcome Center, you'll be able to read about the people who keep the Genealogy Forum running, see how the forum is managed, and find out about upcoming genealogy conferences and events. Most important, you'll be able to read the Genealogy Forum Frequently Asked Question (FAQ) files.

As I've noted before, FAQ files are indispensable reading, not only in forums (which are similar to real-world communities in that they have their own rules of behavior), but also in electronic mailing lists, newsgroups, and at Web sites. The FAQ files are collections of the most commonly asked questions pertaining to the forum, list, newsgroup, or site. Read these files before you start asking questions or posting messages to gain a basic understanding of the forum.

Once you finish with the Member Welcome Center, you have two paths you can follow. One is to head to the Beginners' Center, which is designed for people who are new to genealogy. Or, if you are already a genealogist, you can skip the Beginners' Center, and begin with the Quick Start Guide, which tells you how to start researching your roots with the Genealogy Forum.

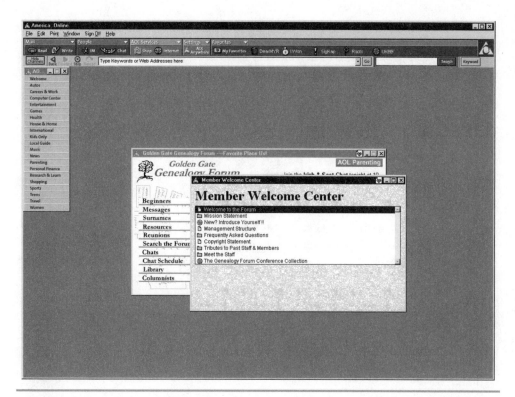

FIGURE 15-2.   *You'll be spending a lot of time in the Genealogy Forum, so visit the Member Welcome Center for background information on the Forum and its staff*

Beginners' Center

To reach the Beginners' Center you click the big Beginners button on the Genealogy Forum main window. This takes you to the Beginners' Center on the www.genealogyforum.com Web site. Click this button and you'll see a window similar to the one in Figure 15-3. Some of the highlights are described in the following.

Beginner's Tool Kit

This is a collection of links to answer the most basic questions about genealogy. They include Information on Getting Started, Making Sense of It All, Obtaining Information, Organizational Ideas, Organizing Information, Other Genealogy Forum Centers, and DearMYRTLE. After you have paged through all these, especially DearMYRTLE's Beginners' Lessons, you will be ready to begin your quest.

FIGURE 15-3. *The Beginners' Center gives you several links to how-to articles on genealogy*

There are all sorts of gems in the tool kit. Do you want to learn about colonial diseases and cures? Can't figure out a genealogical abbreviation? If so, this is the part of the Genealogy Forum for you. Here you'll find guides on getting started in genealogy, organizing your data as you get more experienced, tips on how to get information (who to write, how to ask), and links to related services on America Online.

FAQ/Ask the Staff

Click the FAQ/Ask the Staff link to see a list of Frequently Asked Questions (Figure 15-4). This list is identical to the one you'll find in the Member Welcome Center, except for the last item in the list: ASK THE STAFF. Click it and you'll get to send e-mail directly to one of the Genealogy Forum staff members.

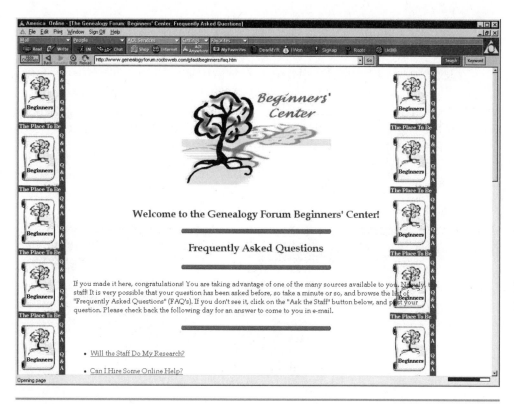

FIGURE 15-4. *Answers to the most common beginner questions are gathered in the FAQ/Ask the Staff area*

The 5-Step Research Process

The 5-step Research Process is a systematic approach to doing any genealogical research. This is an excellent tutorial on how to get started in genealogy. According to the process outline, Family History Research is asking yourself the same questions, in order, and in cycles:

1. What do I already know?

2. What specific question needs to be answered?

3. What records might answer my question?

4. What do the records actually tell me?

5. What conclusions can I reach now?

Click the 5-Step Research Process link to open the window (Figure 15-5) and start applying the process to your research today.

DearMYRTLE's Beginner Lessons

Begun in January 1997, DearMYRTLE's Beginning Genealogy Lessons (Figure 15-6) are weekly text files on aspects of genealogical research for the beginner. They are well worth saving for future reference. The internet center is a collection of links to other Internet sites with beginners' information.

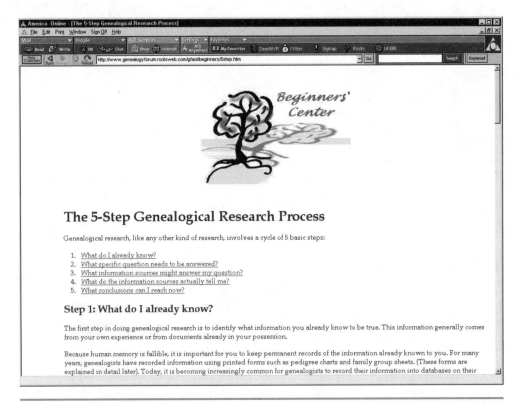

FIGURE 15-5. *The 5-Step Research Process is a system for making your genealogical research fast and efficient*

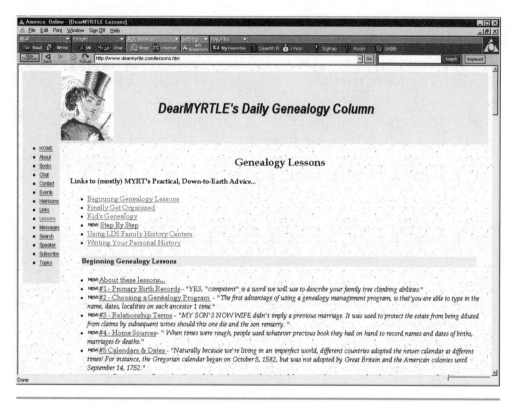

FIGURE 15-6.   *The Beginner's page links you to DearMYRTLE's lessons*

Quick Start

The guide tells you how to put the resources of the Genealogy Forum to work for you immediately. The quick start guide has four sections, each describing specific resources within the forum, and telling you how to use them. The four sections are:

1. SEARCH BY TOPIC—The fastest way to search in the Genealogy Forum. Most people begin by typing in a surname to see what pops up. You can also input a geographical term (Ohio, France) and see what files and articles are returned.

2. SURNAME MESSAGE BOARDS—Use these to look up a surname directly.

3. FILES LIBRARY CENTER—Look in this area to see if other forum members have already uploaded useful material like GEDCOM files that are helpful to your research.

4. SPECIAL CENTERS PROVIDE ADDITIONAL RESOURCES—This is a quick introduction to some of the other useful resources in the Genealogy Forum, some of which are described next, such as the genealogy column DearMYRTLE.

Introduce Yourself Message Board

This is a link to the message board where the topic is member introductions: Who you are, where and what you are searching.

Message Boards

The message boards in the Genealogy Forum are the place to post messages when you need information you can't find elsewhere in the forum. The boards operate on a volunteer basis; you're invited to post any questions you might have and are encouraged to post a reply to anybody else's question should you have information. Also, don't forget to post the family names you're looking for in the message board under the Surname category.

To reach the message boards, click the large Messages button in the Genealogy Forum main window. Using the Message Board Center (Figure 15-7), you can post messages in any of five major subject areas. These are:

♦ Surnames—Post messages asking about specific family names you are researching

♦ US & International—Post messages about research in the U.S., as well as countries other than the United States

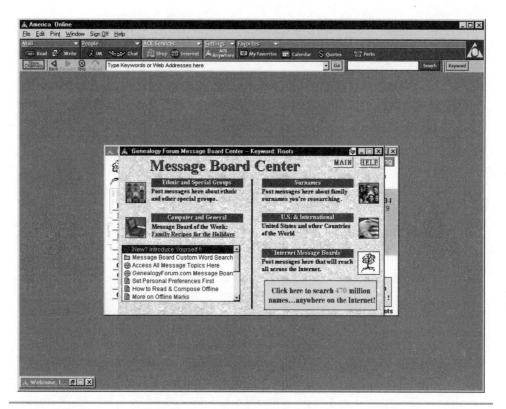

FIGURE 15-7. *The Message Board Center is the place to read and post messages about a wide range of genealogy topics*

♦ Ethnic and Special Groups—Post messages about your research into ethnic or other special groups

♦ Computer and General—Post messages about topics that don't fit into the other message boards

Note

The first four will reach AOL members ONLY.

♦ Internet Message Boards—These will be posted on the Genealogy Forum Web site, and therefore reach people who are non-members of AOL.

Before you start exploring the message boards, it's a good idea to read the messages that appear in the menu on the lower left side of the Message Board Center main window. They explain how the center and the message boards work. In particular, pay attention to the Set Personal Preferences First and How to Read & Compose Offline messages. They can make the Message Board Center much easier to use. Once you've read these messages, you should set your preferences, then start exploring the message boards.

Within each of these message board topic areas, you may find dozens of specific boards. For example, within Surnames there are areas for surnames that begin with each letter of the alphabet. Within those areas are boards for surnames that begin with specific combinations of letters. These finally lead to the actual message boards themselves.

Searching for the surname Mann, you begin with the Surnames topic. Under Surnames, select the M Surnames folder, then the MAN – MBZ Message Board. You'll know when you've reached an actual message board because the icon for it is a green piece of paper with a pushpin through it.

Continuing this example, the MAN – MBZ Message Board (Figure 15-8) is an example of a specific message board. The large directory in the window lists the Subject of each posted message, and the number of postings to each subject. When someone replies to a message that has been posted, it creates a message thread, sort of a conversation on that particular subject. The Postings column tells how many messages are in the thread.

Each board also has a set of controls that make it easy to use and customize. Here is a rundown of the controls and what they do:

♦ Read Post—Displays the contents of the message (or message thread) that is selected in the message list

♦ List Posts—Displays a list of relevant information about the message (or message thread) that is selected in the message list

♦ More—If you selected the More in your preferences, and more messages are available than the message list holds, you can click this button to load more messages into the message list

- Find Since—Click this if you want to do a search of the message list

- Create Subject—Click this to create a new subject in the message board

- Preferences—This button allows you to control how messages appear in the message list

- Mark Read—Click this to mark the selected messages and threads in this list as read. The list will then treat them according to your preferences, as if you actually read them

- Mark All Read—Click this to mark all the messages and threads in this list as read. The list will then treat them according to your preferences, as if you actually read all of them

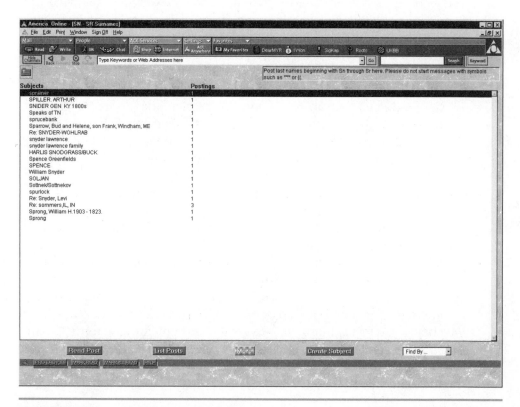

FIGURE 15-8. *Each message board has a set of controls that make it easy to use and customize*

Reading online isn't bad, but I find it much more efficient to read offline, using Automatic AOL and the File Cabinet's Search function. You can only do this with Message Boards that have been converted to Usenet format, and even at the rate of 4,000 boards a day, not all of them have been converted. For those that have, this can be a real time saver.

Here's how to go about it.

Let's say the topic of interest is messages about Powells. First, click "Messages" in the Roots Forum main window. There is a box of links on the left, including "Access all message topics here." Click that link, and you now have the window to search ALL the AOL genealogy message boards.

When the All Genealogy Forum Message Boards window appears (Tip: remember you can use that heart to put this window in your Favorites or on the toolbar!) click the Topic Genealogy Message Boards. For this example, you would click TOP SURNAMES IN THE U.S. When you have that window, keep clicking MORE until you get to the POWELL message board, highlight it and click the button Subscribe. You'll get a message that the board has been added, and to view your list, go to keyword My Boards. At the keyword My Boards (Tip: remember you can add Keyword My Boards to your shortcuts list!) you can click the button that says Read Offline.

Now, when you run an Automatic AOL session, the new messages are retrieved with your e-mail, and placed in the Personal Filing Cabinet. Once a session is done, click on My Files, and then Personal Filing Cabinet. Your message board will be a folder under Newsgroups. To read all the messages, just as you would e-mail or newsgroups, simply open the folder and click on each message (even though you don't really have to look at every one).

To save time, you can use the Find button in the Personal Filing Cabinet and look for messages that interest you. Say you want to learn about Powells in South Carolina. The Find button gives you a choice of searching all folders or only open folders, and either full text or only the subject lines. To make the search faster, open the Powell Folder, closing all others, and choose Open Folders. Then choose Full Text or Titles Only, whichever you feel is most likely to get a hit. Then enter the term "South Carolina" in the text box and click Find Next. If no messages match the search, you can delete all that day's messages, compress the Filing Cabinet, and try another day.

Genealogy Chat Center

The Chat Center (Figure 15-9) is where you go to hold online, real-time conversations with other genealogists. To get to the Chat Center, click the Chats button on the forum's main window. There are Chat rooms for many different topics: Beginning Genealogy Chat, Southern Chat, and War Between the States Chat being three examples. Some chats are continuous, some are active at specific times; schedules and lineups appear in the list on the left of the Chat Center main window.

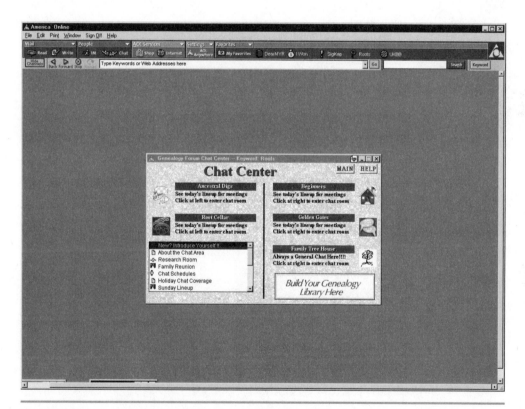

FIGURE 15-9.   *Go to the Chat Center for real-time, live chat sessions with other genealogists from around the world*

As with the Message Board Center, the first order of business is to read the messages in the menu on the lower left of the Chat Center window. Pay particular attention to the Lineup lists. Since chat is a real-time activity, many sessions are scheduled in advance. If you just want to drop in, one of the five main chat rooms usually has someone in it.

Figure 15-10 gives an example of a chat room, showing (at first) an empty room to avoid reproducing anyone's chat without their permission.

The large window on the left is where the chat messages appear. As new ones arrive, they all shift up the screen, so the newest messages are at the bottom.

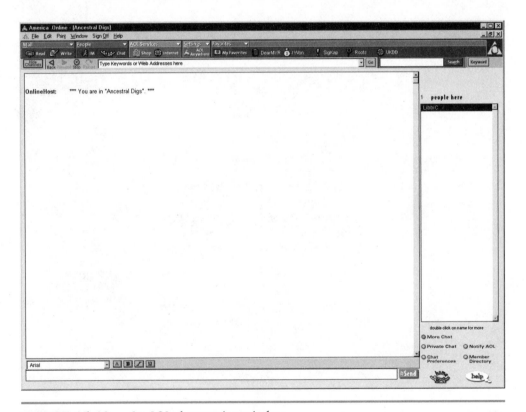

FIGURE 15-10. *An AOL chat session window*

Below the chat window is a box where you enter the text of your message. Click Send to transmit the message to the other participants in the chat.

To the right of the chat window is a list of the people present in the chat room. Right now Bill is the only one there, but the chat rooms can hold dozens of people. To find out more about someone in the chat room, double-click their screen name in this list.

Other controls in the chat window are:

♦ Private Chat—This allows you to invite someone in the chat room to chat with you privately

♦ Chat Preferences—Click this to set the five chat options available

♦ Notify AOL—If someone is misbehaving in the chat, you can click this to report the infraction to AOL

♦ Member Directory—This lets you request the profile of a person, whether they are present in the chat or not

File Libraries Center

The File Libraries Center (Figure 15-11) is a central location for all sorts of computer files of interest to genealogists. Divided into five sections, each containing multiple libraries, the center has thousands of files you can download.

You'll find files here ranging from trial versions of popular genealogy software to GEDCOMs and other genealogy information from members. You can use the new Library Sort feature to make it easier to find specific files in the libraries, or you can click Search the Forum on the main Genealogy Forum window to use the Search Genealogy Forum feature.

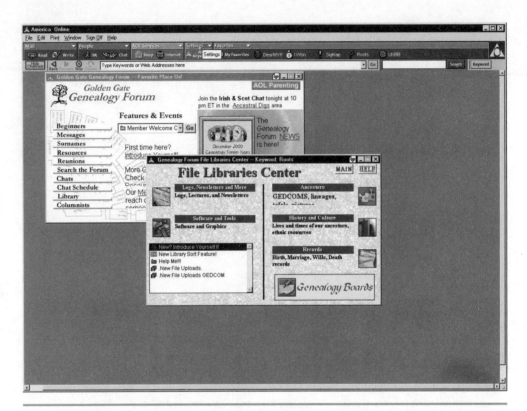

FIGURE 15-11. *Go to the File Libraries Center to find virtually any genealogy-related file you can think of*

Resource Center

Click the button marked "Resources" and you will find The Resource Center chock full of information meant to save you lots of trial and error. There are articles, help texts, and tips under subject headings like Regions of the World, Ethnic Resources, and Vital to make your research more productive.

Internet Center

The Internet Center in the Genealogy Forum is where you'll find Web sites, FTP and gopher sites, newsgroups, and mailing lists that relate specifically to genealogy. This can save you a lot of time, as compared to randomly searching the Internet for the same. However, if you want to go farther afield, be sure to check out Net Help—the Answer Man, where tips, tricks and FAQ's about the Internet in general and AOL's connection in particular are stored. You can subscribe to newsgroups here, or at the keyword: Usenet. Click on Expert Add and type in the soc.genealogy newsgroups you want.

Here's a newsgroup tip. In your FlashSession Settings window, check the box "Retrieve unread NewsGroup messages" and the box "Send outgoing NewsGroup messages." Then, when online, go to keyword: USENET. Click on the "Read offline" button. Your subscribed newsgroups will be listed on the left. Any you add to the box on the right will be put in your filing cabinet during Automatic AOL. This will increase the time of your Automatic AOL with very busy newsgroups, but your online time will still be greatly reduced. You'll just have to remember to erase the old messages regularly to save disk space.

To visit the Internet Center you click Internet on the main Genealogy Forum window.

Note ————————————————————————————

See Chapter 4 for an in-depth discussion of Usenet.

Surnames Center

The Surnames Center (Figure 15-12) is another collection of message boards that's organized by surname. Here, however, individual surnames have their own boards, as opposed to the surname boards you can reach from the Quick Start Guide, which group surnames alphabetically.

The same rules and suggestions discussed earlier apply to these message boards. The only difference is that these message boards are each focused on a single surname, so you will likely find the messages to be more useful than on another board, even though there will be fewer of them.

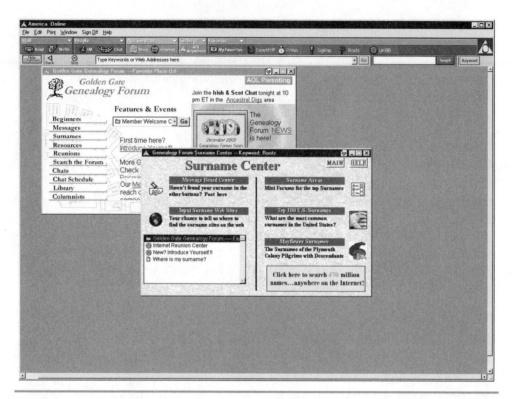

FIGURE 15-12. *The Surnames Center has hundreds of message boards, organized by surname*

Reunions

The Reunions button on the AOL Genealogy Forum main window will take you to http://www.genealogyforum.rootsweb.com/gfaol/reunion/. Here you will find archives of discussions, tips, and articles to help you plan and execute a successful family reunion, either online or in the real world.

Search the Forum

Clicking Search the Forum on the Genealogy Forum main window opens the Genealogy Search window. When you enter a search term in this window, the program will search the file libraries in the forum (the program does not search the messages). The result is a list of files that contain the search term.

GenealogyForum.com

This links you to the Web site of the Golden Gate Genealogy Forum.

So far, you've learned about the main areas of the Genealogy Forum. Beyond those, however, are all sorts of other useful resources. The following sections are short descriptions of some of these resources.

Genealogy Forum News

In the Genealogy Forum News window, you'll find various announcements, the monthly forum newsletter, schedules for chats and classes, and all the other fast changing information in the forum. Several genealogy special interest groups (SIG's) like the U.S. Civil War SIG also post monthly newsletters here.

DearMYRTLE Daily Column

A daily column on genealogy topics, DearMYRTLE Daily, is always helpful and informative. Use the Keyword DearMYRTLE to come here directly. The DearMYRTLE Daily Column area contains Myrtle's columns, as well as a message board, a collection of how-to guides, and much more.

Telephone Search Facilities

The Telephone Search Facilities window gives you access to nine World Wide Web sites that you can use to track down the phone numbers and addresses of people (say, like your long lost cousin).

The best place to start your search is with AOL's own Switchboard (http://www.switchboard.com/), which helps you find people, businesses, Web sites, and e-mail addresses.

Software Search

Start with AOL's Software Center (Keyword: FIND SOFTWARE). Here you have four choices: search for shareware (try-before-you-buy programs such as Brother's Keeper); search for commercial software (such as Family Tree Maker), check out the recommended Daily Download (usually a general purpose program) or the Computing Superstore.

To search for shareware, click the link. You'll get the Software Search window (Keyword: FILESEARCH). You can limit your search according to the time (All dates, Past month, Past week) the file was uploaded, and by categories: applications, operating system and so on. Then type your keywords (genealogy programs, for example). In a few seconds you have a list of matches. You can select one, read its description and decide whether to add it to your Download Manager (the list of files to be downloaded). When you have your list complete, you can just choose Download Manager from the window that pops up when you choose Download Later, and tell it to start.

Golden Gate Store

The Golden Gate store offers books and CD-ROMs on genealogy at good prices. Different delivery and payment options are offered, and they guarantee prompt service.

The Staff of the Genealogy Forum

While the Genealogy Forum is full of interesting and useful treasures, by far the prize jewel of the forum is the people who staff it.

One of the sysops, GFS Judy, said: "The Genealogy Forum provides a sense of family. Not only the 'real' relatives you are searching for, but the sense of family you get entering a chat room and being recognized; the information that total strangers go out of their way to type up and e-mail you, the forwarding of problems to others so that everyone can offer a suggestion or just encouragement to keep on going. I am constantly amazed that people who have spent 20 years of their lives, and countless dollars researching their family lines, will freely give out information just to help another researcher and perhaps get a tidbit in return. The materials people upload into the genealogy libraries save me hours of time traveling around the country, as does the Internet access. Computers truly make genealogy a realistic, global project that anyone can join in on regardless of age or income."

The Genealogy Forum is full of wonderful resources for the beginner, intermediate, and advanced genealogist. One of the best features is the excellent staff of experienced genealogists available to help you.

GFL George is the forum leader. GFA Robin, GFA Terry, GFA Beth, and GFA Drew are some of the sysops. There are over 100 staff members in the forum (anyone with GFS at the beginning of their screen name is a Genealogy Forum staff member), and a list of them, with short bios, can be found in the Welcome Center folder named Volunteers.

GFA Terry is one example. Director of a Mormon Family History center (FHC), she's the Genealogy Forum expert on FHCs and the Family History Library in Salt Lake City.

"I have been working in the Genealogy Club for years," GFA Terry says. "It started in about 1986 when I joined Q-Link (the first network from the owners of AOL—it was designed for Commodore computers). I worked in the genealogy area of Q-Link as a staff member. When AOL came about and when my husband and I upgraded to an IBM, we joined this network. I was already a staff member on Q-Link (owned by the same company), so it was possible to become one here, too.

"My duties cover many things—I greet the new members, answer some of the questions on the message boards, do some librarian duties as I help make files go live, archive message boards, host meetings, and well, there's a lot to do, but I enjoy it very much."

The network has helped her with her genealogy as well, and she says:

"I have made contact with several folks by posting the surnames I was looking for. I even found a distant cousin! This all works on a volunteer principal—folks helping other folks. One of them lived in Connecticut where I had ancestors and looked up some information for me. In turn, I looked up some information for her from Georgia. And the genealogy libraries have helpful text files, too."

Another person you should introduce yourself to is GFL George, the forum leader. A professional genealogist, George Ferguson has over a decade's experience with online genealogy, and is willing to share, help, and inform.

"The Genealogy Forum on AOL has been my love and my passion since its inception in 1988," George said. "With the help of many wonderful and dedicated volunteers, we have guided it to the place it is today. My Great Aunt Gertrude Durham started me on my genealogy work when I was a boy by presenting me with a ten-generation pedigree chart that was partially filled. I knew right then my life's work was to fill in the spaces." George started doing online genealogy research the day after he got his first modem.

George told me, "The best feature of the America Online Genealogy Forum would have to be the ability to get 48 people from all over the country together in one online room and talk about genealogy. It's great because you don't have to leave the comfort of your own home but you can get all kinds of questions answered. We also have an outstanding collection of downloadable files. We have programs and utilities for IBM-compatible systems, Macintosh systems, as well as Apple II systems. We have hundreds of lineage files, GEDCOM database files, genealogical records files, tiny tafel files, alphabetic surname files, as well as logs of past meetings. We have a surnames area where anyone can post a message about someone they are looking for. We also have message boards that are designed to exchange information about computer- and non-computer genealogical subjects.

"We have started several special-interest groups (SIGs), which are becoming quite popular. On different nights we have beginners' classes, an African-American genealogy SIG, a Southern SIG, and a Scot-Irish SIG. In the near future we hope to expand these offerings with expanded beginner services, a New England research SIG, and a reunion software users group."

He points out that the online real-time conversations are a valuable resource. There have been many meetings where somebody finds a cousin or a possible link. It is also an opportunity to chat with people who have similar interests to you. And you don't have to go out at night or drive into a big city to do it. Also, unlike the big genealogy groups that get together only once every month or so, AOL members can get out and talk almost any night of the week.

"We expect people to come and share the passion for genealogy," George said. "We expect nothing, but hope that everyone will share what they have with the rest of us and have fun doing it. What we find is that people freely give of themselves and that we can have a good time while learning different ways of investigating the past."

Another Forum host, GFH Ranch, said, "Long before I assisted with a chat or had any formal involvement with AOL, I was a regular. For me, personally, the chats & message boards have been very instrumental in meeting cousins, which in turn leads to more sources, more information, and more options for research.

"I had used the genealogy newsgroups but prefer working the breakdown of topics that AOL offers. Message boards are broken into portions of the alphabet & geographic locations which dramatically reduces the amount you have to look through to find a possible connection," she added. "Chat sessions are narrowed to geographic areas (as well as general and beginner chats) and historical time periods."

Like many others on AOL, she has had good luck finding real information there. "It is especially fun the first time you find a cousin. One time I helped a lady find a missing link because I had an editor's note in a book. And another contact sent me an ancestor's photograph giving me a rare opportunity to share it with my family. I now have trouble remembering all the cousins I've met. Chats focus on families and heritage with a strong sense of 'helping our brother out.' We have folks in Tennessee offering to assist someone in Texas by calling the court house or photographing a tombstone."

For a beginning genealogist, AOL's Genealogy Forum is a wonderful tool.

Chapter 16

CompuServe's Genealogy Forums

CompuServe is one of the oldest, and best, online services. For years it was based on a text interface: you typed in a command such as GO ROOTS and a text menu would appear containing messages, files, and announcements from its genealogy forum. A graphics interface was introduced in the early 90s, and has continued to evolve. After CompuServe was bought by America Online in 1998, the service's software got a major overhaul. CompuServe still uses GO words to navigate the system's features, but other than that, little remains of the CompuServe interface of 20 years ago.

Despite this, the spirit of CompuServe remains. Although it sports numerous AOL-like features in the new interface, it's still the premier service for serious working professionals who want to do their work (and their hobbies) faster, better, and more cheaply. In other words, there's little nonsense and lots of common sense on CompuServe. CompuServe's online genealogy resources have much to offer:

♦ Social Security Death Records online (link to Ancestry.com)

♦ nearly 2,000 genealogy book reviews available online in the Roots forum

♦ more than 8,000 genealogy-related files available online, including shareware and free genealogy programs for Windows, MS-DOS, Macintosh, Amiga, UNIX, and even older computers

On CompuServe, the part of the service where message boards, files, and chats on a topic are grouped together is called a forum. Each forum, meanwhile, has its own system that sets it apart from its brothers. For instance, each has its own GO word, each has its own chat schedule, and the messages and files of each can be searched for keywords. To join a forum, simply click "Join," then type in your name for that forum along with your preferences as to how you want the files and messages to display.

On all the CompuServe genealogy forums, a "handle" (false name) is strongly discouraged; you are urged instead to use your real first and last name which can be recognized by the forum managers (called "sysops" for "system operators"), who keep things running smoothly.

Note

To get a complete list of the GO words on CompuServe, type in GO SITEMAP.

A Quick Overview

The newest CompuServe software is based on the Microsoft Internet Explorer browser. Getting to the Internet via their latest software is wonderfully easy, and the software's interface hardly changes a whit when you do. You can either establish a local ISP account and use that TCP/IP connection to get to CompuServe, or you can use the dial-up network connection, and surf from CompuServe. Microsoft Internet Explorer is so masterfully integrated into the software that you don't realize you're using it every time you jump from, say, the Genealogy Techniques forum to the Library of Congress site. The only way you can tell if you're still on the service is to look at the page box at the top of the screen to see if CompuServe appears somewhere in the URL name. On installation, the software does a good job of installing the proper dial-up connection, complete with logon script. It worked the very first time I used it.

Note

The CompuServe software will be very familiar if you've ever used AOL. For example, a check mark (instead of a heart) is how a forum or other service is added to your list of "favorites." Otherwise, the process is the same. Click the check mark, and choose from Add to Favorites, Add to an Instant Message, or Add to an E-mail Message (the latter two as links).

Something that's missing from the CompuServe 2000 software as of this writing is the ability to download forum messages so you can read and answer them offline. This has been available on CompuServe since the beginning of the service, right up to the 1999 version (and is even available with AOL's software), but the new CompuServe 2000 requires you to be online to read and answer messages. This is a grave error, in my estimation, and makes the software much less useable. For this reason, many people are choosing to stay with the CompuServe Classic software which allows you to download forum messages and stow them in your filing cabinet. Let's hope future versions put this feature back. Despite this drawback, many useful features have been added in CompuServe 2000:

♦ Instant Messaging, with buddy lists—This works only with other CompuServe members logged on at the same time you are, and is integrated into the Contact List, where you keep e-mail addresses of people you write to often.

♦ Spell Check, special fonts, pictures, and attachments in e-mail— In short, fully multimedia-capable e-mail. It's also POP3-compliant, so you can use Eudora, Outlook, or any other POP3 e-mail reader.

♦ 56K/V.90 access with many admission points in the US and around the world, making it easy to use CompuServe when you travel.

♦ The ability to have several member names listed under your main account.

♦ Ability to download Usenet and e-mail messages, and upload them at specified times. Unfortunately, this does not include messages in forums as of this writing; for this you have to stick with CompuServe Classic.

Go Genealogy

The GO word to get you started is GENEALOGY. Simply type that in the white box at the top of the CompuServe screen and click the green GO button. You'll get the screen in Figure 16-1.

 Note ────────────────────────────────

Capitalization doesn't matter with GO words. GENEALOGY will work as well as genealogy.

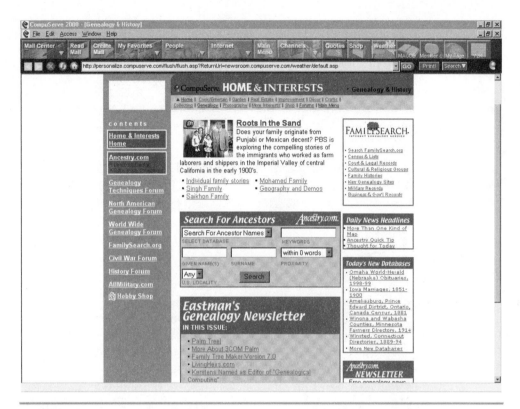

FIGURE 16-1. *The genealogy forums are part of the Hobbies channel on CompuServe*

What used to be one genealogy forum (ROOTS) evolved into several different forums:

- Genealogy Techniques Forum—the place for beginners to share successes or to find out how to get beyond those brick walls when researching. Here you can learn: how to use your computer for genealogy, how to use the World Wide Web, where to find professional genealogists, as well as find out about coats of arms, Adoption Searches, and more. This is the one you get when you use the GO word: ROOTS.

- North American Genealogy Forum—for queries about ancestors in Canada, the U.S., and Mexico. GO word: NAROOTS.

- Genealogy Support Forum—Major genealogy societies and software vendors supply staff at this forum to answer questions, resolve problems, and make announcements about new events, software, patches, and updates. Go word: GENSUP.

- World Wide Genealogy Forum—for queries about ancestors anywhere in the world except North America. GO word: WWROOTS.

- In addition to these, genealogy is often discussed in the Civil War and History forums. The GO words are CIVILWAR and HISTORY (or use the GO word: GENEALOGY, and then look at the links to the left).

Forum Decorum

Regardless of what version of CompuServe you use, with all the Genealogy Forums available to you there, you can exchange information with thousands of other members around the world, from experts and professionals to beginners. Everyone has something to contribute.

The goal of the forums is to create an atmosphere that encourages intelligent interaction and lively debate. The sysops are very insistent on members using common sense and courtesy. If you have questions about how to proceed, you can contact the Forum Managers by posting a message addressed "To: SYSOP" on the message board of any forum.

This is a place that values free expression (you'll often find lively discussions and spirited debates underway). Members hail from all over the world, have diverse ethnic backgrounds, and are widely varied in education—something to keep in mind when reading and answering messages. The give and take can get energetic!

Dick Eastman, the systems operator of the genealogy forums, encourages people of all backgrounds to participate. He is especially eager for members of ethnic minorities to become active in genealogy in order to ensure preservation of both their heritage and those records important to their genealogy.

There are a few rules:

- Keep it clean. No obscenities, slurs, or dirty jokes.

- No flames.

◆ Use smileys if your words could be taken the wrong way. Regardless, choose your words carefully.

◆ Use the spell checker. Also, avoid jargon, because the newbies need to understand your messages, too.

◆ There are specific sections of the forum for posting on different subjects; post yours to the right one. If you simply place all your messages in the "New to Genealogy..." section, the people who can help you might miss it.

◆ Advertising is allowed under specific restrictions, as discussed in the next section.

Advertising on the Forums

Online advertising is a touchy subject. On the one hand, new products and services are a legitimate discussion topic among genealogists. On the other hand, some people feel they are already paying for CompuServe and to have to endure advertisements on top of that is insupportable.

In an attempt at compromise, the Genealogy Techniques Forum (GO ROOTS) has specific sections dedicated to announcements and discussions of commercial genealogy services and products. That way, if you want to see such information, you can find these messages and files quickly and easily. If you don't, you can just ignore those sections.

In the File Libraries, you can look at (and post to) Products/Services for advertising and announcements. The message board has two sections: Professional Genealogists, and Services and Products.

"Professional Genealogists" is a place for professional genealogists to gather and ask questions or discuss the latest issues in their business, so, as you can imagine, it's not strictly an advertising section. Still, you will find a fair number of ads there.

The catch to this permissible advertising: You are allowed to post only one message and only one text file per product. The file stays there until you ask a sysop to delete it; the message may scroll off as all messages eventually do. (You may answer any questions posted by others about your services or products at any time.) The text file should be in a "press release" format, ending with "For further information, contact..." or something similar. You can encourage the reader to contact you online or by conventional means, as appropriate.

On any Genealogy Forum's message board, do not post messages about goods or services you produce or sell without clearly stating your connection. Avoid jumping into threads to recommend products you create or sell. So-called "bombing runs" (posting many messages in different forum sections or by CompuServe Mail to promote your products or services) are rude, as is responding to forum messages by sending private e-mail "advertisements."

In general, don't clutter the genealogy forums with non-genealogy, non-history, or non-adoption traffic without permission of the managers (sysops). An exception is the sale of personal items, which is allowed; even then it should be genealogy-related.

All that said, you are nevertheless encouraged to provide technical support of your customers on the Genealogy Techniques Forum. There is a major difference between providing support and "advertising, soliciting or promoting the purchase of goods or services."

If you see anyone breaking these general rules, you should contact the Genealogy Techniques Forum managers. Just post a message addressed "To: SYSOP" and it will be read by the next manager who enters the forum.

Sysops: The Forum Managers

Forum Managers (also called "sysops" for "system operators") manage the activities of the forums. This involves duties such as checking files and messages for appropriateness, chastising those who break the rules, and sometimes kicking off habitual offenders. The sysops will answer questions about how to use the forum, as well as general questions regarding genealogy—just address your message "To: SYSOP."

Sysops are not employees of the service—they are CompuServe users just like you. They simply have more familiarity with genealogy, as well as greater experience in the use of home computers for genealogy purposes.

A Tour

CompuServe has over two million subscribers, and of those, over 10,000 a week visit the ROOTS Forum, according to Sysop Dick Eastman. True to form for most CompuServe forums, however, only about five percent of those who visit actually leave messages. That's a lot of lurkers!

Nevertheless, the forum sees plenty of action, and the files and messages are valuable and worthwhile.

The members of the forum are varied. There are online assistant sysops and some recognized professional genealogists who drop in, while other members are rank beginners. Many lie in-between. Whatever their experience, members here are just as cooperative, outgoing, and friendly as anywhere online. In fact, in my opinion, this is one of the best online hangouts for genealogists.

Now I'm going to take you on a tour of the Genealogy Techniques Forum (GO ROOTS). You'll find that the North American Genealogy Forum (GO NAROOTS) and the World Wide Genealogy Forum (GO WWROOTS) work in much the same way. Sign onto CompuServe, and use the Go word: ROOTS. That is, type ROOTS in the white box at the top of the screen and click GO or press ENTER. As you can see in Figure 16-2, the opening screen has a lot on it. Let's take it bit by bit.

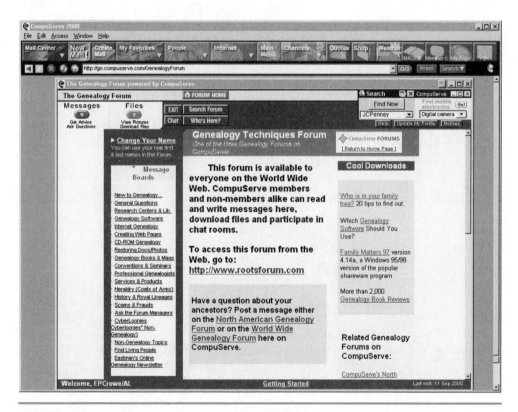

FIGURE 16-2. *The opening screen of the Genealogy Techniques forum has links to everything you can do on the forum*

My username is at the bottom: "Welcome, EPCrowe/AL." The first time you sign on, you are asked to choose a name to use in the forum; often, people put the state they live in as part of their forum name. All genealogy forums ask that you use your real name, not a handle or your CompuServe sign on ID. At the same time, I filled out a profile to tell other members about my interests. The tradition in genealogy forums is to start with the surnames you are searching for, perhaps with geographical locations, along with any other items of interest. My particular profile is shown in Figure 16-3. You get to this screen by clicking "Update My Profile" in the upper right corner of the screen. From there, you can search the forum's member database for surnames.

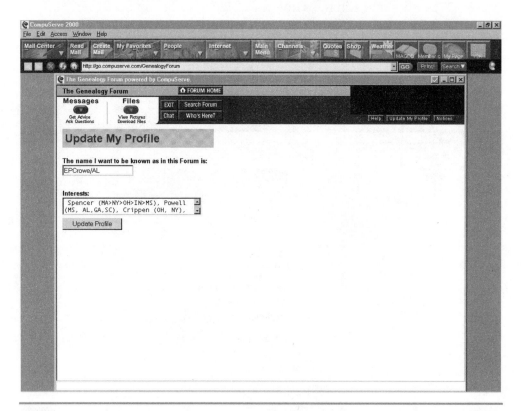

FIGURE 16-3. *List the surnames you are searching for in your profile; you can also search member profiles for the surnames you are interested in*

At the very top of the screen is the menu bar, where you find the usual commands. File, Edit, Window, and Help behave as you'd expect them to. Access allows you to change things like what number you dial to log on, passwords, parental controls, and to check how long you've been on.

Under the Menu bar is the CompuServe toolbar. You can customize it, choosing to have it large or compact, and you can drag the check mark of any window onto it to create a toolbar button.

Under the CompuServe toolbar is the standard Microsoft Internet Explorer toolbar: the round buttons are for forward and back, stop, reload, and home. The URL box is where you type in GO words or WWW URLs. Click the GO button to activate the GO word; Print and Search do what you'd expect.

Just below that you have a window within a window that contains the forum's opening page. The bar across the top (which remains constant, no matter what you're doing in the forum) displays the name of the forum, while the Forum Home button will return you to this page from any of the forum's other screens.

The Forum Home page has links, news, and announcements pertinent to the specific forum. The details on this page will change often.

The two buttons, Messages and Files, have similar functions. They will both change the window to show the various Sections of the forum, to allow you to search or browse their contents. When I searched for "online" in messages, I got several message threads with "online" in the subject. By clicking on "Census Images Online," I got the results in Figure 16-4.

In this view, you can see the topics that matched my search in the upper left; the names of those who posted messages on the selected topic in the lower left; and the text of the first message on the right. By clicking on any message, I can read it in the right pane. Searching Files looks much the same.

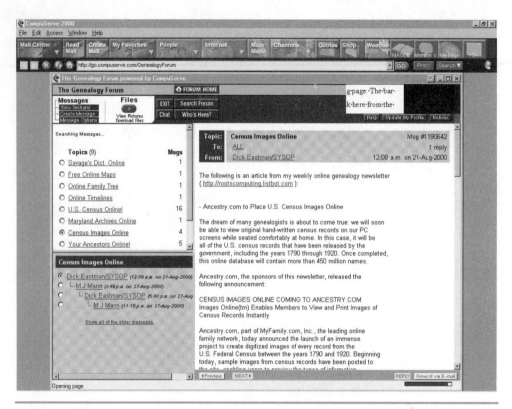

FIGURE 16-4.   *Topics, authors, and messages are read in this window*

So, now I'll click on the Files button and browse instead of search. Clicking on the topic "Internet Genealogy" in the Files section, I get the screen in Figure 16-5.

Browsing Messages looks much the same as browsing Files: click on the Section, look at the topics, read the specific items. You can also right-click and save messages to your file cabinet on disk for later reference. This is a good idea, as messages tend to "scroll off"—that is, the oldest get deleted to make room for the newest.

To contribute a file, click the Contribute button. Choose the appropriate File Section, and then click the Contribute File button. Do not upload anything unless you have the rights (under copyright law, for example) to the files you contribute.

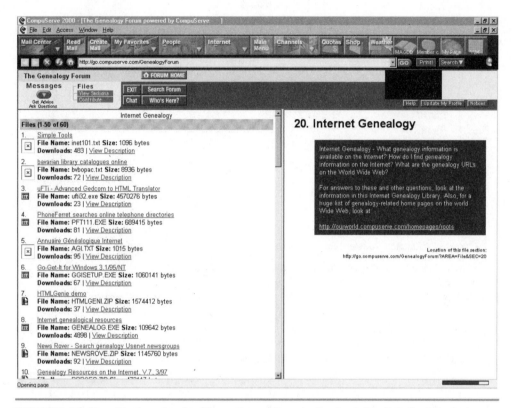

FIGURE 16-5. *To download a file on CompuServe, simply right-click the title and save it to your disk*

The first time you visit this page, CompuServe will attempt to automatically download and install software (an ActiveX control) on your computer. You may be asked for permission to download this control, depending on your security settings. Let it.

As mentioned in Chapter 7, CompuServe has regularly scheduled chats on genealogy in all the forums. Anytime you are on, you can click the Chat Button to see whether any chats are going on. Or you can click the Who's Here? Button and invite someone to an impromptu chat. Figure 16-6 shows you the windows that pop up when you click those buttons. They are separate from the main CompuServe window, so you can click on the main window and send them to the back, cascade the windows, or tile them all.

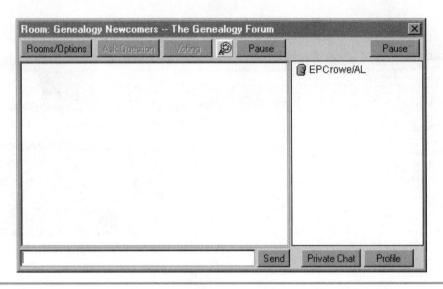

FIGURE 16-6.   *Click CHAT and choose a room for an impromptu chat*

The hosted conferences (chats) on CompuServe are excellent. In one famous case, Sysop Dick Eastman saved the life of a member who was having a stroke during a live chat by noticing that something was wrong and getting help to the member's home. Usually, however, chats are exciting only due to the fun and interesting people who participate! You are free to host one whenever you like—simply announce it in the messages.

The schedule as of this writing is:

♦ The traditional, weekly "free-for-all conference" is held every Tuesday evening at 10 PM Eastern time, 7 PM Pacific (2 AM Wednesday GMT). Join everyone in the Main Conference Room of this forum. (To do this: sign on, go to ROOTS at that time, click "CHAT," then click "Main Conference Room.") The subjects discussed in this chat are wide-open. Genealogy-related conversations and non-genealogy chats mingle together in the Tuesday evening online chats.

♦ A New England Conference is held on the first Thursday of each month at 9 PM Eastern time in the New England Conference Room of NAROOTS. Watch the message board for topics to be covered at each conference.

- Monthly online conferences discussing the excellent genealogy resources of the Daughters of the American Revolution are held on the fourth Sunday of the month at 7 PM Eastern Time.

- Online chats for birth mothers are held every Monday evening at 9 PM Eastern time, 6 PM Pacific in the North American Genealogy Forum at GO NAROOTS. These online conferences are held in the Adoption Searches Conference Room.

- Check out all the new conference rooms in the North American Genealogy Forum (GO NAROOTS) and the World Wide Genealogy Forum (GO WWROOTS). You're likely to find a conference room devoted to one of your favorite topics.

Another important feature is the Notices button (just beyond the Help button). Here is where you'll find text files with the latest information about the workings of the forum. News Flash, Messages, General, and so forth—all have information the sysops want you to know. See Figure 16-7.

Profile: Dick Eastman, Genealogy Sysop

"It's lots of fun, but no money," Dick Eastman says of being a sysop. Along with several other Roots Forum members, he attends all GENTECH conferences to help promote the forum. That's just one of his many functions as sysop. He also manages the files, checks for viruses, keeps the messages where they should be, and offers advice to new genealogists. Eastman recruits assistant sysops as well. He's the buffer between the technical people at CompuServe Headquarters and the CIS user. The goal is to keep problems to a minimum, both in using the service and in doing genealogy.

"We're very much a referral service," Eastman says. "Like a football coach, we won't play the game for you, but we'll help you learn the best game plans." He likes to do that on the forums, but, amazing as it is to him, he says that many people are too shy to post a public message; they send him private e-mail with their questions instead. He'd prefer to answer questions where all can benefit from the answers, though.

"We're a social group," he says, "and we have a lot of fun. We get together at conferences like this [GENTECH] and meet face to face

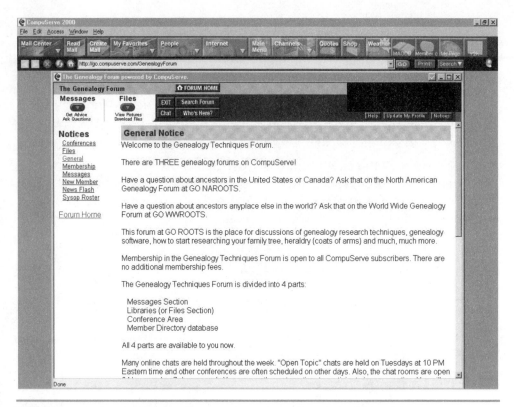

FIGURE 16-7. *The Notices change from time to time. Check them out*

when we can. But I love the online environment. I'm a die-hard techie, and I think it's so much fun!"

Over and over, he says, people have found relatives on the Roots Forum, or because of it. One of the most affecting instances, he says, occurred when he was demonstrating Roots and the Phone*File system at a National Genealogical Society meeting. A woman found a name and number she thought might be her long-lost father's, though she didn't dare hope. Still, she went to the pay phone, and sure enough, was on the phone to him in minutes, arranging a reunion after 30 years. "She had tears running down her cheeks, because she was flying to Philadelphia to see her father that next week. I could hardly talk the rest of the day, I was so choked up," he says.

Gaye Spencer, one of the sysops, had a mysterious Amirilla Eastman in her lineage, whose parents she just couldn't place. That is, until one day when a long message was posted on the Roots Forum about an Eastman family of the right period with all the siblings of that family listed—and there was Amirilla!

Dick Eastman himself found a relative he was able to help online. His French-Canadian Dubay line was hard to find, partly because of variant spellings. But he knew of a history professor of that name, and using Phone*File, Eastman discovered that the fellow lived within 25 miles of where Eastman knew his ancestors to be from.

Calling the gentleman, he discovered the professor had just self-published 1,200 copies of a genealogy of the family, and was having trouble selling them. Eastman sent the professor gummed labels with every Dubay (and variant spelling) he could find on Phone*File. The professor mailed each one a notice of the book, and the result was a wonderful Dubay reunion, as well as a sold-out printing of the genealogy!

Dick Eastman is typical of the sort of person you'll find on CompuServe. The CompuServe genealogy forums were the first online genealogy resources I found—nearly twenty years ago—and I still feel they're among the best online resources available today.

Chapter 17

International Genealogy Resources

Sooner or later, you'll get "back to the boat,"—that is, find your original immigrant in a certain line. Once you reach this point you are in really deep!

Introduction

Of course, the next step is to start researching in "the old country." Can you do this online? Well, that depends on the country. Some countries will indeed have online records for you to search, especially English-speaking ones; but other countries will only have sites with the most general information, places where you'll be lucky just to find the address of the civil records offices. As a result, you'll probably wind up doing a combination of both online and in-person research.

Perhaps you would find the experiences of a real-life genealogist helpful. Denzil J. Klippel had quite a bit of success and was kind enough to share his experiences with me.

A Success Story

"I have had a lot of luck researching my German forebears. And it all started online," Denzil wrote to me. "Klippels all over the world gave me the benefit of their Klippel family history. I was able to put it all together and got a very good idea of the origins of my surname, plus (and better yet) found a lot of 'cousins.' Every Klippel I meet is my 'cousin.' They have all been the greatest people on earth. I am a lucky man to have ventured out on this Klippel Family History quest and found and made such wonderful friends/cousins!"

It did not happen overnight. Klippel started with what he knew, researched back to the boat, and finally found the village of origin of one of his ancestors. How he did it is fascinating.

"About seven years ago I became interested in my roots. I only knew my parents, my grandmother on my mother's side, and her brother and sister. My grandmother had died a few years earlier, and when I got around to writing to my uncle, (I found) he had died a few months before. As for my aunt, she did not reply to my letters, and has since died at 93," he explained.

Note

"In the beginning, I didn't take advantage of the resources on the Net like DearMYRTLE, etc., and ask questions. (See Figure 17-1.) Everyone is willing to help for the asking. We don't need to reinvent the wheel—just ask if anyone has done this or that," Denzil Klippel says.

"A friend of mine who I had worked with before I retired (at 55) was a Mormon and told me to go to the local FHC (Family History Center) in Manhattan, New York City. When I visited the center I was welcomed

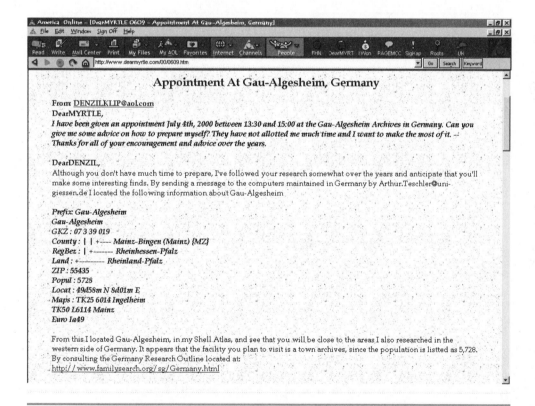

FIGURE 17-1.   *Getting help from people experienced in international genealogy is just one way the online world can make your quest easier*

and shown how to do some lookups. To my surprise I found my grandmother's family but not my grandmother. I requested the tape and the name and address of the submitter. I sent a letter to the submitter of this information and he said he was writing a book on the family," Denzil explained. In his contact information in the letter, he included his e-mail address.

> **Note**
>
> *A complete listing of Family History Centers, searchable by state, is at http://deseretbook.com/browse/family-history/index.html*

Then began the online part. "We shared some information and he must have given my name and e-mail address to another researcher. I was contacted by e-mail by another researcher online and we started sharing contacts and research sites. Everything started to come together then," he continued.

"I still knew nothing about my father's family—not even my grandmother's maiden name. I sent for his death certificate (NY) and found his place and date of birth (CA), his father's place of birth (Upstate, NY) and his mother's maiden name (Settle) and place of birth (CA). I went online and ordered my father's birth certificate, and so on."

> **Note**
>
> *You can find where to write for many vital records at www. vitalrec.com. (See Figure 17-2.)*

"After going back to my great grandfather and finding he came from Germany I hit a brick wall. Not knowing what to do I went to one of the search engines, Yahoo!, and put in the name Klippel—it gave me 6,000 places where the name appeared on the net, most of them being an illness discovered by a Klippel. I captured all of the Klippel e-mail addresses and sent them a message saying I was researching the Klippel family name and if they were interested in working with me, perhaps we could find some common ancestors, and if not that, discover where the Klippels originated."

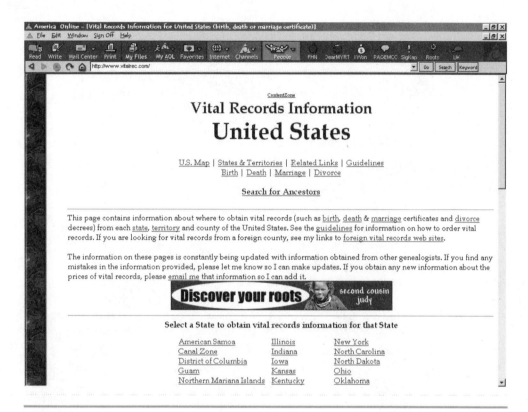

FIGURE 17-2.   *Find where to write for vital records from the U. S. and other nations at VitalRecords.com*

Denzil said he doesn't recommend this approach. "This shotgun approach never works. I still send e-mails to all Klippels I find but refer them to my Klippel site (http://www.channel21.com/family/klippel/) that talks about the origins of the Klippel name and not family lines," he said. What worked was searching for the surname on www.google.com, and looking for the genealogy sites.

After e-mailing people with Klippel genealogy sites, as opposed to just every Klippel he could find online, he heard from others like him who had been researching the line. Several were cousins he didn't know he had, and ever since he calls all Klippels he comes in contact with "cousin."

Origins of Surnames

One of the most fascinating things about genealogy is the meaning and origin of surnames. Denzil found the Klippel surname appears to have more than one origin. Some are listed below:

♦ Locational: "dweller near a small cliff."

♦ German dictionaries of family names: "derber Mensch" (a coarse or rough person)

♦ Eastern Germany: There is a story concerning the origin of Klippel which says the name came into being after the Thirty Years' War. It claims that Klippel deals with an old handicraft—lace-making—that was carried out by women in the area of "Erzgebirge," a low mountain range in eastern Germany close to the border of former Czechoslovakia. Lace-making of this type was carried out by using many thin silk or cotton strings arranged in straight lines that hung down from the ceiling and whose ends were connected to small pieces of wood, called bobbins. The strings were moved by hand in sophisticated ways and fastened with knots to produce regular patterns. The activity of moving the strings was called "klippeln," (a verb) which is local slang; the German verb today is "klöppeln" (meaning: to make lace). The noise raised by the touching of the bobbins during their movements was called "Klippel." There is an old folk song from the "Erzgebirge" area, the "Klippel Lied" (Klippel Song), associated with the practice, that is virtually unknown in Germany today. It has recently been reissued on CD, and Denzil brought a copy back from his trip to Germany.

♦ The theory Denzil believes to be the true origin of the name Klippel, however, is this: From the mid 1400s, the surname Klippel had an occupational genesis. The name is medieval Dutch in origin and derives from the word "clippel," the term for a bell clapper or knocker used by the "Bodebussen" (Sheriff or Guild Master) in Stavenisse on the Island of Tholen in what is today the Netherlands. The name was first used in 1440 when

> Philip of Burgundy desired that his official messenger to the
> town of Stavenisse be sworn into office by the bailiff and
> given permission to attach goods with the force of the rod,
> if necessary. The rod was called the "clippel," thus the holder
> of this office was called Klippel.

"One of these cousins had the name of the town in Germany where
my Klippel line came from (Ober-Hilbersheim). I found that this village
had a web site (see Figure 17-3) and sent a letter to the Mayor. He
responded via e-mail and said he knew of my line and that there were
still Klippels living in the village," Denzil said.

Note

See the village's Web site at: http://www.gau-algesheimvg.de/

"In the meantime, other Klippels in Europe contacted me and before I
knew it, I was planning a trip to visit some of them, and Ober-Hilbersheim.
When they heard I was going to visit, they all said I had to stay with them."

Now he was really into the in-person, off-line mode! Through
electronic and surface mail, he made appointments at all of the archives
he planned to visit in Germany. When he arrived, they were ready for
him, and in most cases had already done all of the lookups. As he
gathered the research material, he mailed it home to himself. This
was important insurance against losing or misplacing any of it during
his sojourn.

"My trip started in Ober-Hilbersheim and I stayed with the
Mayor—he took me to all of the archives and helped me get all of the
Klippel family history back to 1650! My distant cousins in the village
welcomed me with open arms. I then went to the Netherlands and
stayed with the Klippels there and they took me to the Island of Tholen
where the first Klippel came from in the 1400s. Then on to Hamburg to
visit Helmut Klippel and the archive there," he said.

"And last but not least, on to Sweden to stay with Alf Klippel who
had given me a wealth of information about the origins of the Klippel
name via e-mail and done most of the translating of the Old German
documents I had been receiving over the net."

FIGURE 17-3.   *Denzil found his ancestors' village online*

It took some footwork and perseverance, but after seven years, Denzil feels he has accomplished a lot in his international search and that his online resources made it all possible.

The following table lists the sites Denzil Klippel found most useful:

DearMYRTLE	www.DearMYRTLE.com
RootsWeb lists	http://rootsweb.com (HESSE-L; PFALZ-L)
The Telephone Book for Germany	http://www.teleauskunft.de/NSAPI/ &BUAB = BUNDESWEIT
Germany Genealogy Net	http://www.genealogienetz.de/gene/misc/ geoserv.html
Go.com Translator	http://translator.go.com/
Google	http://google.com/
Priceline	http://www.priceline.com/
Deutsche Bahn	http://www.bahn.de/

> *Note*
>
> *Denzil was also able to uncover some family history along with various names and dates. For instance, his great-great-grandfather, Johann Klippel, was the baker in Ober-Hilbersheim, having moved there from Bubenheim. Today, the Klippels there are still bakers in Ober-Hilbersheim, and perform their trade in the same building! Over the years, Johann Klippel was married four times and had 22 children. He was also a member of the village council. You're likely to come upon similar gems of info during your research, so by all means keep a sharp eye out.*

Where to Look

In many of the places covered in previous chapters, you can find links to sites for genealogy beyond the U.S. For online links, you may want to start at Cyndi's List (http://www.cyndislist.com) and RootsWeb (http://www.rootsweb.org).

But before you go, you need to learn how to research in those countries. Each place has its own method of recording vital statistics, history, and other information. Before you start looking for records, you need to know what those records are called, and who keeps them.

LDS Research Guides

The place to begin before you start looking for records beyond the U.S. is the LDS site FamilySearch (see Chapter 14). On the FamilySearch site, click Browse Categories in the navigation bar to the left of the opening page. Then click on Research Support on the Browse page. On the next page, click Research Helps (or go straight to the page http://www.familysearch.com/rg/research/index.html). Click the Sort by Document Type tab, then select Research Guides.

The first one to read is the guide "Tracing Immigrant Origins," a 49-page outline of tips, procedures, and strategies.

On the list of research guides on FamilySearch.com, many are online and printable. (You can also go to any Family History Center and get the research guides on paper for a nominal fee.) Using your browser's "find" function (usually CONTROL + F), simply search for the country you are interested in. For example, search for France, and you'll see there is a guide for researching in France, not to mention a file explaining how to write a letter to France requesting genealogical information. You can find and print out the France Research Outline on FamilySearch, or you can get a printed copy at a local Family History Center for a small fee.

These Research Outlines give you step-by-step pointers on the best way to pursue historical records in a particular state, province, or country. The Letter-Writing Guides tell you what you need to know before you write the letter, where to write, how to address the envelope, how to enclose return postage, and an example letter in the appropriate language. See Figure 17-4.

Arm yourself with the Research Outlines and, if available, Letter-Writing Guide, for the appropriate country before you begin.

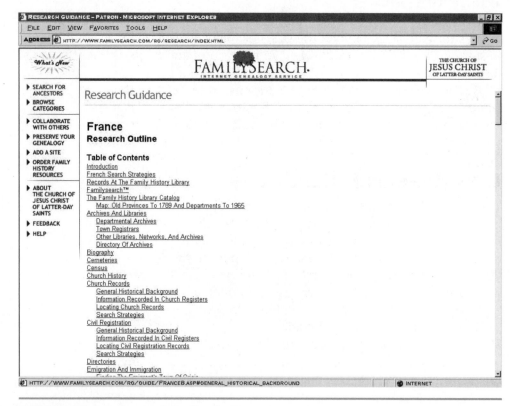

FIGURE 17-4.   *Research Outline for France*

WorldGenWeb

The WorldGenWeb Project was created in 1996 by Dale Schneider to help folks researching in countries around the world. The goal is to have every country in the world represented by an online Web site and hosted by researchers who either live in that country or who are familiar with that country's resources. The site is at http://www.worldgenweb.org (see Figure 17-5).

When the WorldGenWeb Project opened on the Internet in October 1996, volunteers were recruited to host country Web sites. By coordinating with the USGenWeb Project, soon all the world's major countries had Web sites online. Throughout the next year,

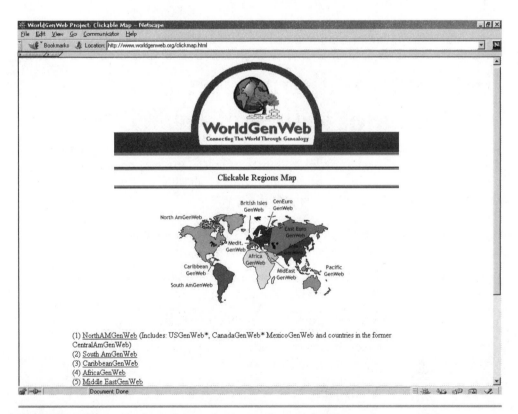

FIGURE 17-5. *The best place to begin any international genealogy search is at WorldGenWeb*

WorldGenWeb continued to grow. On September 17, 1997, the WorldGenWeb Project moved to RootsWeb, and with the support of the RootsWeb staff, WorldGenWeb has expanded to its present size.

Divided into 11 regions (Africa, Asia, the British Isles, Central Europe, the Caribbean, Eastern Europe, the Mediterranean, the Middle East, North America, the Pacific, and South America), it gives links to local sites with the local resource addresses of county/country public records offices, cemetery locations, maps, library addresses, archive addresses, and association addresses, including Family History Centers or other genealogical or historical societies. It also offers some history and culture particular to the region. Other resources may include query pages or message boards, mail lists, historical data including census records, cemetery records, biographies, bibliographies, and family/surname registration Web sites.

Between RootsWeb and WorldGenWeb, you should be able to find out many things, no matter what country your search takes you to.

International Internet Genealogical Society

This all-volunteer effort aims to collect international genealogical material at one site, promote ethics in international genealogy, and promote cooperation among genealogists all over the world. The main features of the site are:

- The list of volunteers involved (an index is available at the Global Village Representatives page)

- The many IRC chats held on a regular basis (including DearMYRTLE's weekly Monday gatherings)

- A library of links to resources all over the world

- Free online courses on how to conduct international genealogy searches

- The IIGS newsletter

Once a lively and active group, as of this writing the pages had not been updated in over six months. The chats still occur regularly, and the how-to lessons are still very applicable, but the last newsletter was posted in March of 2000.

Asia

Chinese Immigrant Files (catalogs of holdings in regional archives and in Washington, D.C.) can be searched at http://www.ins.usdoj.gov/ graphics/aboutins/history/CHINESE.html. This collection of U.S. government records on immigrants is full of good information.

Chineseroots.com (http://www.chineseroots.com/) is a site for searching Chinese genealogy (see Figure 17-6). Through an alliance with Shanghai Library, which holds the world's largest collection of Chinese ancestry records, you can look at a catalog of 90,000 volumes of

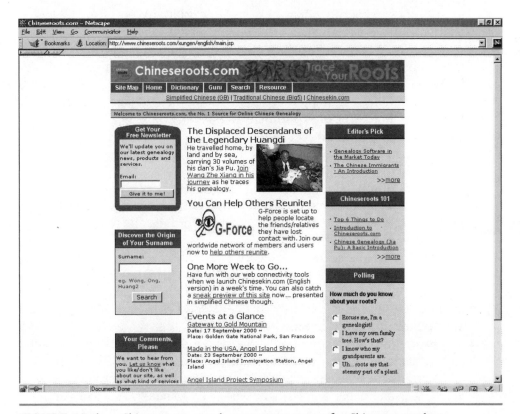

FIGURE 17-6. *Chineseroots.com has many resources for Chinese genealogy*

family details dating back to the 10th century. Other Chineseroots.com partnerships include various world-renowned genealogy organizations such as the Taiwan Surnames Association and the Shanxi Genealogy Centre in China. The text for the Web sites are in English, Chinese Big 5, and Chinese GB. The site has articles, a calendar of events, and message boards.

Other sites to be aware of include AsianGenNet (http://www. rootsweb.org/ ~ asiagw/), which is part of WorldGenWeb and has some sites, but needs hosts for many more, and Chinese Surnames at http://206.184.157.220/names/, a fascinating page with the most common Chinese surnames and their history.

Europe

Most European countries have a page on WorldGenWeb. Also, always check Cyndi's List for links; she updates it daily!

Benelux. At Digital Resources Netherlands and Belgium (http://home.wxs.nl/ ~ hjdewit/links_en.html), you can find resources from the Netherlands and Belgium, including over 350 Internet links to online resources (including more than 150 passenger lists), nearly 900 online resources on Dutch and Belgian bulletin board systems, and hundreds of digital resources.

Also, don't forget the Benelux genealogy discussion groups mentioned in Chapter 5.

Eastern Europe. If you're looking for help regarding Eastern Europe, here are a few sources you may want to check out. The first is *Genealogy for Armenians*—a how-to book—excerpts of which can be read at http://www.itsnet.com/home/gfa/.

Yahoo!, meanwhile, has a category for Czech genealogy discussion and research at http://dir.yahoo.com/Regional/Countries/Czech_Republic/ Arts_and_Humanities/Humanities/History/.

Then there's the Ukranian Roots genealogy Web Ring which begins at http://ukrcommunities.8k.com/ukrroots.html.

France. Besides the usual sites such as Cyndi's List and WorldGenWeb, a good site to explore is FrancoGene, http://www.francogene.com/, which contains links to genealogy sites in former French colonies around the world, such as Quebec and Haiti, as well as the genealogy societies and institutions found there.

Germany. Genealogy.net (http://www.genealogienetz.de/genealogy.html) has how-tos, sample request letters, databases, translations of common terms, and many more tools for researching genealogy in Germany.

GermanRoots (http://home.att.net/~wee-monster/index.html) has tips, links and research helps.

Italy. When searching Italian histories, the Italian Genealogy Homepage (http://www.italgen.com/) is the place to start, with links to how-to articles, discussion groups, and history.

Spain. A personal site, Spanish Genealogy (http://www.geocities.com/CapitolHill/Senate/4593/geneal.html) has tips, data and links about Spain, and more.

Portugal. LusaWeb (http://www.lusaweb.com/genealogy) is a site for Portuguese ancestry, while the Portuguese-American Historical & Research Foundation has a page for genealogy questions and answers at http://www.portuguesefoundation.org/genealogy.htm.

Scandinavia. Scandinavian records are abundant, with many sites to explore. For instance, you can start out with Norwegian Census and Bergen Emigration Information (http://digitalarkivet.uib.no/index-eng.htm), where census records of Norway have been transcribed and posted.

There's also Genealogy Research Denmark (http://www.ida.net/users/really/), a personal page of one woman's collected research, plus links to other resources; Martin's Norwegian Genealogy Dictionary http://www.geocities.com/Heartland/Estates/5536/eidhalist.html which helps you decipher words for relationships, occupations, and so on; the Norwegian Emigration and Genealogy Center, offering information for descendants at http://www.utvandrersenteret.no/index.htm; and Swedish Genealogy (http://sd.datatorget.educ.goteborg.se/) which has queries, data, and a few items translated into English.

United Kingdom. When delving into the lineage of the United Kingdom, UK and Ireland Genealogy, http://www.genuki.org.uk/ is the best starting point. It has transcribed data such as parish records, plus links to individuals' pages where genealogy research (secondary material) is posted. Look at the Index Page, http://www.genuki.org.uk/mindex.html, for specific counties, surnames, etc.

Another site to take a look at is the AncestorSuperSearch, http://www.ancestorsupersearch.com/, which has 1.46 million English birth, marriage, and census events from the years 1755-1891, searchable online.

South America

Genealogy.com has a good list of South American genealogy links at http://www.genealogy.com/links/c/c-places-geographic,south-america.html.

Other spots to explore include H. R. Henly's site, Genealogical Research in Latin America (http://www.saqnet.co.uk/users/hrhenly/latinam1.html) in which he has gathered the links that helped him most in his searches; and the address http://www.hfhr.com/websites.html, created by Rebecca R. Horne and maintained by Salena B. Ashton, which has a good collection of links.

Australia

Australia is rich with genealogy Web sites. Start with Yahoo!'s category, http://dir.yahoo.com/Regional/Countries/Australia/Arts_and_Humanities/Humanities/History/Genealogy/, but don't miss these other pages:

The Society of Australian Genealogists, http://www.sag.org.au/— has materials, meetings, and special interest groups.

The Dead Person's Society (http://home.vicnet.net.au/ ~ dpsoc/welcome.htm) (see Figure 17-7)—a site for genealogy in Melbourne Australia, which headlines a graphic of dancing skeletons on its home page.

Convicts to Australia—a guide to researching ancestry during the time Australia was used as a large prison at http://carmen.murdoch.edu.au/community/dps/convicts/.

The KiwiGen Web Ring—with links to New Zealand genealogy at http://nav.webring.yahoo.com/hub?ring = kiwigen&list.

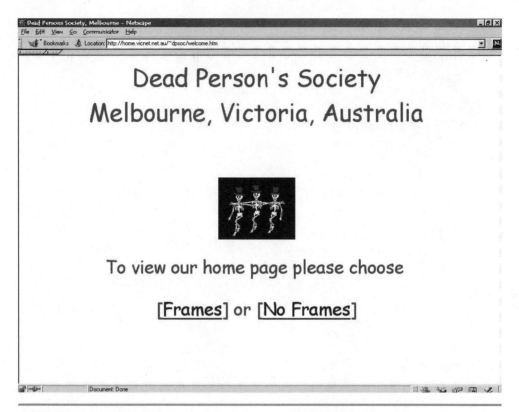

FIGURE 17-7. *Australia has many active genealogy organizations such as the Dead Person's Society of Melbourne*

Africa

If you're looking for leads involving Africa, take a look at Conrod Mercer's page (http://home.global.co.za/ ~ mercon/) a personal collection of tips on doing South African (white) genealogy.

There's also the Africa.com Research page (http://africa.com/research/) which has resources on the culture and history of major African tribes.

North America

Canada. Canadian Genealogy and History at http://www.islandnet.com/
~jveinot/cghl/cghl.html, lists online sites for vital records, genealogies,
and general history, sorted by province.

In Any Language

Certain sites are capable of translating a Web page into English. Here
are a few:

- Alta Vista Babel Fish: http://babelfish.altavista.digital.com/
  translate.dyn

- GO Translator http://translator.go.com/

- Netscape 6 has the Gist-In-Time translation service integrated into it.
  Simply get any page into Netscape 6, then choose View | Translate.

Chapter 18

GenServ

The Original GEDCOM Exchange

GenServ is an idea that was unique at its beginning, but has been copied by several commercial Web sites since. People upload their GEDCOMs, and for a fee of $1 a month are free to search the thousands of uploaded GEDCOMS, finding other researchers to correspond with. Two differences with GenServ: (1) the searches can be done by e-mail. Send in your query, go shopping, come home and get your answers; (2) the cost is minimal (in fact, you can do a trial search for free!). In the end, GenServ at www.genserv.com is more of a co-operative effort than similar commercial Web sites.

The GenServ System contains an international collection of GEDCOM files submitted by the subscribers. The system is based on the idea of sharing your family history information with others by using your GEDCOM data. To become a member, you must send in a GEDCOM file; the money is only to help support the people who are using their computers, hard drives, and Internet service provider accounts to run GenServ.

You don't download GEDCOMs from GenServ; instead, you search them for specific data, and then get reports on the data, including the name and address of the person who contributed it. Then you can start corresponding with the people whose data matches your family.

> **Note**
>
> *Do not send in a check without sending your data.*

Loading your data to the system is key. Although you can find out if you have matches in GENSERV without contributing either money or data, to get the names and addresses of submitters on the system, you must be a contributing member of GenServ. And that means, data.

Let me remind you again: the information in GEDCOMs should always be considered secondary source information. Even if the GEDCOM has cited sources, you should verify the information yourself in case of inadvertent errors.

If you need to write to a real live person about all this, Cliff Manis is the guy. You can contact him at:

Cliff Manis
Attn: GenServ System
P. O. Box 33937
San Antonio, Texas 78265-3937 USA

Or

ADMIN@genserv.com

GenServ is the Greatest!

I've been using GenServ for about six or seven years and I still think it's the best Internet genealogy service I've ever used. Even though there have been upgrades to the system and now there's a Web site for searches and queries, they still have the old e-mail search and query system in place—which is the system that I like.

I was trying to find some of the people in the same area I found my 18-year-old great-great-grandfather. In the search, I found that two different users had submitted the same individual. I wrote to both of them telling each about their common family member. Neither one knew about the other. In fact, it turned out I'd introduced two cousins. In the process, I gained a friend who has given me a tremendous amount of data about my great-great-grandfather's neighbors. Through this information, I was able to carry that line back one generation.

Maybe one generation is not so exciting to you, but try to imagine looking for an 18-year-old living in a particular county where there isn't one other person with that surname in the whole state! Nor could I find anyone with the same surname in the neighboring states. He had listed his parents as being born in the state of Georgia (where he was living), but he was the only one in the state with that surname.

--Nancy B.

Four Easy Steps to Join GenServ:

Create a GEDCOM file.

Every commercial genealogy program can do this. Usually, it's under FILE or EXPORT on the Commands menu. An example can be seen in the box. GENSERV has a very helpful file on how to make sure your GEDCOM comes out well. To get it, send an e-mail to: gedmake@genserv.com. Instructions will be returned to you via e-mail.

GenServ's site also has a list of Genealogy Software Programs on the system showing links to different programs which have been used by subscribers to send in GEDCOM data.

How to export your GEDCOM

Exporting a GEDCOM is usually easy. For example, the GENSERV site shows you how to do it in the Family Tree Maker:

1. Open the family file you'd like to use to make the GEDCOM.

2. Select File, then Copy/Export Family File.

3. Click the Save as Type drop-down list and select GEDCOM (*.GED).

4. In the File name field, type a name for the GEDCOM file. It must have the extension .GED.

5. In the Save In fields, select the drive and folder where you want to place your file.

6. Click Save and the File Type screen will be displayed. In the Destination field, if available, choose FTW. This offers the most complete selection. If the program you are exporting to is not listed, choose FTM. In the GEDCOM field, select Version 5.5. In the Character Set field, select ANSI. (Be sure to leave the Indent Tabs check box unselected. The Abbreviate Tags check box, on the other hand, *should* be selected.)

7. Click OK and Family Tree Maker creates the GEDCOM file. (Protect the privacy of living persons in your database. You can do this in two ways. You can copy the original Family Tree Maker file and remove the vital statistics for your living relatives from this copy OR you can use a utility program to delete that information for you. Please remember to use the utility on the COPY of your original Family Tree Maker file.)

8. There is a very easy GEDCOM utility—available free—to remove living people's vital statistics from your GEDCOM file. This utility should be run after you've created your GEDCOM file. It's available for download from the following Internet address: http://www.rootsweb.com/ ~ gumby/ged.html.

9. Run the GEDCOM utility. In the From field, Browse and select your new GEDCOM file. In the To field, save this new GEDCOM file (with living people's data removed) with a new name. Select Remove Details in the Processing Options and select the Cut-off year. Then click Process.

10. Now you're ready to send your GEDCOM file to GenServ. Open your e-mail program and compose a message to gedcom@genserv.com

11. Attach the GEDCOM file to this e-mail and click Send.

Fill-in and submit the GenServ Information Request Form on the Web page: http://www.genserv.com/gs3/inforeq.html. (See Figure 18-1.) This form gives them your name and address, and allows GenServ to collect some profile data on their users to help them fine-tune the site or add better features.

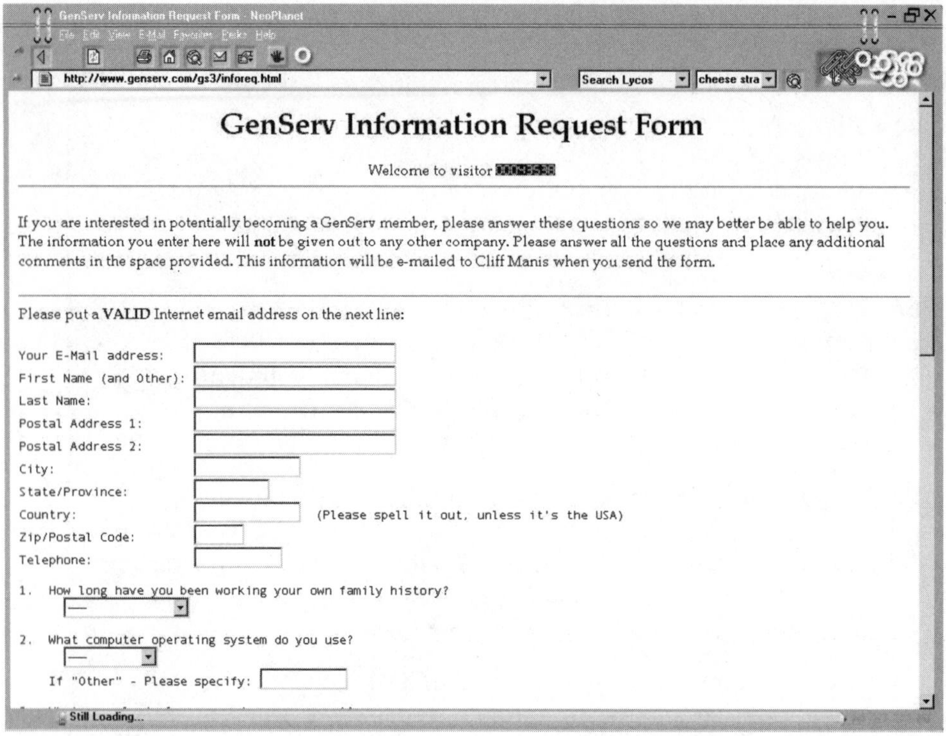

FIGURE 18-1. *The registration form on GenServ is part of the sign-up process*

Send your GEDCOM file to GenServ. You will receive confirmation within 24 hours that your file was received. For information regarding the different ways to send the file, e-mail them asking for one of these explanations:

- How to send a GEDCOM E-Mail—send an e-mail to: genem@genserv.com

- How to send a GEDCOM FTP—send an e-mail to: genftp@genserv.com

- How to Postal Mail a GEDCOM—address your e-mail to: genpostal@genserv.com

Choose your type of membership:

FREE—You can try GenServ for free for two months after submitting your GEDCOM. You get 12 requests per hour to the system. Trial subscriptions do not include access to the Web pages or submitter info with the reports from the databases. One trial access per person/e-mail address regardless of the number of GEDCOM files submitted. Also, members over the age of 80 are given complimentary memberships!

$12.00—Regular subscription (8 UK Pounds) per year. Regular subscription maximum: 12 requests per hour.

$6.00—Senior (over 60) & student subscription (4 UK Pounds) per year. Maximum: 12 requests per hour.

$20.00 or more—A Sponsor account gives you up to 25 requests per hour.

$35.00 or more—Prime Sponsor accounts get up to 60 requests per hour while using the GenServ system.

Note

Use this address only for postal mail to GenServ or Cliff Manis. Cliff Manis - GenServ System P. O. Box 33937, San Antonio, TX 78265-3937 USA. Those living in Europe should use this address: Jon Rees, Church Cottage, Ringsfield, Beccles, Suffolk, NR34 8JU UK. E-mail: J.M.Rees@cefas.co.uk

How soon you hear back depends on how you sent in your GEDCOM—from 24 hours for FTP to a couple of weeks for surface mail. As soon as your GEDCOM file is tested and successfully uploaded to GenServ, you will be sent an ID and instructions on how to use e-mail to access GenServ.

Note

Questions or problems? Send them to ADMIN@genserv.com with the following information: Your name, your e-mail address, HOW, WHEN & WHERE you sent your GEDCOM file, and what you named it.

Please remember that the staff members at GenServ are all VOLUNTEERS. Most of them have full-time "real" jobs, and a family, too. They are all addicted to Genealogy and do the best they can to get your files uploaded as fast as possible in order to help you learn the system.

Freebies

You should at least give the one free search a try at http://www.genserv. com/gs3/samplesearch.html. (See Figure 18-2.)

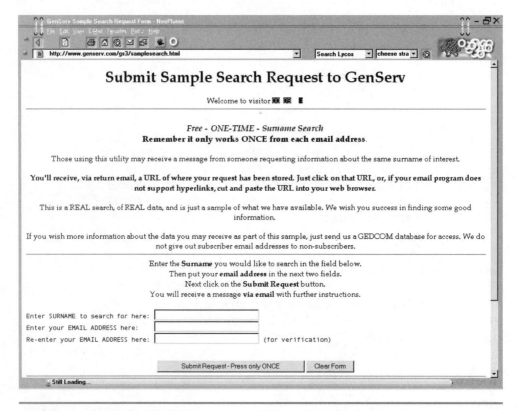

FIGURE 18-2. *You can have one free sample search of the GenServ GEDCOM database by filling out this Web form*

You can try out all the GenServ functions during a free two-month trial after you submit a GEDCOM, or you can sample some of the free services GenServ offers (that don't require a GEDCOM submission), including:

Queries—Fill out a simple form at http://www.genserv.com/gs3/guestbook.html to tell others who and where you are searching.

Queries Search—Put in a keyword at http://raven.genserv.net/ to search all the query messages posted at this page.

Chat Board—By filling out a quick form, you can become a member of the chat board on GenServ for free. Most messages here are queries, too.

GenServ Demo—This demonstration system has only a tiny sample of the data available on the full GenServ system. It is designed for non-members who want to sample the full range of searching and reporting capabilities available to GenServ members.

How Does GenServ Work?

The simple answer: you send an e-mail message with your GenServ ID number, and a search command, with or without limiters. Within minutes, you will get back a formatted reply with the information you asked for.

The detailed explanation, of course, is a little more involved. The details are in the file GenHow2. The latest version of this file may be obtained any time by sending a message (even a blank one) to:genhow2@GenServ.COM.

The file, as of this writing, includes these topics:

Rules for Subscribers

For best results in using this system, read these instructions all the way through before trying it. Subscribers in REGULAR, SENIOR or STUDENT GenServ Subscription Categories may send up to 12 commands per any one hour. You can upgrade your category at any time by sending the difference in subscription amounts. Subscribers over age 80 get access free; e-mail cmanis@genserv.com for details.

Subscribers in the PRIME SPONSOR category may send up to 60 requests to the server per any one hour. (Please note: this used to be only 50 per hour, but has since been changed to 60.) For your own benefit, read the GenServ DISCLAIMER page and remember new information will be seen first by Subscribers in the "fileset" file.

SEARCHCOUNT

SEARCHCOUNT tells you how many hits you have in all the databases. It's a quick way to see what's there. All SEARCHCOUNT commands go to: SEARCHCOUNT@GenServ.com.

```
ID: CM12345
```
(Instead of CM12345, use your own ID#.)
```
SEARCH NAME: manis
```
(Instead of Manis, you may put any surname.)

> *Note* ———————————————————————————————
>
> *The options listed under 4) SEARCH NAME COMMAND EXPANDED can be used with SEARCHCOUNT.*

Search Name Command Basics

All search name commands go to: SEARCH@GenServ.com. ID: and SEARCH NAME: and ID: are the ONLY required fields, everything else is optional. Names with apostrophes (like "O'Brian") will be found with SEARCH NAME.
You may send the command:
```
ID: CM12345
```
(Instead of CM12345, use your own ID#.) Only those subscribers who have sent in a GEDCOM datafile will have access to this system.
```
SEARCH NAME: manis
```
(Instead of manis, you may put any surname.)
or
```
ID: CM12345
SEARCH NAME: Spencer, A
```
or
```
ID: CM12345
SEARCH NAME: Spencer, Abraham
```
You then will get something like that shown in Table 18-1:
Please DO NOT REPLY to this message. Requests for HUMAN INTERVENTION should be addressed to < ADMIN@GenServ.COM >.

-Cut----- > Cut on this line and at the end of this message < ------Cut-
This is request number 1 of 12 allowed for this hour.
Your account expires on 31 December, 2001.
***** 16 entries found for name: "spencer, abraham" *****

Last Name	First Name	INDI#	Spouse Name	SNDX	Birthdate	Death Date	Dbase
Spencer	Abraham	10037	Patty	S152			THOC8JR
Spencer	Abraham	12729	Comer, Mary	S152	1827	1880	STEC7NF
Spencer	Abraham	12958	Christena	S152	1811		STEC7NF
Spencer	Abraham	13170		S152			STEC7NF
Spencer	Abraham	2089	?, Nancy L.	S152	1808	1850	SMIN8DA
Spencer	Abraham	2369	Donaldson, Grazi	S152	1801	1861	STEC7NF
Spencer	Abraham	2771		S152	04 Jul 1753	26 Jan 1766	WILQ7NA
Spencer	Abraham	5050		S152	1616	1655	STEC7NF
Spencer	Abraham	5404	Cross, Mary A	S152	Jun 1786		EAGB6EA
Spencer	Abraham	589		S152	17 Oct 1738	1741	STOC8CM
Spencer	Abraham	6066	Bush, Tabatha	S152	1779		SMIN8DA
Spencer	Abraham	638		S152			FORCE1
Spencer	Abraham	9236	Dickerson, Lucy	S152			SMIN8DA
Spencer	Abraham	13164		S152	1837		STEC7NF
Spencer	Abraham	12749	Fisher, Rebecca	S152	19 Jul 1851	1934	STEC7NF
Spencer	Abraham	13181		S152	07 Oct 1871	06 Nov 1894	STEC7NF

TABLE 18-1. *Index of Surnames Found (SNDX = Soundex, S = Sex, P = Parents known, F = #families, Chi = #children)*

SEARCH COMMAND EXPANDED

ID: and SEARCH NAME: are the ONLY required fields, everything else is optional. Say you want to exclude your own database, or your cousin's, or databases that you know from past searches don't have what you want. Then you use the EXCLUDE command with the database name (that last column in the example).

```
ID: AA12345
EXCLUDE: smittd1, bruq6na
```

You can put in up to ten EXCLUDEs, separated by commas, spaces, or commas and spaces. If you want to be sure to search a particular database:

```
INCLUDE: mb5
```

This command has the same limitations as EXCLUDE. However, you cannot have both INCLUDE and EXCLUDE in the same message.

To search for specific names:

```
SEARCH NAME: Abbott
```

(or)

```
SEARCH NAME: Abbott, J
```

(or)

```
SEARCH NAME: Abbott, John
```

OPTIONAL COMMANDS

```
BORN BEFORE: 01 Jan 1960
BORN AFTER: 01 Jan 1940
DIED BEFORE: 01 Jan 1960
DIED AFTER: 01 Jan 1940
LOADED SINCE: 10 Feb 1996
```

Of course, you would put in your wanted date after the colon in each example.

LIST FIELDS COMMAND

LIST FIELDS: With this command, you can have only specific fields of a match sent back to you. The field numbers and their associated data are:

1. Name

2. INDI#

3. Spouse Name

4. SOUNDEX

5. Birth date

6. Death date

7. Database name

8. S = Sex (M or F)

9. P = Parents (Y or N)

10. F = Family (# of generations)

11. Chi = Children (# of)

12. Birthplace

13. Death place

14. Last update of this database

If you use LIST FIELDS : All, then you will get all this information on a certain name. If you omit it, you get the results shown in the example, 1 through 8 shown previously. So, the command:

```
LIST FIELDS: 1 2 3 4 5 8
```

will give you those fields, and the records will be sorted by the first field. The command:

```
LIST FIELDS: 5 1 2 3 7
```

would show ONLY the Birth date, Name, INDI, Spouse Name and database, in that order, sorted by the first field (birth date).

You can also control the look of the output. Using the LIST WIDTH COMMAND tells GenServ where to put the right margin on your reports. There is a minimum of 60, a maximum of 200, and a default of 80.

If your e-mail account has limits on the size of a message, you can use the SPLIT COMMAND to control the length of reports. It can be set as high as 5000k or as small as 16k. (Note: Before using any split size over 100k, ask your Internet provider if they have any limitations on e-mail message size.) Omitting SPLIT leaves your messages at the default limit of 50k.

By default, your original request is appended to the end of the message sent from GenServ. If you want to disable this feature, add the following line to any request you send:

```
SHOW REQUEST: NO
```

Send Command

To get files from GenServ, send a message with your ID: on one line and SEND: <fileid> in the next.

 Note ────────────────────────────────

ALL SEND COMMANDS GO TO: SEND@GenServ.com

SEND: datadate—Current listing and time each database was loaded
SEND: datatot—Name and date/time/size of last few databases loaded
SEND: genhow2—The how-to file
SEND: geninfo—The latest current documentation for the GenServ system
SEND: genrpts—Samples of all available reports. Get this and print it out. It's very handy.
SEND: idinfo—You will receive back your own name/address info.
SEND: fileset—Current listing of files, plus late-breaking news.

Some older files are also listed in the fileset file. To get them, send a blank message to the following addresses:
geninfo@GenServ.comLatest info about GenServ
genhow2@GenServ.com—How to format requests
genrpts@GenServ.com—Sample reports; a must have!
gedmake@GenServ.com—How to make a GEDCOM file
genem@GenServ.com—How to send a GEDCOM email
genftp@GenServ.com—How to send a GEDCOM ftp
genpostal@GenServ.com—How to send a GEDCOM postal mail
disclaimer@GenServ.com—GenServ Disclaimer

There are many more detailed searches you can do with GenServ; be sure to get the GENRPTS file to learn about them.

As I said at the beginning of this chapter, GenServ is not the only GEDCOM exchange, but it's the most reasonably priced, and it's a co-operative venture. Furthermore, updating your GEDCOM twice a year on GenServ is a good way to back up your data.

Appendix A

Forms of Genealogical Data

One of the reasons to get involved in the online genealogy world is to share the information you have, as well as find information you don't. To do that, standards have been set up for transmitting that information.

Ahnentafels, Tiny Tafels, and GEDCOMs

Ahnentafels, tiny tafels, and GEDCOMs. They are all designed to put information in a standard format. The last two are readable by many different genealogical database programs, and many utilities have been written to translate information from one to another.

Ahnentafels

Ahnentafels are not big tiny tafels. The word means ancestor table in German, and the format is more than a century old. It lists all known ancestors of an individual, and includes the full name of each as well as dates and places of birth, marriage, and death. It organizes this information along a strict numbering scheme.

Once you get used to ahnentafels, it becomes very easy to read them, moving up and down from parent to child and back again. The numbering scheme is the key to it all. Consider this typical pedigree chart:

```
                              8. great-grandfather
            4. paternal grandfather, |
            |                 9. great-grandmother
  2. Father, |
  |         |                 10. great-grandfather
  |         5. paternal grandmother, |
  |                           11. great-grandmother
1. Person, |

  |                           12. great-grandfather
  |         6. maternal grandfather, |
  |         |                 13. great-grandmother
  3. Mother, |
  |                           14. great-grandfather
  7. maternal grandmother, |
            15. great-grandfather
```

Study the numbers in the above chart. Every person listed has a number, with a mathematical relationship between parents and children. The number of a father is always double that of his child's. The number of the mother is always double that of her child's plus one. The number of a child is always one-half that of its parent (ignoring any remainder).

In this example, the father of person #6 is #12, the mother of #6 is #13, and the child of #13 is #6. In ahnentafel format, the chart reads like this:

1. person

2. father

3. mother

4. paternal grandfather

5. paternal grandmother

6. maternal grandfather

7. maternal grandmother

8. great-grandfather

9. great-grandmother

10. great-grandfather

11. great-grandmother

12. great-grandfather

13. great-grandmother

14. great-grandfather

15. great-grandmother

Notice that the numbers are exactly the same as in the pedigree chart. The rules of father $= 2 \times$ child#, mother $= 2 \times$ child# $+ 1$, child $=$ parent/2, ignore remainder, etc., remain the same. This is an ahnentafel chart.

In practice, ahnentafels are rarely uploaded as text files, but it's one way to show what you do know about your tree quickly, and in few characters. Just clearly state that it's an ahnentafel. Some Web sites list genealogies as Ahnentafels.

Tiny Tafels

Despite the similar name, a tiny tafel (TT) is a different animal. It provides a standard way of describing a family database so that the information can be scanned visually or by computer. It was described in an article entitled "Tiny-Tafel for Database Scope Indexing" by Paul Andereck in the April-May-June 1986 issue (vol. 5, number 4) of *Genealogical Computing*.

The concept of TTs was adopted by COMMSOFT first in their popular program, Roots-II, and later in Roots-III. It has since been adapted by other genealogical programs, such as Brother's Keeper and GED2TT.

A TT makes no attempt to include the details that are contained in an ahnentafel. All data fields are of fixed length, with the obvious exceptions of the surnames and optional places. A TT lists only surnames of interest (with Soundex) plus the locations and dates of the beginning and end of that surname. Tiny tafels make no provision for first names, births, marriages, deaths, or multiple locations.

The format of the tiny tafel is rigidly controlled as you can see in the following table and in Table A-1. The following table shows the specifications as released by CommSoft:

Column	Description
1	Header Type
2	Space delimited
3	n Text (n < 38)(n + 1) Carriage Return

Header Type	Description	Remarks
N	Name of person having custody of data	Mandatory first record
A	0 to 5 address lines, address data	Optional
T	Telephone number including area code	Optional
S	Communication, service/telephone number	0 to 5 service lines (MCI, ITT, ONT, RCA, ESL, CIS, SOU, etc, e.g., CIS/77123,512
B	Bulletin Board/telephone number	Optional

TABLE A-1.   *Defined types*

Header Type	Description	Remarks
C	Communications nnnn/X/P nnnn maximum baud rate X = O(riginate only), A(nswer only), B(oth) P = Protocol (Xmodem, Kermit, etc.)	Optional
D	Diskette format d/f/c d = diameter (3, 5, 8) f = format MS-DOS, Apple II, etc. c = capacity, KB	Optional
F	File format	Free-form, optional ROOTS II, ROOTS/M, PAF Version 1, etc.
R	Remark	Free-form, optional
Z	Number of data items with optional text	Required last item

TABLE A-1.   *Defined types* (Continued)

In the COMMSOFT Tiny Tafel, the name of the database, the version of the database, and any special switches used when the Tiny Tafel was generated are shown on the Z line. The definitions of the special switches are shown next.

D DATEFILLDISABLED—Tiny Tafel normally suppresses the output of data for which the birth dates necessary to establish each line of output are missing. When this switch is on, the Tiny Tafel generator has estimated missing dates. The Tiny Tafel program applies a 30 year per generation offset wherever it needs to reconstruct missing dates.

N NOGROUPING—Tiny Tafel normally "groups" output lines that have a common ancestor into a single line containing the most recent birth date. Descendants marked with an interest level greater than zero, however, will have their own line of output. Alternatively, when this switch is enabled, one line of output is created for every ultimate descendant (individual without children).

M MULTIPLENAMES—Tiny Tafel normally lists a surname derived from the descendant end of each line. Specifying this option lists all unique spellings of each surname (up to five) separated by commas.

P PLACENAMES—Tiny Tafel will include place names for family lines when this switch is enabled. Place names will be the most significant 14 to 16 characters of the birth field. When this option is enabled, the place of birth of the ultimate ancestor and the place of birth of the ultimate descendant of a line of output, respectively, are added to the end of the line.

S SINGLEITEMS—Tiny Tafel normally suppresses lines of output that correspond to a single individual (that is, in which the ancestry and descendant dates are the same). This switch includes single-person items in the output.

#I INTERESTLEVEL—Tiny Tafel normally includes all family lines meeting the above conditions no matter what its interest level. An interest level may be specified to limit the lines included to those having an interest level equal to or greater than the number specified. For example, with the interest level set to 1, all lines which have an ancestor or descendant interest level of 1 or higher will be listed.

Table A-2 shows how Tiny Tafel data is arranged.

The Soundex code for any given line is obtained from the end of the line that has the highest interest level. If the interest level is the same at each end, however, the name at the ancestor end will be used. If the application of these rules yield a surname that cannot be converted to Soundex, however, the program will attempt to obtain a Soundex code from the other end of the line.

Col	Description
1 through 4	Soundex Code (note 1)
5	Space delimiter
6 through 9	Earliest ancestor birth year
10	Interest flag, ancestor end of family line (note 2)
11 through 14	Latest descendant birth year
15	Interest flag, descendant end of family line (note 2)
16 through 16 +	SL Surname string area (SL = total surname length)
	above + PL Place name area (PL = total place name length)
	above + 1 Carriage return

TABLE A-2. *Tiny Tafel Data*

Interest flag: The codes for interest level are
[space] No interest (level 0)
. Low interest (level 1)
: Moderate interest (level 2)
* Highest interest (level 3)

Up to five surnames can be on one line where the surname has changed in that line. If more than five surnames are found in a line, only the latest five will be shown. The inclusion of additional surnames is enabled by the M switch.

Place names for the birth of the earliest ancestor and the latest descendant may be included by using the P switch. If a place name is not provided for the individual whose birth year is shown, the field will be blank. The place for the ancestor is preceded by a backslash (\), and for the descendant by a slash (/).
Terminator:
W Date Tiny Tafel file was generated, DD MMM YYYY format.

That's how you build one manually. Most genealogical software packages now have a function to create and accept either a TT or GEDCOM, or both, from your information in the database. Always be certain a downloaded GEDCOM or TT has verified information before you load it into your database, because taking it back out isn't fun.

The best way to use computers is to take some of the drudgery out of life, and the best way to use tiny tafels is to compare and contrast them with as many others as you can. Thus the Tiny Tafel Matching System was born. It's a copyrighted software program from CommSoft, Inc., and is on many BBSs, which have to be on The National Genealogy conference (FidoNet) to carry the program. You have to be a qualified user of a BBS and submit your own TT file (which can have more than one tafel in it) to be allowed to use TTMS to the fullest.

To find a TTMS near you, call the CommSoft BBS at 707-838-6373, register as a user, and look at the Files section under genealogy-related files. You can also get a description of the system there. Or call Brian Mavrogeorge's board Roots(SF!) at 415-584-0697, which has an eight-page article about the system. Send him an e-mail message at brian.mavrogeorge@p0.f30.n125.z1.fidonet.org to ask for a copy.

The TTMS system has three main functions:

- Collecting and maintaining a local database of TTs
- Presenting "instant" matches on the local database
- Allowing "batch" searches of all other databases on the NGS

In this context, "instant" means while you sit waiting at your keyboard, hooked onto the BBS (which could take some time—with you and your line both tied up). For this reason, some BBSs will limit the time of day you can try this. A "batch" search means that your query is sent out on the NGS and, in a few hours or days, you'll receive messages about other TTs that match yours. Then you can contact the persons who submitted the data.

Anyone who can sign onto a BBS can look for instant matches, but you have to submit a TT file of your own to do a batch search. The searches can be limited by dates, soundex, interest level, and so on to make the hits more meaningful.

Your TTs should be machine-generated (by Brother's Keeper, for example) to avoid formatting errors. Keep the TT as concise as possible and submit to only one board; for the batch system to be most efficient, redundancies have to be minimal. And be sure to experiment with the date overlap features to keep the reports short. As you find new information, you can replace your old TT file with new information; this is especially important if your address changes.

GEDCOMs

In February 1987, The Church of Jesus Christ of Latter-Day Saints (Mormon church) approved a standard way of setting data for transfer between various types of genealogy software, including its own Personal Ancestral File, or PAF. The standard (a combination of tags for data, and pointers to related data) has been adopted into most major genealogical database programs, including MacGene, Roots, Family Roots, Family Ties, Brother's Keeper, and so on.

If data from one database doesn't fit exactly into the new one even with GEDCOM's format, the program will often save the extraneous data to a special file. A good program can use this data to help you sort and search to determine whether it has what you're looking for. Which is why so many people upload GEDCOMs to BBSs; perhaps someone somewhere can use the data. But, as GEDCOMs tend to be large, many BBSs have a policy against uploading them. Instead, you upload a message that you're willing to exchange for the price of the disk, or some other arrangement.

Appendix B

Internet Error Messages

The Information Superhighway is full of potholes, dead ends, and wrong turns. You know you've hit one when a message pops up saying "404 not found" or "Failed DSN lookup." Scratching your head you wonder, "40what? Failed who? What do these cryptic messages mean anyway?"

They mean the Internet is trying to tell you something. Here's a short guide to some of the most common ones, their probable cause, and what you can do about them.

Browser Error Messages

403 forbidden—The Web site you're trying to access requires special permission—a password at the very least. No password? You'll probably have to give up or find out how to register for the site. Your browser has made it as far as the remote host computer, but it can't find the page or document you want.

404 not found—Your browser found the host computer but not the specific Web page or document you requested. Check your typing, make sure you have the address (URL) right, and try again. If this doesn't work, shorten the address, erasing from the right to the first slash you encounter. For example, if http://www.benchley.com/pub/dottie isn't working, try http://www.benchley.com/pub/. If that doesn't work, keep erasing the address back to the first single slash.

Bad file request—The problem: you're trying to fill out an on-screen form, and you get this message. Cause: either your browser doesn't support forms or the function isn't turned on. Another possibility: the form you filled out or the HTML coding at that Web site has an error in it. If you are sure your browser isn't the problem, send e-mail to the site administrator and surf on.

Cannot add form submission result to bookmark list—A script—say, from a WebCrawler search—returns variables, such as the results from a query. You can't save the results as a bookmark because it's not a permanent file on the Internet. It's just a temporary display on your computer at this moment. You can save only the address of a page or document that's stored on some computer on the Internet. You can, however, save the result of a search to your own hard disk and create a bookmark that points to that.

Connection refused by host—See 403 forbidden.

Failed DNS lookup—The Web site's address couldn't be translated into a valid IP address (the site's officially assigned number). Either that, or the domain name server (DNS) was too busy to handle your request. What does this all mean? Well, the vespucci.iquest.com site I visit is also known as 199.170.120.42. The computer that translates the site's name into that number is a domain name server. If I see this message, the DNS couldn't take the word-based URL and translate it into an IP address (numbers). First, check your spelling and punctuation. If you still get the message, try to ping the site. Or, assume the DNS was busy and try again later.

File contains no data—The browser found the site but discovered nothing in the specific file. If you typed in a URL and got this message, check your spelling and punctuation. If you got this message after using an interactive page, perhaps you didn't finish the form, or the script on the page is faulty. Try again, at least once.

Helper application not found—Your browser downloaded a file that needs a viewer (like a video clip), but can't find the program to display it. Go to your browser's Option menu (or similar menu) and make sure you've properly specified the necessary helper program, its correct directory, and executable file name. Then try again. Note: You can usually ignore this error and download the file to view it later.

NNTP server error—You tried to connect to your Internet service provider's newsgroup server—the computer that handles messages going to and from all newsgroups supported by your ISP. The problem: your browser couldn't find it. This could be because the server is down or because you typed in the wrong server. Be sure you entered the news server correctly in the Preferences or Options dialog. Try again.

Another cause could be that you have tried to access one Internet service provider's news server from your account on another Internet service provider. You can't use CompuServe's network to read Usenet off Prodigy Internet and vice versa.

Not found—The link to a page or document or some other site no longer exists. Shorten the URL back to the first single slash and try again. If you still can't find the site, access a Web-search program like WebCrawler or Lycos and see if you can find the site's new address.

TCP error encountered while sending request to server—Some kind of erroneous data got in the pipes and is confusing the easily confused Internet. This could be due to a faulty phone jack, line noise, sunspots, or gremlins. Try again later and if the problem persists, report it to your system administrator.

Too many users—Many servers, especially ftp servers, have a limit on the number of users that can connect at one time. Wait for the traffic to die down and try again.

Unable to locate host—Your browser couldn't find anything at the URL you specified. The address could have a typo, the site may be unavailable (perhaps temporarily), or you didn't notice that your connection to the Internet service provider has ended.

FTP Error Messages

There are probably hundreds of FTP programs for the PC and Mac, and the error messages will vary. Nevertheless, here are some errors, their causes, and resolutions.

Invalid host or Unable to resolve host—This is FTP's equivalent to "404 not found." It doesn't mean the site isn't there, it just means your FTP program couldn't find it. First, check your syntax and try again. If you still run into a brick wall, run a PING program and see what's going on. Most ISPs have a PING program on their server; in fact, Windows 95 comes with one. Just type **PING < <sitename> >**. If the site exists, PING will tell you how long it took a signal to travel there and back. If PING couldn't get through, then assume the site is down, at least temporarily. Try another day.

Another way to find out if a site exists is to run nslookup, a program available from many ISPs. It looks up a server's IP address in a master Internet directory. When you are logged onto your ISP, just type **nslookup hostname**.

Your FTP program connects then suddenly freezes—If this happens shortly after you log in, try using a dash (-) as the first character of your password. This will turn off the site's informational messages, which may be confusing your FTP program.

Too many consecutive transmit errors—This means line noise has confused your FTP program and it can't continue.

It could be your modem. If you got a bargain 28.8Kbps modem for $99, it's possible that modem has less configurable options and cheaper interface circuits between the modem's real guts, the chipset, and the phone line. Modem connections above 9600bps require real care in these circuits, and cheaper modems cut corners. Call your manufacturer to see if they have some workarounds.

Another possibility is you're choking Windows, the communication program, or the modem by setting the COM port's speed to higher than 38.4 or 57.6Kbps. Even though most 28.8Kbps modems claim to handle communications at speeds up to 115Kbps, something in the link may not be able to. Reset the COM port speed and try again.

This could also be a problem with the command string sent to your modem before dialing. Check with your vendor and be prepared to supply the model number, the current initialization string sent to the modem, and settings for hardware flow control, error correction, and so on.

Usenet Error Messages

Reading and participating in newsgroups is one of the Internet's oldest and most enjoyable pastimes. But to avoid glitches and online faux pas, read some FAQ files first. You can find a good set at http://www.cs.ruu.nl/wais/html/nadir/usenet/faq/part1.html.

Usenet error messages are usually specific to your news reader, but there are some common traps.

Invalid newsgroup—This jarring note can appear for various reasons. You may have spelled the newsgroup name wrong. It's easy to put periods in the wrong place. Or maybe the newsgroup no longer exists. This is very common with the alt.* groups. Search your provider's list of all newsgroups. You can also find a list of active newsgroups at http://www.cis.ohio-state.edu/hypertext/faq/usenet/active-newsgroups/top.html.

If you try to "add" a Newsgroup, but get the address wrong, you'll get this message. Finally, your news server may not carry this group. Talk to the sysop about adding it or find the archived messages of the group via FTP at rtfm.mit.edu in the /pub/usenet, /pub/usenet-by-group, or /pub/usenet-by-hierarchy directory. If all else fails, search for the newsgroup (or its archives) with DejaNews (http://www.dejanews.com) or the Excite searcher (http://www.excite.com/).

No such message—Sometimes, especially if you are using a browser, you'll get a list of messages that is out of date. The message you wanted to read is still listed in the index, but it has "scrolled off" the server. This means it has been erased to make room for newer messages. Go to DejaNews or one of the archive sites to search for that message. Some archives are:

- ftp.uu.net/usenet/news.answers

- ftp.seas.gwu.edu/pub/rtfm

Could not connect to server—Either the news server is busy (you can try again later), down (you should notify your ISP), or you are not allowed access to the news server. Another possible cause is that you have set up your browser or newsreader client incorrectly. Check your typing in your configuration screen.

A Usenet message looks like gibberish—This isn't really an error. It is a binary file, such as a picture, sound, movie, or program that has been uuencoded into ASCII characters. You can copy the message to a file and use a decoding program to restore it; however, the newest and best newsreaders come with automatic decoding. Read the instructions for getting coded messages for your newsreader.

E-Mail Error Messages

E-mail is what the Internet was originally designed for and it's very dependable. Most mail errors are user syntax errors. When addressing a message, you must get the syntax exactly right. Commas and spaces are never allowed in e-mail addresses. The first thing to do when an e-mail you've sent is "bounced" back is to check your typing.

Unknown user—Usually you have typed the name wrong. Sometimes you have the wrong address. Call the person and ask for the correct e-mail address.

Mail from a mail list stops coming—If delivery from one of your favorite mail lists suddenly stops, it could be caused by a temporary glitch in that site or the Internet. If you are not getting mail from anywhere else, the latter is probably the case. If you are, you may have been involuntarily "unsubscribed" by the mail list program at the site. (The usual reason is because the mail it sent you was bounced back with an error.) The solution is to resubscribe.

Another possibility is that the list may have been discontinued and you weren't reading the messages closely. If you suspect this, send an e-mail to the site with just this in the body of the message: review listname with listname being the name of the list. You should get back the list's current status, including the address of the owner, whom you may want to query.

Message undeliverable Mailer Daemon—You've just met the mail program that parses all messages. If something is wrong, the header will try to tell you what. Read the whole header and you'll probably find the problem. Usually, it's the spelling.

WARNING: Message still undelivered after xx hours—Sometimes, the Internet is kind enough to warn your when you mail isn't getting through. This message is typically followed by one saying the mailer will keep trying for so many hours or days to deliver the message. You don't have to do anything about this message, but you might want to call the recipient and tell her the e-mail will be delayed.

Glossary

Ahnentafel—   The word means "ancestor table" in German, and the format is a more than a century old. It lists all known ancestors of an individual and includes the full name of each ancestor as well as dates and places of birth, marriage, and death. It organizes this information along a strict numbering scheme.

anonymous FTP—   (File Transfer Protocol) - The procedure of connecting to a remote computer, as an anonymous or guest user, in order to transfer public files back to your local computer. (See also: *FTP* and *Protocols*) Anonymous ftp is usually read only access; you often cannot contribute files by anonymous ftp.

Archie—   An Internet program for finding files available by anonymous FTP to the general public.

backbone—   A set of connections that make up the main channels of communication across a network.

baud—   A measure of speed for data transmission across a wire. It is not equivalent to bits per second, but to changes of state per second. Several bits may go across the wire with each change of state, so bits per second can be higher than the baud rate.

bitnet—   Originally, a cooperative computer network interconnecting over 2,300 academic and research institutions in 32 countries. Originally based on IBM's RSCS networking protocol, BITNET supports mail, mailing lists, and file transfer. It eventually became part of the Internet, but some colleges restrict access to the original BITNET collection of computer.

browser—   An Internet client for viewing the *World Wide Web.*

Bulletin Board System (BBS)—   A set of hardware and software you can use to enter information for other users to read or download. In this book, a BBS is usually a stand-alone system that you dial up with the phone, but many are now reachable by telnet. Most bulletin boards are set up according to general topics and are accessible throughout a network.

catalog—   A search page for the web where only an edited list is covered, not the "whole Internet".

chat— When people type messages to each other across a host or network, live and in real time. On some commercial online services this is called "conference".

client— A program that provides an interface to remote internet services, such as mail, *Usenet*, *telnet* and so on. In general, the clients act on behalf of a human end-user (perhaps indirectly).

compression— A method of making a file, whether text or code, smaller by various methods. This is so that it will take up less disk space and/or less time to transmit. Sometimes the compression is completed by the modem. Sometimes the file is stored that way. The various methods to do this go by names (followed by the system that used it) such as: PKZIP (DOS), ARC (DOS), tar (UNIX), STUFFIT (MacIntosh) and so on.

conference— (a) live, online chat. (b) a forum or echo (which see) of email messages.

CREN— Computer Research and Education Network is the new name for the merged computer networks, BITNET and Computer Science Network (CSNET). It supports electronic mail and file transfer.

data base— A set of information organized for computer storage, search, retrieval, and insertion.

default— In computer terms, not a failure to meet an obligation, but instead the "normal" or "basic" settings of a program.

directory— **1.** A level in a hierarchical filing system. Other directories branch down from the root directory. **2.** A type of search site where editors choose the Web sites and services in the catalog, instead of a robot collecting them indiscriminately.

Domain Name— The Internet naming scheme. A machine on the Internet is identified by a series of words from more specific to more general (left to right), separated by dots: microsoft.com is an example (See also: *IP address*)

Domain Name Server (DNS)— A machine with software to translate a Domain Name into the corresponding numbers of the IP address. "No DNS entry" from your browser means a name such as first.last.org was not in the domain name server's list of valid IP addresses.

door—   A program on a BBS, which allows you to perform specific functions, e.g., download mail, play a game, scan the files, etc. The BBS software shuts down while you are in a door, and the door's commands are in effect.

downloading—   To get information from another computer to yours.

echo—   A set of messages on a specific subject sent to specific BBS, which have requested those messages.

email—   An electronic message, text or data, sent from one machine or person to another machine or person.

firewall—   Electronic protection against hackers and other unauthorized access to your files while you are connected to a network or the Internet.

flame—   A message or series of messages containing an argument or insults. Not allowed on most systems. If you receive a flame, ignore the message and all other messages from that person in the future.

flash ROM—   A chip in a modem that can be used to upgrade the unit if new technology comes along after you bought it. The upgrade comes in the form of a program, which when run, rewrites the read-only memory in the modem with the new standard, protocol, or whatever else has been improved.

forum—   A set of messages on a subject, usually with a corresponding set of files. Can be on an open network such as ILINK, or restricted to a commercial system such as CompuServe.

FTP—   File Transfer Protocol allows an Internet user to transfer files electronically from remote computers back to the user's computer.

gateway—   Used in different senses (e.g., Mail Gateway, IP Gateway), but most generally, a computer that forwards and routes data between two or more networks of any size or origin. It is never, however, as straightforward as going through a gate; it's more like a labyrinth to get the proper addresses in the proper sequence.

GEDCOM—   The standard for computerized genealogical information that is a combination of tags for data and pointers to related data.

Gopher—   An Internet program to search for resources, present them to you in a menu, and perform what ever Internet program (telnet, ftp, etc.) is necessary to get the resource. See *Veronica* and *Jughead*; all three are read only access.

host computer—   In the context of networks, a computer that directly provides service to a user. In contrast to a network server, which provides services to a user through an intermediary host computer.

hot key—   When a BBS systems responds to one-keystroke commands, without an < ENTER > or < RETURN > key, that option is called "Hot Key". Some BBS software enables it with no option to turn it off; others let you set your user configuration to choose this or not. Without hot key, to make a command take effect, you must press an < ENTER > or < RETURN > ; also without hot key, some systems let you string together several commands on one line.

HTML—   Hypertext Markup Language, a coding system to format and link documents on the *World Wide Web* and *intranets*.

hub—   A BBS which collects email regionally and distributes it up the next level; collects the e-mail from that level to distribute it back down the chain.

Internet—   The backbone of a series of interconnected networks that includes local area, regional, and national backbone networks. Networks in the Internet use the same telecommunications protocol (TCP/IP) and provide electronic mail, remote login, and file transfer services.

Internet Relay Chat (IRC)—   Real-time messages typed over an open, public server.

Internet presence—   A type of chat program that requires users to register with a server. Users build "buddy lists" of others using the same program and are notified when people on their "buddy list" are available for chat and messages. Also called "instant message".

Internet service provider (ISP)—   A company that has a continuous, fast and reliable connection to the Internet and sells subscriptions to the public to use that connection. The connections may use *TCP/IP, shell accounts,* or other methods.

INTERNIC— The company that has contracted to administer certain functions of the Internet such as maintaining *domain names* and assigning *IP addresses.* Its home page is at http://rs1.internic.net/

Intranet— A local network set up to look like the *World Wide Web,* with *clients* such as *browsers,* but self-contained and not necessarily connected to the *Internet.*

IP (Internet Protocol)— The Internet standard Protocol that provides a common layer over dissimilar networks, used to move packets among host computers and through gateways if necessary.

IP Address— The alpha or numeric address of a computer connected to the Internet; also called Internet address. Usually the format is user@someplace.domain; but also seen as ###.##.##.##

Jughead— An Internet program that helps *Gopher* (which see) build menus of resources, by limiting the search to one computer and a text string.

list (Internet)— Also called **mail list.** listserv lists (or listservers) are electronically transmitted discussions of technical and nontechnical issues. They come to you by electronic mail over the Internet using LISTSERV commands. Participants subscribe via a central service, and lists often have a moderator who supervises the information flow and content.

lurk— To read a list or echo without posting messages yourself. It's sort of like sitting in the corner at a party without introducing yourself, except it's not considered rude online; in fact, in some places you are expected to lurk until you get the feel of the place.

mail list— Same as *list.*

MNP— A data compression standard for modems.

modem— A device to modulate computer data into sound signals, and to demodulate those signals to computer data.

moderator— The person who takes care of an echo, list, or forum. This person takes out messages that are off-topic, chastises flamers, sometimes maintains a database of old messages, and sometimes handles the mechanics of distributing the messages.

navigation bar— A set of words and/or images that appear on every page of a web site, with links to other sections or pages of the same web site.

NIC (Network Information Center)— A NIC provides administrative support, user support, and information services for a network.

NREN— The National Research and Education Network is a proposed national computer network to be built upon the foundation of the NSF backbone network, NSFnet. NREN would provide high speed interconnection between other national and regional networks.

offline— The state of not being connected to a remote host.

online— To be connected to a remote host.

OPAC— Online Public Access Catalog, a term used to describe any type of computerized library catalog.

OSI— (Open Systems Interconnection) - This is the evolving international standard under development at ISO (International Standards Organization) for the interconnection of cooperative computer systems. An open system is one that conforms to OSI standards in its communications with other systems. As more and more genealogical data becomes available online, this standard will become increasingly important.

PPP— Point-to-Point Protocol. A type of Internet connection. An improvement on *SLIP* (which see), it allows any computer to use the Internet protocols, and become a full-fledged member of the Internet, with a high speed modem. The advantage to SLIP and PPP accounts is that you can usually achieve faster connections this way than a *shell account*.

protocol— A mutually determined set of formats and procedures governing the exchange of information between systems.

remote access—   The ability to access a computer from outside another location. Remote access requires communications hardware, software, and actual physical links, although this can be as simple as common carrier (telephone) lines or as complex as *Telnet* login to another computer across the Internet.

RAM—   The working memory of a computer. RAM is the memory used for storing data temporarily while working on it, running application programs, etc. "Random access" refers to the fact that any area of RAM can be accessed directly and immediately, in contrast to other media such as a magnetic tape data is accessed sequentially. RAM is called volatile memory; information in RAM will disappear if the power is switched off before it is saved to disk.

ROM—   Read Only Memory. A chip in a computer or a peripheral that contains some programs to run the unit; the memory can be read, but not changed under normal circumstances. Unlike RAM, it retains its information even when the unit is turned off.

search engine—   A program on the World Wide Web that searches parts of the Internet for text strings. It may search for programs, for Web pages, or for other items. Many claim to cover "the whole Internet" but that's physcially impossible. Getting more than 50% of it is a good lick.

server—   A computer that allows other computers to log on and use its resources. A client (which see) program is often used for this.

shareware—   Try-before-you-buy concept in microcomputer software, where the program is distributed through public domain channels, and the author expects to receive compensation after a trial period. Brother's Keeper, for example, is shareware.

shell account—   A method of connecting to the Internet. You dial an *Internet service provider* with regular modem software and connect to a computer there that is connected to the Internet. Using a text interface, usually with a menu, you use the Internet with this shell, using commands such as *telnet*. In this system, the Internet clients do not reside on your computer, but on the ISP's.

signature— A stored text file with your name and some information such as names you are searching or your mailing address, to be appended to the end of your messages. Should contain only ASCII characters, no graphics.

SLIP— Serial Line IP; a system allowing a computer to use the Internet Protocols with a standard telephone line and a high-speed modem. Most ISPs now offer PPP or SLIP accounts for a monthly or yearly fee.

Social Security Death Index— Often referred to as SSDI, this is a searchable database of records of deaths of Americans with Social Security numbers, if that death was reported to the Social Security Administration. It runs from the 1960s the present, although there are a few deaths prior to the 1960s in it. The records give full name, place and date of death, where the card was issued, and birth date. Many Web sites have online searches of the SSDI, some with SOUNDEX (which see).

SOUNDEX— An indexing system based on sound rather than spelling of a surname.

spider— A program that gathers information on Web pages for a database, usually for a search engine.

SSDI— Social Security Death Index (which see).

sysop— The SYStem OPerator of a *BBS*, *forum*, or *echo*. The sysop sets the rules, maintains the peace and operability of the system, and sometimes moderates the messages.

tagline— A short, pity statement tagged onto the end of a BBS email message. Example: "It's only a hobby, only a hobby, only a . . . " Taglines are rarely seen on commercial networks such as AOL, MSN and CompuServe.

TCP/IP— Transmission Control Protocol/Internet Protocol is a combined set of protocols that performs the transfer of data between two computers. TCP monitors and ensures correct transfer of data. IP receives the data from TCP, breaks it up into packets, and ships it off to a network within the Internet. TCP/IP is also used as a name for a *protocol* suite that incorporates these functions and others.

telnet—   An Internet client that connects to other computers, making yours a virtual terminal of the remote computer. Among other functions, it allows a user to log in to a remote computer from the user's local computer. On many commercial systems, you use it as a command, e.g., telnet "ftp://ftp.cac.psu.edu". Once there, you are using programs, and therefore commands, from that remote computer.

terminal emulation—   Most communications software packages will permit your personal computer or workstation to communicate with another computer or network as if it were a specific type of terminal directly connected to that computer or network. For example, your terminal emulation should be set to VT100 for most online card catalog programs.

terminal server—   A machine that connects terminals to a network by providing host TELNET service.

thread (message thread)—   Discussion made up of a set of messages in answer to a certain message and to each other. Sometimes very worthwhile threads are saved into a text file, as on CompuServe's Roots Forum. Some offline mail readers will sort by "thread" that is according to subject line.

tiny tafel (TT)—   A TT provides a standard way of describing a family database so that the information can be scanned visually or by computer. All data fields are of fixed length, with the obvious exceptions of the surnames and optional places. Many TTs are extracted from GEDCOMs.

TN3270—   A version of *telnet* providing IBM full-screen support, as opposed to VT100, or some other emulation.

Trojan horse—   A type of malicious code. It is usually a program that seems to be useful and harmless. In the background, however, it might be destroying data or breaking security on your system. It differs from a virus in that it propagates itself as a virus does.

upload—   To send a file or message from one computer to another. See *Download*.

USENET— A set of messages and the software for sending and receiving them on the *Internet*. The difference between USENET and a *mail list* lies in the software and the way you connect to them.

V.32— A data compression standard for modems.

Veronica— A search program for *gopher*.

virus— A program that installs itself secretly on a computer by attaching itself to another program or email, and duplicates itself when that program is executed or email is opened. Some viruses are harmless, but most of them intend to do damage, such as erasing important files on your system.

World Wide Web (WWW or the Web)— A system to pull various Internet services together into one interface called a *browser*. Most sites on the WWW are written as pages in *HTML*.

worm— A computer program that will make copies of itself, and spreads through connected systems, using up resources in affected computers or causing other damage.

Z39.50 Protocol— Name of the national standard developed by the National Information Standards Organization (NISO) that defines an applications level protocol by which one computer can query another computer and transfer result records, using a canonical format. This protocol provides the framework for OPAC users to search remote catalogs on the Internet using the commands of their own local systems. Projects are now in development to provide Z39.50 support for catalogs on the Internet. SR (Search and Retrieval), ISO Draft International Standard 10162/10163, is the international version of Z39.50. protocol.

Smiley (Emoticon) Glossary Because we can't hear voice inflection over email, a code for imparting emotion sprung up. These punctuation marks used to take the place of facial expressions are called Smileys or emoticons. Different systems will have variations of these symbols. Two versions of this Unofficial Smiley Dictionary were sent to me by Cliff Manis (Internet: "mailto:cmanis@csf.com"; ROOTS-L Mailing List Administrator), and I have edited and combined them.

Several versions are floating around, but I think this one sums up the ones you are most likely to see.

:-)   Your basic Smiley. This Smiley is used to show pleasure, or a sarcastic or joking statement

;-)   Winky Smiley. User just made a flirtatious and/or sarcastic remark. Somewhat of a "don't hit me for what I just said" Smiley.

:-(Frowning Smiley. User did not like that last statement or is upset or depressed about something.

:-I   Indifferent Smiley. Better than a Frowning Smiley but not quite as good as a happy Smiley

:->   User just made a really biting sarcastic remark. Worse than a :-).

>:->   User just made a really devilish remark.

>;->   Winky and devil combined.

Those are the basic ones...Here are some somewhat less common ones.

Note: A lot of these can be typed without noses to make midget smilies.

- -:-)   Smiley is a punk rocker

- -:-((real punk rockers don't smile)

;-)   wink

,-}   wry and winking

:,(crying

:-:   mutant Smiley

.-)   Smiley only has one eye

,-)   ditto...but he's winking

:-?   Smile smoking a pipe

:-/   skepticism; or consternation; or puzzlement

:-\   ditto

:-'   Smiley spitting out its chewing tobacco

:-~)   Smiley has a cold

:-)~   Smiley drools

:-[un-Smiley blockhead

:-[Smiley is a Vampire

:-]   Smiley blockhead

:-{   mustache

:-}   wry smile, or beard

:-@   Smiley face screaming

:-$ Smiley face with its mouth wired shut

:-*   Smiley after eating something bitter or sour

:-&   Smiley is tongue tied.

:-#   braces

:-#| Smiley face with bushy mustache

:-%   Smiley banker

:-<   mad or real sad Smiley

:-=)   older Smiley with mustache

:->   hey hey

:-| "have an ordinary day" Smiley

:-0   Smiley orator

:-0   No Yelling! (Quiet Lab)

:-1	Smiley bland face
:-!	(see above)
:-6	Smiley after eating something sour
:-7	Smiley after a wry statement
:-8(	condescending stare
:-9	Smiley is licking his/her lips
:-a	lefty smiley touching tongue to nose
:-b	left-pointing tongue Smiley
:-c	bummed out Smiley
:-C	Smiley is reaally bummed
:-d	lefty Smiley razzing you
:-D	Smiley is laughing
:-e	disappointed Smiley
:-E	bucktoothed vampire
:-F	bucktoothed vampire with one tooth missing
:-I	hmm
:-i	semi-Smiley
:-j	left smiling smilely
:-o	Smiley singing national anthem
:-O	uh oh
:-o	uh oh!
:-P	disgusted or nyah nyah

:-p   Smiley sticking its tongue out (at you!)

:-q   Smiley trying to touch its tongue to its nose

:-Q   smoker

:-s   Smiley after a BIZARRE comment

:-S   Smiley just made an incoherent statement

:-t   cross Smiley

:-v   talking head Smiley

:-x   "my lips are sealed" Smiley

:-X   bow tie

:-X   Smiley's lips are sealed

::-)   Smiley wears normal glasses

:'-(Smiley is crying

:'-)   Smiley is so happy, s/he is crying

:^)   Smiley with pointy nose (righty). Sometimes used to denote a lie, myth or misconception.

:^)   Smiley has a broken nose

:(sad midget Smiley

:)   midget Smiley

:[real downer

:]   midget smiley

:*   kisses

:*)   Smiley is drunk

:<   midget unSmiley

:<)   Smiley is from an Ivy League School

:=)   Smiley has two noses

:>   midget Smiley

:D   laughter

:I   hmmm...

:n)   Smiley with funny-looking right nose

:O   yelling

:u)   Smiley with funny-looking left nose

:v)   left-pointing nose Smiley

:v)   Smiley has a broken nose

':-)   Smiley shaved one of his eyebrows off this morning

,:-)   same thing, other side

~~:-(net.flame

(-:   Smiley is left handed

(:-(unSmiley frowning

(:-)   Smiley big-face

):-)   (see above)

(:I   egghead

(8-o   it's Mr. Bill!

):-(unSmiley big-face

)8-)   scuba Smiley big-face

[:-)   Smiley is wearing a walkman

[:]   Smiley is a robot

[]   hugs

{:-)   Smiley with its hair parted in the middle

{:-)   Smiley wears a toupee

}:-(toupee in an updraft

@:-)   Smiley is wearing a turban

@:l   turban variation

@=   Smiley is pro-nuclear war

*:o)   Bozo the Clown!

%-)   Smiley has been staring at a green screen for 15 hours straight

%-6   Smiley is braindead

+-:-)   Smiley is the Pope or holds some other religious office

+:-)   Smiley priest

<:-l   Smiley is a dunce

<:l   midget dunce

<|-(Smiley is Chinese and doesn't like these kind of jokes

<|-)   Smiley is Chinese

=)   variation on a theme...

>:-l   net.startrek

|-)   hee hee

|-D   ho ho

|-l   Smiley is asleep

|-O   Smiley is yawning/snoring

|-P   yuk

|^o   snoring

|I   asleep

0-)   Smiley cyclops (scuba diver?)

3:[mean pet Smiley

3:]   pet Smiley

3:o[net.pets

8 :-)   Smiley is a wizard

8 :-I   net.unix-wizards

8-)   glasses

8-)   Smiley swimmer

8-)   Smiley is wearing sunglasses

8:-)   glasses on forehead

8:-)   Smiley is a little girl

B-)   horn-rims

B:-)   sunglasses on head

C=:-)   Smiley is a chef

C=}>;*())   Mega-Smiley... A drunk, devilish chef with a toupee in an updraft, a mustache, and a double chin

E-:-)   Smiley is a Ham radio operator

E-:-I   net.ham-radio

g-)   Smiley with ponce-nez glasses

K:P   Smiley is a little kid with a propeller beenie

O :-)   Smiley is an angel (at heart, at least)

O |-)   net.religion

O-)   Megaton Man On Patrol! (or else, user is a scuba diver)

X-(Smiley just died

Index

A

About.Genealogy scheduled chats, 167, 170
Abraham Lincoln Papers, 247
Acadian Genealogy Homepage, 120
Adoptee Search Center, 120
Adoptees Internet Mailing List, 99
ADOPTION mailing list, 100
ADSL (Asymmetric DSL), 11, 13
Advertising, on CompuServe forums, 305
Africa.com Research page, 333
African ancestry, 102, 120-121, 135-138, 245, 255, 333
African-American Genealogical Society of N. California, 120
African-American Odyssey page (LOC), 245
African-American research, 255
African-American Web Ring, 120
AfriGeneas, 121, 135-138
AfriGeneas Home Page, 121
AFRIGENEAS mailing list, 102
Ahnentafels, 350-351

AIM (AOL Instant Messenger), 151, 153, 155-157
    privacy features, 156
    version 4 enhancements, 157
Alabama Department of Archives and History, 121
Allen County Indiana Public Library, 121-122
AltaVista Advanced Search, 178-179
AltaVista Babel Fish, 334
ALT-GENEALOGY mailing list, 79
America Online. See AOL
American Civil War Home Page, 122
American Memory (LOC), 244-246
    collection items, 246
    maps, 246-247
Ancestor tables, 350-351
Ancestors' village found online, 323-324
AncestorSuperSearch, 331
Ancestral Files, 57, 261-262, 266-268
Ancestry.com family of sites, 211-221
    Daily News, 110
    features, 212

GenPage Finder, 179-180
levels of membership, 212
merger with RootsWeb, 210
Society Hall, 217
World Tree, 213, 216
Ancient Faces, 122
AND (Boolean), 176-177
Anonymous FTP, 118
AOL (America Online)
 chat session window, 288-289
 and CompuServe, 79
 Favorite Places, 276
 FileGrabber, 82
 free trial membership, 274
 Genealogy Chat Center, 287-288
 Golden Gate Genealogy Forum,
  275-297
 Instant Messenger (AIM), 151,
  153, 155-157
 keywords, 273
 Mail Controls, 34
 main screen name, 275
 Netfind, 86-87, 180-181, 193
 off-line reading of newsgroup
  articles, 78
 Parental Controls, 82
 Personal Filing Cabinet, 286
 sign-up process, 275
 slow response time, 274
 using Find to look for
  messages, 286
Archives Project (USGenWeb), 147
Ariadne browser, 25
Armenian ancestry, 330
Articles (Usenet), 76
ASCII character set, 39-40
ASDL, 11
ASDL light, 11
AsianGenNet, 330
AskJeeves, 181
Australian ancestry, 332

B

Bad file request (error), 360
BBS echoes, 17
Beginner tries the shot-gun approach, 66

Beginners' Center, Golden Gate
 Genealogy Forum, 277-278
Beginning Genealogy Lessons
 (DearMYRTLE), 280-281
Belgian ancestry, 330
Bergen Emigration Information, 331
Bible records, 237
BigFoot, 193
Binaries (binary files), 82-83, 119
BINHEX encoders and decoders, 40
Biography Guide, 181
Bookmarks (browser), 28
Boolean terms, using in searches,
 176-177
Bounty survivors, 131
Branching Out Online, 122
BRAZIL mailing list, 102
British Heraldic Archive, 122
Browser toolbars, 28
Browser-based chat, 168
Browsers, 21-29
 choosing, 23-26
 to connect to library card
  catalogs, 233-238
 error messages, 360-362
 FTP programs in, 118
 mail readers in, 31
 reading newsgroups with, 77-78
 tips and tricks, 115-117
 tour of, 26-29
Bulletin Board Systems (BBSs), 20
Bureau of Land Management Land
 Patent Records, 61-62, 122-123
Byzantine.net, 122

C

Calendars Through the Ages, 122
Canadian Genealogy and History, 334
Canadian Heritage Information
 Network, 122
Card catalogs. See Library card catalogs
Catalog, explained, 174
CD-ROM Catalog (Everton's), 225
Cello browser, 24
Cemetery Junction: The Cemetery
 Trail, 122

Census Bureau (census.gov), 62, 122-123
CERN research group, 22
Chat, 149-172
    on AOL, 287-289
    based on Java, 153
    browser-based, 168
    on CompuServe, 311-312
    vs. e-mail, 151
    on Excite, 168
    on Gen Forum, 168
    on Genealogy Online, 168
    Golden Gate Genealogy
        Forum, 296
    hosted (moderated), 151
    how to, 163-166
    on Infoseek, 169
    on MyFamily.com, 220
    one-on-one, 151
    scheduled, 141, 166-167, 170
    security of, 153-154
    on Snap, 169
    un-moderated (drop-ins), 151
    warnings about, 152-153
    where to, 166-169
    without a chat program, 168-169
    on Yahoo!, 169
Chat Board (GenServ), 343
Chat etiquette, 169-171
Chat room lurking, 170
Chat rooms, 150-151, 170, 287-289
Chat servers, public (IRC), 153
Chat shorthand, 172
CHEROKEE-L mailing list, 102
Chinese Immigrant Files, 329
Chineseroots.con, 329-330
Christine's Genealogy Website, 123
Church of Jesus Christ of Latter-day
    Saints. See LDS
Civil War forums, 304
CIVIL-WAR mailing list, 104
Clients, 20
Closed lock (browser), 29
C|Net Search, 181-182
Collection Finder (LOC), 245-246
Commercial online services, 272-297
CommSoft BBS, 355
Communications programs, types of, 20

Compressed files (FTP), 119
CompuServe
    AOL and, 79
    blocking UBE, 35
    downloading a file, 311
    genealogy forums, 299-315
    GO words, 273
    and Internet Explorer, 301
    scheduled chats on genealogy,
        311-312
CompuServe Classic software, 302
CompuServe Forum Managers (sysops),
    304, 306
CompuServe forum messages
    downloading, 302
    reading, 301-302
CompuServe forums
    advertising on, 305
    decorum on, 304-306
CompuServe genealogy forums, list of,
    303-304
CompuServe toolbar, 309
CompuServe 2000, new features, 302
Computer viruses, 47-48
Congressional biographies, 181
Connect to server error, 364
Connecting to the Internet, what you
    need, 4, 18
Connection refused by host (error), 360
Convicts to Australia, 332
Cybertree Genealogy Database, 123
Cyndi's List of Genealogy Sites, 14,
    110, 123
Cyrillic alphabet browser, 25
Czech genealogy, 330

D

Danish ancestry, 331
Dead Persons Society, 332-333
DearMYRTLE Beginning Genealogy
    Lessons, 280-281
DearMYRTLE Daily Column (AOL), 293
DearMYRTLE newsletter, 109
DearMYRTLE scheduled chats, 166-167
DearMYRTLE's Place, 138-142
Decoding e-mail-attached files, 41

Dedicated newsreader, 75
Definitions of terms in this book,
    367-377
Deja.com, 74, 86, 196
Dial-up networking in Windows 98, 21
Digests, from ROOTS-L, 95
Directories, explained, 174
Directory of Royal Genealogical
    Data, 124
Documentation, supporting data
    with, 60
Downloading CompuServe forum
    messages, 302
Downloading a file on CompuServe, 311
Downloading files from an FTP
    server, 30
Draft registration from NAIL, 253
Drop-ins (un-moderated chat), 151
DSL (Digital Subscriber Line), 8, 10-13
    incompatibility of versions of, 13
    from Internet Service Providers, 10
    types of, 11
DSL information pages, local phone
    company, 12
DSL modems, 10
DSL speeds, 13

E

Eastern European ancestry, 330
Eastman, Dick, 313
Eastman's Genealogy Index, 108
Eastman's Online Genealogy
    Newsletter, 124
Edit menu (browser), 28
Electronic card catalogs, 232-242
ELIJAH-L mailing list, 100
E-mail, 31-41, 273
    vs. chat, 151
    file attachments, 39-41
    mail reading programs, 31,
        41-47, 74-77
    sorting, 32
    spam, 32-39
E-mail Abuse FAQ, 36
E-mail accounts, public and private, 33
E-mail error messages, 364-365
E-mail filters, 31-32

E-mail from a mail list stops coming,
    364-365
E-mail headers show message origin, 35
E-mail lists, searching for on
    FamilySearch, 264
Emoticon glossary, 377-385
Encoded binary files, broken up, 82
Encoding of e-mail-attached files, 40-41
Eppstein, David, 124
Error messages (browser), 360-362
Error messages (e-mail), 364-365
Error messages (FTP), 362-363
Error messages (Internet), 359-365
Error messages (Usenet), 363-364
Errors in genealogy data, 61
Ethnic groups genealogy, 102-103
Etiquette for chat, 169-171
Eudora 4.3, 42-45
    account personalities, 43
    custom stationery, 43-44
    filters, 44-45
    instant messaging, 155
    scheduled pick-ups, 42-43
    signatures, 43-44
Everton's Guide to Genealogy on the
    Web, 125
Everton's Web site, 223-229
    databases, 225-227
    online classes, 227
    Family History Newsline, 110
    Genealogical Helper, 224
    Reference Library, 227-228
    subscribing to, 228
    workshop locations, 227
Excite, 168, 182
Exhibitions (LOC), 248
External modems, 5-7

F

Failed DNS lookup (error), 361
Family Chronicle, 125
Family group sheets, 56
Family History Centers (FHCs), 57, 227,
    259, 265, 267-268
    list of, 269, 320
    visit to, 269-270
Family History Library, 265

Family History Library Catalog, 258
Family names. See Surnames
FamilyHistory.com, 214-217
    How Do I Begin, 125
    message boards, 214-215
FamilySearch.com, 57, 258-270,
    325-326
        Ancestral Files, 261-262, 266-268
        databases and Web sites, 258
        interactive elements, 262
        opening page, 260
        pedigree chart form, 260
        registering your site with, 265
        research guidance, 261-263
        searching for e-mail lists, 264
        sharing your research, 263
        uploading your GEDCOM to,
            265-266
Family Tree, on MyFamily.com,
    218-219
Family Tree Finders at SodaMail
    Archives, 125
Family TreeMaker Online, 126
FAQ files
    E-mail Abuse FAQ, 36
    Golden Gate Genealogy Forum,
        278-279
    newsgroup, 70-71, 83, 86
FastSearch, 182
Favorite Places (AOL), 276
Fax capabilities of modems, 6
Featured Attractions (LOC), 248
Federal Records in African-American
    Research, 255
Federal Register Publications
    (NARA), 254
Federation of Genealogy Societies
    (FGS), 217
Fetch for Macintosh, 118
File attachments to e-mail, 39-41
File contains no data (error), 361
File Libraries Center, Golden Gate
    Genealogy Forum, 289-290
File menu (browser), 28
File Transfer Protocol (ftp), 29-31
FileGrabber (AOL), 82
FileMine, 194-195
Files, from online services, 273-276

Filters
    for e-mail, 31-32, 34
    Eudora 4.3, 44-45
    for newsgroup messages, 76
Firewalls, 48
Flame wars, 70
Flames (insulting messages), 70, 72, 83
Flash upgrade modem technology, 6
Form submission to bookmark list
    error, 360
Forums (genealogy), 273
    AOL, 275-297
    CompuServe, 299-315
404 not found (error), 360
403 forbidden (error), 360
FrancoGene, 330
FreeBMD, 126
French ancestry, 326, 330
Frequently Asked Questions (FAQ files)
    E-mail Abuse FAQ, 36
    Golden Gate Genealogy Forum,
        278-279
    newsgroup, 70-71, 83, 86
FTP conventions, 119
FTP error messages, 362-363
FTP (File Transfer Protocol), 118-119
FTP program connects then freezes, 362
FTP server, downloading files from, 30
Fuller and Gaunt's genealogy mail
    lists, 111

G

Gathering of the Clans Home Page, 126
GEDCOM-L mailing list, 107
GEDCOMS (GEDCOM files), 336,
    356-357
    exporting, 338-339
    sending, 340
    translated into HTML, 52-53
    uploading to FamilySearch,
        265-266
GedPage program, 52
GEDPalm program for personal digital
    assistants, 14-15
Gen Forum chat, 168
GENCMP-L mailing list, 107

GenConnect message board suites, 206
GenConnect (RootsWeb), 206-207
GEN-DE-L mailing list, 80, 103
GENDEX, 127
Genealogical Helper, The, 229
Genealogical software lists, 107
Genealogy Chat Center (AOL), 287-288
Genealogy data
    accuracy of yours, 264
    errors in, 61
    forms of, 349-357
    translated into HTML, 48
Genealogy Dictionary, 127
Genealogy and Family History
    (NARA), 250
Genealogy Forum (AOL), 275-297
Genealogy Forum News (AOL), 293
Genealogy forums (CompuServe),
    299-315
Genealogy Home Page, 127, 142-144
Genealogy Links.Net, 127
Genealogy mailing lists. See Mailing
    lists (genealogy)
Genealogy newsgroups. See
    Newsgroups (genealogy)
Genealogy Online chat, 168
Genealogy Page (NARA), 249-250
Genealogy Pages, 127, 184
Genealogy program, web publishing
    with, 51-52
Genealogy project, beginning, 55-66
Genealogy Support Forum, 304
Genealogy sysops, 304, 306, 313-315
Genealogy for Teachers, 127
Genealogy Techniques Forum (GO
    ROOTS), 303, 305
    contributing to, 310
    messages and files, 309-310
    notices, 313-314
    opening screen, 307-309
Genealogy Today newsletter, 108, 127
Genealogy on the Web Ring, 127
Genealogy web sites
    evaluating, 63-64
    list of, 119-135
GenealogyForum.com, 293-294
Genealogy.net, 331
GenealogyPortal.com, 184-185

GenealogySearch.com, 186
GeneaSearch.com, 184
GEN-FF-L mailing list, 80, 103
GEN-FR-L mailing list, 80
GenGateway, 185
GEN-IRC-L mailing list, 166
GEN-MEDIEVAL-L mailing list, 81, 105
GENMSC-L mailing list, 81, 100
GENMTD-L mailing list, 81, 100
GEN-NEWBIE-L mailing list, 100
GenPage Finder (Ancestry.com),
    179-180
GenSeeker (RootsWeb), 204-205
GenServ, 185-186, 335-348
    Chat Board, 343
    free trial of, 343
    freebies, 342-343
    how it works, 343
    Information Request Form,
        339-340
    joining, 338-339
    LIST FIELDS command, 346-347
    LIST WIDTH command, 347
    Queries, 343
    Queries Search, 343
    rules for subscribers, 343
    search name commands,
        344-347
    SEARCHCOUNT, 344
    SEND command, 348
    SHOW REQUEST command, 347
    SPLIT command, 347
    surnames search results, 345
    types of membership, 341
GenSource, 186
GENUKI-L mailing list, 81, 127
GenWeb Database Index, 128
Geographic area mailing lists, 105-107
German ancestry, 318-325, 331
GermanRoots, 331
Getting online, what you need, 4, 18
Gist-In-Time translation service, 334
Global Genealogy Supply web site, 128
Glossary of terms used in this book,
    367-377
GO GENEALOGY, 302
GO NAROOTS, 307
GO ROOTS, 305, 307

GO Translator, 334
GO words (CompuServe), 273
GO WWROOTS, 307
Golden Gate Genealogy Forum (AOL),
    275-297
        Beginners' Center, 277-278
        Beginners' page, 280-281
        chat, 296
        FAQ/Ask the Staff, 278-279
        File Libraries Center, 289-290
        5-step research process, 279-280
        GenealogyForum.com, 293-294
        Golden Gate store, 294
        Internet Center, 290-291
        Member Welcome Center,
            276-277
        Message Board Center, 283-284
        Message board controls, 284-285
        message boards, 282-286
        quick start guide sections,
            281-282
        reading messages offline, 286
        Resource Center, 290
        reunions, 292
        Search the Forum, 292
        SIGs, 296
        staff, 294-297
        Surnames Center, 291-292
Google, 187
Granite Mountain Records Vault, 264
Greater Manchester Integrated
    Library, 232
Greater than sign (>), 85

H

Handle (nickname) for login id, 154, 169
Hardware hogs, 23
Hauser-Hooser-Hoosier Theory, 128
HDSL (high-bit-rate DSL), 11
Headstone Hunter, 128
Heirloom quilts (DearMYRTLE), 140
Help menu (browser), 28
Helper application not found (error), 361
HIR-Hungarian Information
    Resources, 128
Hispanic Genealogy Special Interest
    Group, 122

Historical Collections of the National
    Digital Library, 244
Historical group mailing lists, 104-105
History forums, 304
HistorySeek! History Search Engine,
    128-129
Hosted (moderated) chat, 151
HotBot, 187
Hotmail, 160
How to Get Past Genealogy Road
    Blocks, 128
HTML, 22
        GEDCOM files translated into,
            52-53
        genealogy data translated into, 48
HTML editor, using, 54
HTTP (hypertext transfer protocol), 22
Humor, in genealogy newsgroups, 84
Hypertext, 23
HYTELNET Library Catalog, 241

I

ICQ, 157-159
ICQ 2000, 157
INDIAN-ROOTS-L mailing list, 103
InfoSeek, 86-87, 182-184
        chat on, 169
        InfoSeek Guide, 87
        Search Options page, 183
Instant messages, 151
Instant Messenger (AOL), 151, 153,
    155-156
Internal modems, 5
International Genealogical Index (IGI),
    57, 267
International genealogy resources, 57,
    166, 267, 317-334
International Internet Genealogical
    Society, 166, 328-334
International Telecommunications
    Union (ITU), 5
Internet, 67-196
        continuous connection to, 8
        publishing on, 48-54
        searching, 174-196
        what you need to get connected,
            4, 18

Internet appliances, 13-14
Internet Center, Golden Gate Genealogy
    Forum, 290-291
Internet error messages, 359-365
Internet Explorer, 23, 115-116, 239
    CompuServe and, 301
    page in, 27
Internet Family File (Everton's), 226
Internet mail clients, 41-47
Internet presence, 151, 157
Internet Service Providers. See ISPs
Internet Tourbus, 128
Invalid host (error), 362
Invalid newsgroup (error), 363
IRC (Internet Relay Chat), 150
    chat servers, 153
    common commands, 164-165
    default channel (Lobby), 165
    security risks, 154
    server channels, 167-168
ISDN channels, 8
ISDN connection costs, 9
ISDN (Integrated Services Digital
    Networks), 8-10
ISDN line installation, 9
ISDN line supporting two phone
    numbers, 8
ISPs (Internet Service Providers)
    busy signals during prime
        time, 17
    choosing, 14-18
    digital access in your
        neighborhood, 16
    DSL accounts, 10
    e-mail box capacity, 17
    56kbps access, 16
    file collections, 17
    flat fee or hourly connect
        charges, 18
    questions to ask them, 16-18
    Usenet newsgroup message
        readers, 17
Italian Genealogy Homepage, 331
ITU V.90 standard, 5

J

Janyce's Root Digging Dept, 128
Java-based chat, 153
Java-based Quick Buddy, 155
JewishGen, 128
JEWISHGEN mailing list, 80, 103
JFK Assassination Records
    Collection, 254
JOG: The Journal of Online
    Genealogy, 109
Juliana's Links, 214
Junk e-mail, 32-39

K

Keywords (AOL), 273
KiwiGen Web Ring, 332
Klippel, Denzil J., 318-325

L

Land patents, 61-62, 122-123
Latin American ancestry, 332
LDS (Church of Jesus Christ of
    Latter-day Saints), 257-270
    giving permissions to, 265
    how to use information from,
        266-267
    Letter-Writing Guides, 326
    research guides, 325-326
LDS genealogy, background to,
    267-268
Libbi's Spammer Twit List, 36-39
Library card catalogs, 231-242
    connecting by Telnet, 239-240
    connecting to, 232
    sample search, 234-238
    Web connection, 233-238
    where to find, 240-242
Library Catalog (NARA), 254-255
Library of Congress (LOC), 128-129,
    244-249
Library of Virginia card catalog, 237-238

Library of Virginia Digital Collections, 129
Lightning strikes, 4
Lineage Project (USGenWeb), 147
Lineages Inc, 129
Link (pointer to another file), 23
Lobby (IRC), 165
LOC (Library of Congress), 128-129, 244-249
Local History and Genealogy page (LOC), 247
Local phone company DSL information pages, 12
Location box (browser), 28-29
Login id nickname (handle), 154, 169
LookSmart, 187
Lurking in chat rooms, 170
Lurking in CompuServe forums, 306
LusaWeb, 331
Lycos, 188-189

M

Mac browsers, 25
Mail clients (stand-alone), 31
Mail Controls (AOL), 34
Mail lists. See Mailing lists (genealogy)
Mail reading programs, 31, 41-47, 74-77. See also E-mail
Mailing list server vs. mailing list, 93
Mailing lists (genealogy), 89-111
    automated, 90
    directory of, 110
    ethnic groups, 102-103
    e-mail addresses of, 90
    family name, 103-104
    finding, 110-111
    historical groups, 104-105
    hosted by RootsWeb, 110
    losing contact with, 97-98
    mail stops coming, 364-365
    vs. mailing list servers, 93
    message posting address, 90
    moderated, 90
    regional groups, 105-107
    subscribing tips, 91
    subscription address, 90
    unsubscribing to, 33, 91
Manis, Cliff, 337
Marston Manor, 129-130
MAYFLOWER mailing list, 105
Mayflower Passenger List, 60
Mayflower Web Pages, 130
McAfee Anti-Virus, 47
Medal of Honor Citations, 130
MegaBit 7Mbps download/1Mbps upload, 13
MegaHome ADSL residential service, 13
Member Welcome Center, Golden Gate Genealogy Forum, 276-277
Menu bar (browser), 28
Message boards (FamilyHistory.com), 214-215
Message boards (Golden Gate Genealogy Forum), 282-286
Message boards (RootsWeb GenConnect), 206-207
Message body, newsgroup, 76
Message of the Day (MOTD), 165
Message headers, newsgroup, 76
Message posting address (mailing lists), 90
Message readers for Usenet newsgroups, 17
Message threads, 284
Message undeliverable Mailer Daemon, 365
MetaCrawler, 189
Metasearch engine, 175
MetaSearch (RootsWeb), 203-204
MIAs from the Vietnam War (LOC), 248-249
Microfilm publications search (NAIL), 254
Microsoft Chat, 151, 153, 160-161
    cartoon character layout, 161
    in text mode, 162
Microsoft Internet Explorer (MIE), 23, 115-116, 239
    CompuServe and, 301
    page in, 27
Microsoft Meeting, 151

Microsoft's security page, 154
MIME encoding scheme, 40
mIRC, 153, 162-163
mIRC text display, 163
Missing Links, 109, 208
Modems, 4-7
    DSL, 10
    fax capabilities, 6
    flash upgrade technology, 6
    internal or external, 5-6
    selecting, 6
    two computers using one, 6-7
    and UARTs, 7
Moderated chat, 151
Moderated mailing lists, 90
Moderated newsgroups, 72
Mormon Church. See LDS
Mosaic browser (NCSA), 24-25
MSD.EXE (Microsoft System
    Diagnostics), 7
MSN Messenger Service 2.2, 159-160
Multipurpose Internet Mail Extensions
    (MIME), 40
MyFamily.com, 217-221
    chats on, 220
    Family Tree, 218-219
    My Sites page, 218
    Our Family History, 219-220
MyRoots database for Palm Pilot, 14

N

NAIL (NARA), 252-254
    draft registration from, 253
    Digital Copies Search, 253
    Expert Search, 252
    microfilm publications search, 254
    Physical Holdings Search, 253
    Standard Search, 252
NARA (National Archives and Records
    Administration), 244, 249-256
    Library Catalog, 254-255
    NAIL, 252-254
    Prologue magazine, 249, 255-256
    Web databases, 250-255
National Genealogical Society, 130,
    144-145

research standards, 57-58
standards for sharing
    information, 64-65
technology standards, 59-60
web publishing standards, 49-51
National Genealogy conference
    (FidoNet), 355
National Union Catalog of Manuscript
    Collections (NUCMC), 242
Native American Genealogy, 130
Net etiquette, 83-86
Netfind (AOL), 86-87, 180-181, 193
Netherlands ancestry, 330
Netscape Navigator, 23, 115-116, 239
    browsing history in, 117
    Gist-In-Time translation
        service, 334
    instant messaging, 155
    news-reading window, 77
    page in, 26
    screen, 27-29
NetSearch, 29
New England Conference, 312
New England Historic Genealogical
    Society, 130
NEW-GENLIST mailing list, 101
NEW-GEN-URL mailing list, 101-102
News server, explained, 76
news.admin.misc, 70
news.announce.newusers, 70
news.answers, 70
news.compuserve.com, 76
Newsgroup articles, searching, 76
Newsgroup FAQ files, 83, 86
Newsgroup message readers, 17,
    74-79, 273
Newsgroup messages
    gibberish in, 364
    message body, 76
    message filters, 76
    message headers, 76
    subject lines, 85
    surnames uppercase in, 85
Newsgroup servers, 77
Newsgroups (genealogy), 69, 71-72,
    79-81. See also Usenet
    ISP access to, 17
    moderated vs. unmoderated, 72

quoting in responses, 85
reading with a Web browser,
    77-78
searching within, 86-87, 195-196
staying on topic, 83
topics welcomed in, 83
Usenet categories of, 72
using humor in, 84
Newsletters (e-mail), 107-110
Newsletters (RootsWeb), 207-209
News.prodigy.com, 76
Newsreaders, 17, 74-79, 273
Newton palm devices, Relations 2.3
    database, 14
NNTP server error, 361
No such message (error), 363-364
North American Genealogy Forum (GO
    NAROOTS), 303, 307
Northern Light, 189-190
Norton Anti-Virus, 47
Norwegian Genealogy Dictionary, 331
NO.SLEKT mailing list, 80
NO.SLEKT.PROGRAMMER mailing
    list, 80
NOT (Boolean), 177
Not found (error), 361

O

Obituary Search Pages, 189-190
OfficeConnect 56K LAN modem
    (3Com), 6
One-on-one chat, 151
Online Genealogy Classes, 130
Online library card catalogs (OCCs),
    231-242
Online services (commercial), 272-297
    channels or sections, 272-273
    e-mail, 273
    files, 273-276
    forums, 273
    front end software, 272
    newsgroup readers, 78
    Usenet newsreader, 273
Open look (browser), 29
Opera 2.1 browser, 25
OPR (Old Parochial Register), 57

OR (Boolean), 176
Oregon History and Genealogy
    Resources, 130
Original documents, 60
Original source document, scanned
    image of, 61
Our Family History, on MyFamily.com,
    219-220
Our Spanish Heritage, 130
Outlook Express, 75-76
    newsgroup message filters, 76
    searching newsgroup articles, 76
    three-pane layout, 75-76
Outlook 2000 (Microsoft), 45-47
Outlook 2000 stationery, 46
OVERLAND-TRAILS mailing list, 105

P

PAF mailing list, 107
Palm Pilot, MyRoots database for, 14
Palm-top computers, 13-14
Parental Controls (AOL), 82
Pedigree chart form, 260
Pedigree charts, 56, 260, 350-351
Pegasus Mail, 45
Permissions, giving to LDS, 265
Personal Ancestral File (PAF), 107, 356
Personal digital assistants, GEDPalm
    program, 14-15
Personal Filing Cabinet (AOL), 286
Personal toolbar (browser), 29
PhotoFind Database (Everton's),
    226-227
PIE mailing list, 103
PING program, 362
Pitcairn Island Web Site, 130-131
Pocket Family Researcher, 14
Points of Presence (POPs), 18
Poland Worldgenweb, 131
Portals, 174, 272
Portuguese ancestry, 331
Posting on the Web, 49
POWs and MIAs from the Vietnam War
    (LOC), 248-249
PPP, 17
Presidential Libraries (NARA), 252

Primary and secondary sources, 60-63
Private e-mail accounts, 33
Prologue magazine (NARA),
    249, 255-256
Proof, 59-64
Protocols, 5
Public vital records, 61
Public (IRC) chat servers, 153
Publicly Accessible Mailing List web
    site, 110
Publishing on the Internet, 48-54

Q

Quick Buddy, 155
Quick Guide to Genealogy in Ireland, 131

R

RADSL (rate-adaptive DSL), 11
Read-only memory (ROM), 6
Regional group mailing lists, 105-107
Registering your site with
    FamilySearch, 265
Relations 2.3 database, for Newton
    palm devices, 14
Repositories of Primary Sources, 131
Research, sharing yours, 263
Research Guidance tool, 261
Research Guides (LDS), 325-326
Research help from FamilySearch,
    262-263
Research outline for France, 326
Research Room (NARA), 250
Research standards, National
    Genealogical Society, 57-58
Research Tools page (LOC), 248
Resource Center, Golden Gate
    Genealogy Forum, 290
Reunion story, 200-201
Reunions, Golden Gate Genealogy
    Forum, 292
Roots Cellar (Everton's), 225-226
ROOTS Forum, 305
        members of, 307
        tour of, 306-313
RootsComputing, 132
Roots-II and Roots-III, 352
RootsWeb, 199-210

automated keyword search,
    204-205
database search engines, 205
e-mail newsletters, 207-209
finding mailing lists on, 110
GenConnect, 206-207
genealogy chats, 166
genealogy Web site hosting, 207
GenSeeker, 204-205
HelpDesk, 207
mailing lists, 209
merger with Ancestry.com, 210
MetaSearch, 203-204
project missions, 200
searching for surnames on,
    201-205
State Resource pages, 207
RootsWeb chat room (Microsoft Chat),
    160-161
RootsWeb E-zines, 132
RootsWeb Review newsletter, 108,
    207-208
RootsWeb Surname List (RSL), 202
RootsWeb/IIGS chats, scheduled, 166
ROOTS-L
        digest mode, 95
        files and databases, 94
        index mode, 96
        losing contact with, 97-98
        mail mode, 96
        messages with attachments, 96
        putting to work, 94-95
        rules, 92-93
        sending commands to, 93
        sending messages to
            subscribers, 93
        visit to, 91-98
ROOTS-L Library, 94
ROOTS-L Resources, 208
Royal Family of the Netherlands, 127

S

SBt Genealogy Resources, 132
Scandinavian ancestry, 331
Scanned image of original source
    document, 61
Scheduled chats (About.Genealogy),
    167, 170

Scheduled chats (DearMYRTLE), 141,
    166-167
Scheduled chats (RootsWeb/IIGS), 166
Scottish ancestry, 126
Screen name (AOL), 275
SDSL (single-line DSL), 11
Search engines, 174
Search page (NARA), 251
Search sites, 174, 178-192
Search tips, general, 175
Searches
        narrowing, 175
        using Boolean terms, 176-177
        using WITH operator in, 177-179
Searching
        for e-mail lists on
            FamilySearch, 264
        the Internet, 174-196
        newsgroup articles, 76
        for surnames, 308
        for surnames on RootsWeb,
            201-205
        within newsgroups, 86-87,
            195-196
Secondary sources, 62-63
Secure sites, 29
Security features of chat, 153-154
Security risks in IRC, 154
Serial communications programs, 20
Servers, 20
Shanghai Library, 329
Shanxi Genealogy Centre, 330
Shareware, ZDNet library of, 196
Shareware search
    (GenealogyForum.com), 293-294
Shareware.com, 195
Sharing information, NGS standards
    for, 64-65
Sharing your research, 263
Shields Up, 48
Shortcuts to a site, 28
Signatures (Eudora 4.3), 43-44
Slave data, 137
SLIP, 17
Smiley glossary, 377-385
Snap, 169, 191
Social Security Death Index,
    204, 213, 227
Society Hall (FGS), 217

Soc.roots, 79, 81
Software, 19-54
Software Center
    (GenealogyForum.com), 293-294
Software lists (genealogical software), 107
SOFTWARE.GENCMP-L mailing list, 80
Somebody's Links (RootsWeb), 110, 209
Sorting e-mail, 32
Soundex codes (Tiny Tafel), 354-355
Source document, scanned image of, 61
Sources, primary and secondary, 62-63
Sources cited in detail, 60
Sources and proof, 59-64
South African (white) genealogy, 333
South American ancestry, 332
South Carolina State Library card
    catalog, 132, 239-241
Spam protection, 32
Spam (unsolicited bulk e-mail), 32-39
Spammers, 32
Spanish Genealogy, 331
Spanish heritage, 132, 331
Special-interest groups (SIGs), 296
Spiders, 174
SSDI (Social Security Death Index), 204,
    213, 227
State Resource pages (RootsWeb), 207
StateGenSites, 132-133
Status line (browser), 29
Stroud's Consummate Winsock
    Apps page, 25
Subject lines, newsgroup message, 85
Subscribing tips, mailing list, 91
Subscription address (mailing lists), 90
Successful Links (RootsWeb), 208
Surname mailing lists, 103-104
Surname Search (Everton's), 225
Surname Web, 190
Surnames
        mailing lists, 103-104
        origins of, 322-323
        searching for, 308
        searching for on RootsWeb,
            201-205
        sites listing, 132
        uppercase in newsgroup
            messages, 85
Surnames Center, Golden Gate
    Genealogy Forum, 291-292

SURNAMES-CANADA-L mailing list, 103
SurnameSite, 191
Swedish ancestry, 331
Swiss Genealogy Project, 132
Switchboard, 193
Systems operators (sysops) of
genealogy forums, 304, 306,
313-315

T

Taiwan Surnames Association, 330
Task Force Russia database (LOC), 248
Tasks menu (browser), 28
TCP error, 361-362
TCP/IP, 20
TCP/IP stacks, 20-21
Technology, NGS standards for use of,
59-60
Telephone Search Facilities
(GenealogyForum.com), 293
Telnet connection to library card
catalogs, 239-240
Telnet LION system menu, 240
Terms of Service statements, 152
Terms used in this book, 367-377
Thermometer bar (browser), 29
Threads (message), 284
Tiny tafel data, 354
Tiny tafel defined types, 352-353
Tiny tafel specifications (CommSoft),
352-354
Tiny tafel (TT), 352-354
Tiny-Tafel for Database Scope
Indexing, 352
Title bar (browser), 27
Tombstone Project (USGenWeb), 148
Too many consecutive transmit errors,
362-363
Too many users (error), 362
Toolbar (browser), 28
Transcribing original documents, 61
Translating Web pages into English,
167, 334
Traveller Southern Families, 132-134
Treasure Maps newsletter, 108-109

Treasure Maps/The How-to Genealogy
Site, 132-133
Trojan horses, 47
TTMS (Tiny Tafel Matching System),
355-356
TUCOWS, 25, 195
Tuffsearch's Ancestor's Attic, 133

U

UART (Universal Asynchronous
Transmitter and Receiver), 7
UBE (unsolicited bulk e-mail), 32-39
UK and Ireland Genealogy, 331
Ukrainian Roots genealogy, 330
Ultimate Collection of Winsock
Software (TUCOWS), 25, 195
Ultimate White Pages, 193-194
Unable to locate host (error), 362
Unable to resolve host (error), 362
United Kingdom ancestry, 122, 331
Universal DSL, 11
University of Alabama in Huntsville
LCC, 235
University of Minnesota Genealogy
Resources, 240
University of Texas at Austin
UTNetCAT, 234
UNIX, Usenet and, 73
Unknown user (error), 364
Unmoderated chat, 151
Unmoderated newsgroups, 72
Unsubscribing from a mail list, 33, 91
URL (uniform resource locator), 22, 28
URL box (browser), 28
U.S. Census Bureau, 62, 122-123
U.S. Civil War Center, 134
U.S. Gazetteer, 133
U.S. Presidents, public papers of, 254
Usenet, 69-87. See also Newsgroup
messages; Newsgroups (genealogy)
articles, 76
binary files, 82-83
error messages, 363-364
FAQs, 70-71
genealogy newsgroups, 79-81
history of, 73-74

newsgroup categories, 72
software needed for, 74-79
structure, 71-73
tips on, 83-86
viruses on, 82
USGenWeb library card catalogs, 242
USGenWeb Project, 62, 134, 145-148
Utah State Archives, 134
UTNetCAT, 234
Uudecode programs, 41
Uuencoded files, 40-41
UUE.ZIP, 41

V

VDSL (very-high-bit-rate DSL), 11
Vietnam Database (Everton's), 225
Vietnam Era POWs and MIAs (LOC),
248-249
View menu (browser), 28
Virtual Bouquets (RootsWeb), 209
Virus protection, 47-48
Viruses, 47-48, 82
VitalRecords.com, 321
V.90 ITU standard, 5

W

Web browsers. See Browsers
Web page translations into English,
167, 334
Web pages, 22
Web publishing standards, NGS, 49-51
Web site address, entering in a
browser, 28
Web sites
creating, 217-218
list of genealogy, 119-135

Web (the World Wide Web), 113-148
connection to library card
catalogs, 233-238
and mobility-challenged
genealogist, 114
posting on, 49
publishing on, 48-54
terms used on, 22-23
White Page directories, 193-194
WinZIP, 41
WITH operator, using in searches,
177-179
World Connect Project, 191, 202-203
World Tree (Ancestry.com), 213, 216
World Wide Genealogy Forum (GO
WWROOTS), 304, 307
WorldGenWeb Project, 327-328
Worms, 47
WS_FTP, 30-31
WS_FTP32, 118

X

xDSL, 10-13
Xerox Map Server, 135
XXENCODE encoding scheme, 40

Y

Yahoo!, 174, 191-192
Yahoo! chat, 169
Yahoo! Genealogy Page, 135

Z

ZDNet Software Library, 195-196

INTERNATIONAL CONTACT INFORMATION

AUSTRALIA
McGraw-Hill Book Company
Australia Pty. Ltd.
TEL +61-2-9417-9899
FAX +61-2-9417-5687
http://www.mcgraw-hill.com.au
books-it_sydney@mcgraw-hill.com

CANADA
McGraw-Hill Ryerson Ltd.
TEL +905-430-5000
FAX +905-430-5020
http://www.mcgrawhill.ca

GREECE, MIDDLE EAST, NORTHERN AFRICA
McGraw-Hill Hellas
TEL +30-1-656-0990-3-4
FAX +30-1-654-5525

MEXICO (Also serving Latin America)
McGraw-Hill Interamericana Editores
S.A. de C.V.
TEL +525-117-1583
FAX +525-117-1589
http://www.mcgraw-hill.com.mx
fernando_castellanos@mcgraw-hill.com

SINGAPORE (Serving Asia)
McGraw-Hill Book Company
TEL +65-863-1580
FAX +65-862-3354
http://www.mcgraw-hill.com.sg
mghasia@mcgraw-hill.com

SOUTH AFRICA
McGraw-Hill South Africa
TEL +27-11-622-7512
FAX +27-11-622-9045
robyn_swanepoel@mcgraw-hill.com

UNITED KINGDOM & EUROPE (Excluding Southern Europe)
McGraw-Hill Publishing Company
TEL +44-1-628-502500
FAX +44-1-628-770224
http://www.mcgraw-hill.co.uk
computing_neurope@mcgraw-hill.com

ALL OTHER INQUIRIES Contact:
Osborne/McGraw-Hill
TEL +1-510-549-6600
FAX +1-510-883-7600
http://www.osborne.com
omg_international@mcgraw-hill.com